T0325476

Steel Town

Steel Town

The Making and Breaking of Port Kembla

Erik Eklund

MELBOURNE UNIVERSITY PRESS

MELBOURNE UNIVERSITY PRESS
(an imprint of Melbourne University Publishing)
PO Box 1167, Carlton, Victoria 3053, Australia
mup-info@unimelb.edu.au
www.mup.com.au

First published 2002
Text © Erik Eklund 2002
Design and typography © Melbourne University Publishing 2003

This book is copyright. Apart from any use permitted under the
Copyright Act 1968 and subsequent amendments, no part may be
reproduced, stored in a retrieval system or transmitted by any
means or process whatsoever without the prior written
permission of the publisher.

Typeset in Meridien Roman 10/13 pt
by Syarikat Seng Teik Sdn. Bhd., Malaysia
Printed in Australia by Ligare Pty Ltd

National Library of Australia Cataloguing-in-Publication entry

Eklund, Erik Carl.
   Steel town: the making and breaking of Port Kembla.

   Bibliography.
   Includes index.
   ISBN 0 522 85026 X.

   1. Steel industry and trade – New South Wales – Port Kembla.
   2. Port Kembla (N.S.W.) – History. 3. Port Kembla (N.S.W.) –
   Social conditions. I. Title.

994.46

1901-2001
Centenary of Federation

This project has been supported by the National Council for
the Centenary of Federation and the Australian Historical
Association.

Contents

Illustrations

Plates

Maps

Tables

Acknowledgements

I would like to thank Stephen Garton, Stuart Macintyre, Greg Patmore, John McQuilton, and Mendo Trajcevski, all of whom offered valuable assistance, comments and constructive criticisms at different stages. Michael Organ from the University of Wollongong facilitated access to original records, as did Anna Francis from BHP–Billiton Archives in Melbourne, Emma Jolley from the Noel Butlin Archives in Canberra, and Roger Stockins from Wollongong City Council. More than one idea came to me via the very perceptive and supportive Antoinette Holm. Her intellectual and emotional support ensured that this book was completed. From Melbourne University Press I would like to thank Teresa Pitt, Gabby Lhuede and Janet Mackenzie. David Roberts drew the maps with great skill and at short notice. A perusal of the references will demonstrate the extent to which I have relied upon the work of past and present scholars of Port Kembla and Illawarra history. Responsibility for the final interpretation presented here is mine alone.

The manuscript was largely completed while on sabbatical leave at the Center for Australian and New Zealand Studies, Georgetown University, Washington, DC. I would like to thank Richard Teare and Grace Tompkins for this opportunity. The Australian Academy of Humanities provided a Travelling Fellowship that enabled me to visit industrial sites in the United States and Britain. The Australian Historical Association and the School of Liberal Arts at the University of Newcastle both offered subsidies that made publication feasible. Thanks also to all my history colleagues in the School of Liberal Arts for providing such a congenial and productive workplace. The University of Newcastle provided sabbatical leave and research funding necessary to complete the work in a timely manner.

The original research was a doctoral thesis completed through the History Department at the University of Sydney in 1995, where I benefited from the expert supervision of Stephen Garton. Readers interested in following footnotes and references are directed to this earlier work. A general thank-you to my labour history colleagues who encouraged and nurtured this study from its tentative beginnings more than ten years ago.

This book would not have been possible without the generous assistance of current and former residents of Port Kembla. I thank them for sharing their memories, and for all the tea and biscuits a researcher could care for. Two of those former residents include my mother and father, to whom I owe a very special debt for their encouragement and assistance over many years.

Erik Eklund

Abbreviations

AAM	Australian Aborigines' Mission
AI&S	Australian Iron and Steel Ltd
APB	Aborigines' Protection Board
AWU	Australian Workers' Union
BHP	Broken Hill Proprietary Company Ltd
CRA	Conzinc Rio Tinto Australia Ltd
CRM	Commonwealth Rolling Mills Pty Ltd
EEA	Electrolytic Employees' Association
ER&S	Electrolytic Refining and Smelting Company of Australia Ltd
FEDFA	Federated Engine Drivers' and Firemen's Association
FIA	Federated Ironworkers' Association
MM	Metal Manufactures Ltd
OBU	One Big Union
PKC	Port Kembla Copper Ltd
TCF	Telephone Cable Factory, Metal Manufactures
UWM	Unemployed Workers' Movement
WWF	Waterside Workers' Federation

Conversions

Weights and Measures

1 pound	=	454 grams
1 ton	=	1.02 tonnes
1 foot	=	30.5 centimetres
1 mile	=	1.61 kilometres
1 acre	=	0.4 hectare

Currency

On 14 February 1966 Australian currency changed from pounds, shillings and pence (£, s, d) to dollars and cents at a rate of £1 = $2. Twelve pence made up one shilling and twenty shillings made up one pound.

Introduction

A DISTINCTIVE BLUE-GREEN MOUNTAIN RANGE defines a narrow coastal strip on Australia's east coast. The morning sun touches the top of the range, known locally as 'the escarpment', sharpening and defining its contours, and then illuminates the foothills, ridges and higher suburbs. Sunlight moves across the narrow coastal plain that borders the range to the north and then creeps southwards, embracing a lake and the southern suburbs. It shows once separate places now merged into one suburban entity, a ribbon of residential, commercial and industrial development. The suburbs are roughly arranged around two centres. There is a commercial centre whose tall, metallic and glass structures reflect the light, and celebrate an industrial heritage. And to the south, an area where a mass of industrial buildings converge around a large harbour. This area stands as a telling symbol of the region's golden industrial age.

By midday the sun's illumination is indiscriminate. All points are brought into focus in an overwhelming crowd of detail. Yet this book focuses on one crucial area of this coast. A distinctive town developed in the twentieth century whose history is now subsumed within a regional suburban identity. By spotlighting this town and its residents, the place that experienced the full effects of industrialisation can be better understood.

At the end of the day the escarpment, between 250 and 660 metres high, cuts off the late afternoon light. By evening, twilight sits high above the coast, while the suburbs gather a murky dark punctuated by pinpricks of streetlight. Another sign of human industry joins these lights, as the fires of huge furnaces light up the night sky above the town of Port Kembla.

From the first decades of the twentieth century large industrial factories were established throughout Australia. In towns like Newcastle, Lithgow, Port Kembla in New South Wales, Mount Isa in Queensland and Port Pirie in South Australia, as well in the major capital cities, highly mechanised

1

factories employing up to a thousand workers heralded twentieth-century industrialisation. Industrial change created distinctive physical and social landscapes, which in turn shaped the communities that developed around these new factories. Industrialisation often brought major urban development to otherwise sleepy country regions. Some 85 kilometres south of the New South Wales capital of Sydney, white settlers knew the area that became Port Kembla variously as Illawarra Farm, the Five Islands or Red Point for most of the nineteenth century. It contained a mix of leased and owner-occupied dairy farms. In the early 1880s the Mount Kembla Coal Company began using the partly sheltered beach area to ship coal from its nearby mine on the escarpment. The name Port Kembla became widely adopted by settlers, who were largely unaware of the traditional Koori name of Nitoka.[1] In 1898 a government decision to construct an extensive artificial harbour initiated the industrial development of the area. Major industries were established. A copper refinery and smelter set up in 1908, and a related manufacturing company arrived in 1916. By this time a distinct town had emerged through industrial growth, residential subdivision and commercial development. In 1927 the arrival of the Hoskins iron and steel works changed Port Kembla's status from an 'industrial town' to a 'steel town'. By the 1930s Port Kembla was a nationally significant industrial location.

Port Kembla was the first Australian town whose origin and growth was solely linked to the process of industrialisation. To the north of Sydney, Newcastle was a convict colony and then the centre of a coalmining district well before the arrival of large-scale industrial production in the late nineteenth century. Port Pirie in South Australia existed as a centre for wheat export before the harbour facilities and smelters expanded in the late 1880s to cater for the Broken Hill trade. The mining and later processing town of Mount Isa, in north-western Queensland, was not established until the 1920s. Unique in Australian terms, Port Kembla was an urban environment where industrial society shaped local life and politics like nowhere else.

A history of Port Kembla is important in light of powerful and homogenising national discourses that equate Australian history with capital-city history. Australian capital cities did indeed dominate the urban hierarchy. But one effect of an exclusive focus on capital cities is to remove spatial and historical diversity from Australian history. Places beyond the capital cities such as Port Kembla, Newcastle, Wonthaggi, Whyalla and Port Pirie are left at the historical margins even if they represented the centre for significant numbers of Australians. These towns, like their overseas equivalents, have characteristic industrial experiences and social structures that are not easily incorporated into analyses that centre on capital cities. Australians who have never been to Port Kembla still carry a fifty-year-old image of a dirty, polluted industrial wasteland. Industrial society created a powerful national image of such areas that still informs national perceptions. Yet these perceptions, often sweeping assumptions or stereotypes, effectively function as replacements for a historical understanding of the experience of living and working in an industrial town.

The history of Port Kembla highlights the local manifestation of important global forces. Industrial towns are places where the global and local collide in an often tumultuous fashion. In Australia, Britain and the United States these towns have distinctive images among outsiders; they bear witness to the power of investment decisions made in distant boardrooms; and they experienced rapid population influx through immigration in periods of growth and expansion. Yet these towns also exhibit powerful moments of collective mobilisation and generalised place-based loyalty, where a sense of locality sharpened the edges of local culture while mediating the forces of the outside world.

In this analysis, however, the focus is on the Port Kembla experience and the way locals negotiated a changing world. As Canadian scholar Ian Angus suggests, locality is not the opposite of global but rather where we begin both in personal and methodological terms. Moving beyond a simple local/global dichotomy may help us think more clearly and critically about the process of economic and social change, especially as deindustrialisation proceeds across many so-called First World industrial towns.[2]

The experience of this Australian industrial town can be related to major international examples from Britain and the United States. These countries had their own industrial towns and cities, and a consideration of their histories sheds light on the unique dimensions of the Port Kembla experience. Britain and the United States stand out as the two most important international influences. Expertise, capital and, in the case of Britain, large numbers of migrants, came from these nations. In comparison to major British and US steel centres, Port Kembla's twentieth-century transformation was modest in terms of dimension, but more wide-ranging in terms of impact. British centres such as Sheffield and Birmingham, or US sites like Pittsburgh, Pennsylvania, and Gary, Indiana, dwarfed Australian industries. Yet at Port Kembla there was no existing workshop-style manufacturing industry or pig iron industry, characteristic of most British and US industrial sites. Birmingham, England for example, even as early as the 1840s was a rich industrial amalgam of specialist workshops, tool makers, jewellery producers, engineering equipment firms, copper and copper alloy producers, as well as toy and carriage makers.[3] In Pittsburgh, the most important steel centre in the United States, the steel industry of the late nineteenth century grew out of the existing iron industry. Even Gary, the industrial city built on the shores of Lake Michigan on old farming land by the US Steel Corporation, was largely populated by workers who had prior experience of industrial employment and had lived in industrial communities.

The essentially rural context for industrial development at Port Kembla heightened the impact of industrial society. The regional economy leaped from dairying and coalmining to the widespread deployment of the technology and social relations of twentieth-century industrialisation within the space of thirty years. Overall, Port Kembla's living and working environment provides the opportunity for a case study of the advent and implications of industrial society that is unprecedented in Australian terms.

Industrialisation proceeded at uneven speeds across the Western world from the early nineteenth century, while its characteristic features (factories, manufacturing employment, the bifurcation of management and ownership) arrived at Port Kembla from the beginning of the twentieth century. Industrialisation also brought a 'rational', 'calculative' mode of thinking that was applied beyond the factory to social and home life. Industrial society was the most powerful expression of the dominance of industrialisation where the technology, methods and values of this mode of production held together a powerful consensus. At Port Kembla this consensus held sway from 1945 through to at least 1970 and probably much longer.

In Australia a number of important 'community studies' of local areas have been carried out.[4] Community studies, originating in the disciplines of sociology and anthropology, usually highlight themes of social stratification, power and authority, patterns of leadership, and social interaction. However, community studies are less useful for analysing the historical dimensions of localities. Many focus on contemporary society, and are often restricted to the years in which participant observation was undertaken. Moreover, while cities have been the preserve of urban anthropologists and urban historians, community studies have focused on the small towns of rural Australia, or occasionally on isolated working-class mining communities.[5]

Rather than community, I employ the concept of 'locality' to develop a historical understanding of Port Kembla. Originating in the discipline of human geography, the term became widely accepted in English sociology and cultural history from the 1980s.[6] The concept of locality represents one part of the considerable body of work on the role of space in social relations; it offers insights for historians, and provides both a point of departure and an inspiration for this study of Port Kembla.[7] As economic geographer Doreen Massey argues, it is no longer tenable for research and theorising to 'proceed blithely ... as though the world existed on the head of a pin, as though it were distanceless and spatially undifferentiated'.[8] The work on locality, with its examination of spatial diversity and its recognition of the geographically uneven nature of capitalist development, can help the historian of locality refine notions of 'urban' and 'rural', and present a more subtle and encompassing picture of the living environments inhabited by Australians. Labour historians have already begun to explore the wealth and diversity of the individual histories of Lithgow, Broken Hill, and Wagga Wagga, among other places.[9]

The locality of Port Kembla was the creation of a specific type of capitalist development interacting with the existing contours of human settlement. The locality's boundaries were the limits of industrial, commercial and residential development as Port Kembla grew. Yet the nature of these boundaries, their importance for society and politics and the way they were perceived by locals and non-locals, was very much a subjective matter.[10] The nature of the locality was redefined and contested by the efforts of locals to boost and diversify their locality, and the power of surrounding interests to undermine this self-sufficiency. Such political conflict occurred in the context of other economic and social processes like new transport technology, the changing labour market, and the rhetoric of an ascendant industrial society, which in turn influenced the localised or exposed status of the locality.

Any theorisation of place, then, needs to be dynamic and appreciate the changing regional context. Port Kembla was located within the well-populated and growing Illawarra region, and was only 6 kilometres south of the large commercial centre of Wollongong. The increasing integration of the Illawarra region, as well as competition from near-neighbour Wollongong, are a vital part of the Port Kembla story. By the 1940s there was a high level of interaction between towns in the region, and this represented a significant challenge to a self-sufficient town like Port Kembla. The Illawarra region is defined as the coastal area between the town of Helensburgh in the north and Shellharbour in the south.[11] The larger contemporary definition of the Illawarra, extending south to Nowra, has been largely adopted for planning purposes. Helensburgh and Shellharbour form the geographical and political boundaries marking the northern and southern edges of the region. There were also strong economic and political links between the towns within this area, and the region was characterised by the economic interrelationships between coalmining, dairying and later heavy industry, centring on the commercial hub of Wollongong. Wollongong-based politicians and businessmen also looked south towards the new industrial town with considerable interest, eyeing the opportunities it presented but also wary of the challenges emanating from its rapid development.

Wollongong's dominance of the Illawarra region, well established by the late twentieth century, has been uncritically accepted by historians. Histories of the Illawarra region are presented as histories of 'Wollongong', using the name of the largest city of the region to represent, however problematically, the geographical and social diversity of the region. This book makes no such assumption and in fact reveals a crucial period in which the dominance of Wollongong, and the ability of other town-based interests to articulate their own concerns, were highly contested aspects of regional life. By the 1990s the idiom Steel Town with reference to Port Kembla was rarely heard or seen. The common phrase now is Steel City and that is almost always associated with Wollongong. Port Kembla is now often called a 'suburb' of Wollongong, or 'the industrial area' of the Illawarra region; the town's centrality to those who lived and worked there are relegated to the margins of other places. This history of Port Kembla shows that this situation was not always the case.

Oral history, both the interviews I completed and the tapes and transcriptions from the work of other researchers, is an important source of information and insight for the chapters that follow. The oral record, however, should be approached with caution. Memory is fallible and can be selected and ordered according to the present-day perspective and concerns of the respondents. The interviewing process can subtly influence the nature and content of the interviews. In using oral history, contradictions, pauses, and omissions can be an important part of the story. I have corroborated, where possible, individual memories with other sources. Diversifying the number and nature of the sources ideally should add certainty and reliability to the interpretations offered. The interviews undertaken for this project were never designed to be 'representative' of the local population. Instead, interviews were ways to tap into a shared, and remarkably consistent, collective memory. The interviews were a valuable source that often shed new light on the written records. Despite these potential problems, the various interviews by myself and other researchers all demonstrated one point very strongly. Memory is a highly individualised expression, yet the common stories, collective language and shared history contained within the oral record is a remarkably powerful historical tool, and has greatly enriched this study.

Behind every book is an author with their own history. While I was writing this book my dreams were full of half-forgotten friends and childhood experiences. Consciously and unconsciously, my family history has shaped the story that follows. My maternal great-grandparents came to Port Kembla from the Sydney suburb of Strathfield in the early 1920s, searching for the commercial opportunities that the new industrial town offered. Family legend has it that they were inspired by the announcement by Charles Hoskins, the Lithgow-based steelmaker, that he was to build a new steel works at Port Kembla. My great-grandparents ran a small mixed business and carrying firm in Military Road, Port Kembla. My mother's parents, who were married in 1917 and lived in suburban Sydney, followed them a few years later. Shortly thereafter my mother was born in Port Kembla. My maternal grandfather, a farrier by trade, worked variously for the local copper smelter, or on public works projects.

My father, a Swedish migrant who 'came ashore' in 1951, married my mother in 1953 and worked for a local engineering firm until retirement in 1984. I and my sister and brothers lived in Port Kembla until 1969. Although my personal and family links to the town have inspired me to tell the Port Kembla story, this is not a family history. The aim of this book is to explore the boundaries and meanings of Port Kembla, a place that was a central focus for many during this period of rapid change.

The following chapters discuss local experiences and responses to industrial society at an economic, political and cultural level. Industrial society initiated the development of Port Kembla at the turn of the century, and industry became closely bound to this specific locality. By the 1920s Port Kembla was the epitome of 'industrial town', where the lives and experiences of the majority of local residents interlocked with the fate of local industry. This interlocking relationship encouraged the development of class politics and workplace-centred class conflict. At the same time, town development and an inward-looking society encouraged localist politics based on cross-class coalitions and calls for local unity. These developments occurred in a crucial regional context with Wollongong interests, as well as the general process of regional integration, opening the locality up to greater outside influences.

After 1945, the links between industry and locality began to unravel as the monumental scale of industrial development had growing regional and later national consequences. Class politics were increasingly played out through organisations and by major actors who had few links to the locality, while the scale and the dominant rhetoric of industrial society overwhelmed localist politics. The political conflicts surrounding the place of the town within the region reveals a series of battles over the organisation and administration of industrial society. These battles were ultimately won by Wollongong-based interests as, by the 1960s, the Steel City of Wollongong replaced the Steel Town of Port Kembla. Strong social and emotional investments in locality were, however, largely unaffected by the changing political scene.

In contrast to white inhabitants and their increasing attachment to place, Koori inhabitants were further displaced and marginalised throughout the twentieth century. The role and place of Kooris within a local history of Port Kembla is a fraught issue as the construction of an Anglo-Australian town simultaneously involved the attempted eradication or denial of a local Koori topography. Local histories, as they are typically conceptualised, focus on the very Eurocentric space of the built environment, yet Koori history lies at the margins of the town's boundaries, and follows its own path through the twentieth century.

Such issues are further complicated by the spectre of a non-Aboriginal historian writing Aboriginal history. The analysis is more than likely limited by a lack of cultural capital and inside knowledge, and incorporating Aboriginal history into a wider analysis of Port Kembla society and culture may blur the distinctiveness of the local indigenous experience. Whilst recognising these issues, the alternative—to omit Koori history all together—is even more problematic. Ultimately, indigenous and non-indigenous history cannot be so easily separated since many of the structures and individuals from white society affected, both negatively and positively, Koori lives at Port Kembla. The two stories weave together and give to each other greater meaning. The Aboriginal experience of dislocation is given greater poignancy when contrasted to the growing local connections that non-Aboriginal people developed over the same period.

In a range of contemporary debates historians sometimes struggle to highlight the historical dimension to a mainstream culture and society that privileges the short-term, superficial analysis over a longer, more considered viewpoint. This work is written as an antidote to the kind of world view that reports the daily, sometimes hourly, shifts in monetary and share value as if this means something significant. It aims to chart the relationship between economic change and the human experience of it in one place. For an evaluation of industrial society requires not one hour or one day but a century. Even then, as the following chapters reveal, the legacy of industrial society is a mixed one; its experiences and consequences are full of contradictions. And that, of course, is the beauty of history.

1

Port Kembla: The Global and the Local

FROM THE END of the nineteenth century the swirling currents and tides of circulating investment capital washed upon the shores of Port Kembla. Outside forces created the town and shaped its character, as investment in infrastructure encouraged local development and construction. Yet how these waves of outside influence washed over the lie of the land was influenced by the physical and social contours of existing human settlement. Industrial towns are remarkable composites of this interplay between outside influences and local distinctiveness. A global and local framework provides a context for understanding Port Kembla during the formative period of industrial society.

Before the area attracted significant attention from distant investors, interest came from regional sources, especially the regional coal companies. In 1900 the Illawarra region was split into a north/south economic divide, with the north from Mount Keira to Helensburgh dominated by coalmining, while the south from Figtree to Shellharbour was 'dairying and nothing but dairying from one end of the place to another'.[1] Port Kembla and the nearby towns of Figtree, Unanderra, Brownsville, Dapto and Mount Kembla formed the principal towns of the Central Illawarra Municipality. The municipality's population had grown from 3247 in 1891 to 4464 in 1901, and was a substantial portion of the Illawarra's regional population of 19 111.[2] Rich grazing pastures, along with proximity to Sydney markets for butter and milk, had brought some prosperity for large dairy farmers and cattle breeders in the 1890s.

These established dairying families dominated the Central Illawarra Council through long-serving (and occasionally related) aldermen such as John Brown (an alderman from 1859 to 1911), Frank O'Donnell (1890 to 1906; mayor eight times) and J. W. Gorrell (1908 to 1935; mayor twelve times). Not all the local dairy farmers were so well off, and a large number of farming families struggled on properties leased from large landowners. The Board of Health had continual trouble in the municipality with insanitary dairies, and many were without clean water supplies or proper water closets. Leaseholders usually operated family-run farms of 8 to 12 hectares and had a high rate of failure.[3]

At the hub of this economic divide between north and south Illawarra was Wollongong, with a population of 3545 in 1901. Wollongong dominated the Illawarra because of its importance as a service centre. One correspondent found Wollongong stores were a 'very busy picture indeed' on mine pay-days, 'with people in them from the mines at Keira, Kembla and Bellambi'. Wollongong's commercially minded middle class was active in real estate, accountancy, law and medicine. Storekeepers, tinsmiths, blacksmiths, bootmakers, tanners and watchmakers also enjoyed local and regional trade, making Wollongong the middle-class and petit-bourgeois stronghold of the Illawarra.[4]

To the north of Wollongong, along the narrow coast plain between the sea and the escarpment, small villages such as Mount Pleasant, Balgownie, Corrimal, Bellambi, Bulli and South Clifton clustered around coalmines. In 1900, 1300 men worked in the region's eleven mines (all but one north of Wollongong), while many others were employed in related industries such as shipping, the coke industry and the government railway.[5] Mining towns were essentially working-class towns and inhabitants were strongly parochial. In 1894, Helensburgh, a mining town on the northern edge of the Illawarra, formed the first Progress Association in the region. Many town-based union lodges had strong local traditions and proved difficult to co-ordinate, hampering the regional development of the coalminers' union.

Like the land-owning dairy farmers, the mine owners were active in regional politics. Henry McCabe, owner of the Mount Keira mine, served as alderman on the Wollongong Municipal Council and was mayor in 1899. Owner and manager of the Mount Kembla mine, Ebenezer Vickery, was a member of the New South Wales Legislative Council. As a devout Methodist, he was best remembered for his trips to Port Kembla by company train, where he would hand out religious tracts to his employees.[6]

The mine owners encouraged the New South Wales government to improve Port Kembla because the port had become crucial to the local coal trade. By the mid-1890s almost 40 per cent of all the coal mined in the Illawarra was shipped through two private jetties at Port Kembla.[7] Yet the port only had limited natural protection. Coal ships moored at Port Kembla would ride the ocean swells and pitch dangerously in the seas whipped up by winter gales or strong summer north-easterly winds. The mine owners and their parliamentary allies secured the passage of the *Port Kembla Harbour Act* in December 1898.[8] The Act authorised the construction of a deep-water

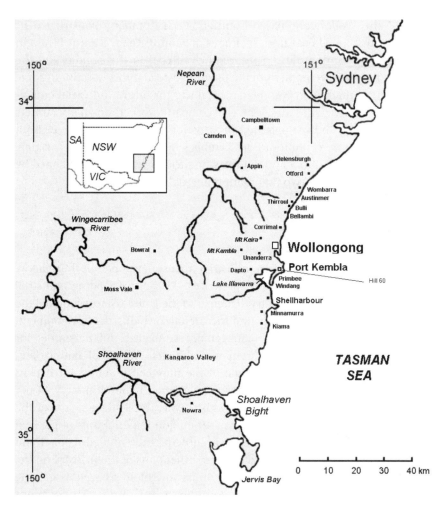

South-east New South Wales, showing the principal towns of the Illawarra region

harbour at Port Kembla with an eastern breakwater (at the southern side of the port), and the resumption of two private jetties and land belonging to the Wentworth estate, which covered much of the land surrounding the port. The rival ports of Wollongong and Bellambi were considered more costly and less suitable than Port Kembla. Construction work began in January 1900. It was in this regional context that the industrialisation of Port Kembla began.

The initial waves of investment capital were small and regional in origin. The Mount Kembla Company, which operated a coalmine at Mount Kembla, south of Wollongong, developed the port as a coal shipping facility from the 1880s. In 1883 the company completed a coal loading jetty and railway from the port to its mine at a cost of between £25 000 and £30 000.[9]

In 1887 the Wollongong-based Southern Coal Company constructed its jetty, which shipped coal from its mines at Mount Keira, Mount Pleasant, Corrimal and South Bulli.[10] The presence of coal in the region, and the potential for the development of the open roadstead into a harbour of some consequence, made Port Kembla an ideal site for future industrial expansion. In the following decades, local coal company workers and dairy farmers were joined and then supplanted by a major industrial workforce. Both the process and perception of Port Kembla's industrialisation, increasingly underwritten by national and overseas financial interests, were shaped by the prior expansion of two dominant industrial nations.

Global Context

Port Kembla, like all Australian industrial towns, developed in the shadow of British and North American experiences. As the two leading industrial powers at the turn of the century, Britain and the United States supplied the vast majority of the technology and the capital for industrial development. At times they also provided management strategies and personnel for Australian industrialisation. Britain was the first industrial nation, and its dominance peaked in the middle of the nineteenth century, when its share of the world's manufactured exports averaged approximately 44 per cent. In the 1860s, when the iron industry was the leading sector of the economy, Britain produced more than 40 million imperial tons of pig iron per annum.[11] Britain's experience was subsequently studied, copied and exported around the world, particularly to other parts of the British Empire. Australian managers undertook study tours to Britain as well as gaining ideas through the process of trade and investment. 'British' innovations (sometimes borrowings from continental engineers and inventors) were re-exported to Europe or transferred to the New World by entrepreneurs who looked to copy or adapt British successes.[12] Britain enjoyed extensive foreign trade, principally with parts of her own Empire. Colonial outposts like Australia and Canada supplied the raw materials and in turn imported British manufactured goods.

This domination of trade and industrial activity had a powerful impact in the colonies of the British Empire. In South Africa, British technology and capital underpinned the gold and diamond mining industry. In New Zealand, British shipping companies and banks supported the trade in butter and wool. In Australia, the British invested in pastoralism, construction, pockets of manufacturing, gold and metal mining. Australian or Australian-based companies often directly borrowed British expertise and even imported

British personnel, working in Australia according to directions given by British boards of directors. After 1871 telegraphic communication between Australia and Britain made absentee investment and distant management more feasible, though not necessarily straightforward. In the mining industry, for example, British boards controlled the British Broken Hill Pty Ltd, while similar British investors and directors managed the British-registered Sulphide Corporation, which owned a Broken Hill mine and a smelting facility at Boolaroo, south of Newcastle, New South Wales.[13]

From the turn of the century, however, the British began to invest more substantially in industrial activities in Australia and other peripheral resource economies. This had important implications for industrial towns as regional capital was joined and then surpassed by interstate and international investors. British investment, British migrants and British ideas, altered the very fabric of local life in parts of Australia as elsewhere.

British capital, in the form of British Helsby and Insulated Cable Ltd, subscribed one-third of the investment behind the Port Kembla-based manufacturing firm Metal Manufactures when it was founded in 1916. In 1928 when the Hoskins brothers, iron and steel makers from Lithgow, floated Australian Iron and Steel Pty Ltd to build and manage its Port Kembla works, British firms Dorman and Long and Howard Smith were prominent partners. John Lysaght, a steel fabrication company based in Bristol, England, constructed a large plant in Newcastle, New South Wales, which began production in 1921, and later established a plant at Port Kembla in 1937.

Increasing British investment in Australia was partly a result of fierce competition from the United States, Germany and other industrialising countries. British capital retreated to the confines of the Empire behind the protective barriers of imperial preference and the British Navigation Acts. As Peter Cochrane remarked, the Empire 'became a haven for a battered old power'.[14] By 1920 Australia exported over £80 million worth of goods to Britain (mostly wool, agricultural products, and gold), which was over 40 per cent of Australia's total exports. In turn that same year, almost 39 per cent of Australia's imports, valued at £35 million pounds, came from the United Kingdom.[15]

Despite losing its status as a world leader, Britain remained central to the health of the Australian economy throughout the 1920s and 1930s, and decisions made in its distant boardrooms, clubs and stock markets had major implications for Australia, its economy and its urban make-up. British investment capital, increasingly unable to compete on the world stage, was channelled into particular imperial industries in particular locations. It was in this context that Australia industrialised, with the United States, Germany and other industrial nations becoming more influential as initial British dominance faded.

As well as British investment, British migrants, both skilled and un-skilled, were a vital part of Australia's new industrial workforce. After a net loss of migrants from the 1890s depression to 1906, net gains in migration resumed, and increased again after World War I. In 1921 Australia gained 17 525 migrants, a number which increased every year until the onset of the Great Depression. Many of these migrants were British. Indeed, only British migrants were actively encouraged, and non-British migrants faced the discriminatory dictation test under the White Australia policy. One measure of this British influence was the rates of British-born in the region. The 1911 Census surveyed such figures for the county of Camden, which covered the Illawarra from Bulli in the north to Kiama in the south. In this area, approximately 13 per cent of the total population of 43 097 were born in the British Isles. By 1947 in the Central Illawarra Municipality, a smaller area which included Port Kembla and the surrounding rural towns of Dapto, Figtree, and Mount Kembla, the British-born still made up 10 per cent of the total population of 14 121.[16]

These workers and their families brought with them the cultural tra-ditions of their places of origin. Australian industrial and mining towns were distinctive social formations that included many of the institutions that characterised their British counterparts. In the coalfields of Newcastle and the Illawarra the coalminers' lodges, brass bands, Masonic clubs, and retail co-operatives were central to local social and political life.[17] A culture of respectability—with strong though not universal adherence—emphasised sobriety, self-help and thrift. These strategies enabled working-class people to survive materially and psychologically against the brutalising experience of wage labour. These traits also underpinned a more proactive labour politics that sought to reorganise or at least moderate the workings of the waged economy.[18] At a community level, these political and cultural expres-sions often came together as a powerful unifying force during industrial action, or economic hardship.

Other British migrants, fewer in number and from the management or 'staff' hierarchy, had a specific regional impact upon the structure of industrial communities and the nature of labour management in Australia. Companies imported British professional and technical staff to provide the necessary skills and personnel for new industries. At Port Kembla, Metal Manufactures imported British managers, engineers and accountants. Con-sequently, locals sometimes called the management houses in Private Lane 'Pommy Lane', thus equating Englishness with middle-class management, not an unfamiliar experience in many industrial workplaces of the period.

The movement of people, as well as capital and technology, had distinctive social ramifications for industrial communities.

In the period 1870 to 1914 the United States and Germany challenged and then surpassed British industrial hegemony. At the beginning of this period, American industrial entrepreneurs named their cities in honour of their British equivalents. In 1871 the soon-to-be-established iron and steel city of Birmingham, Alabama, was so named by one of the town's promoters in honour of Birmingham, England, a city he had recently visited.[19] British patents like the open hearth furnace and the Bessemer process were transferred to the United States. By 1913, however, the United States had surpassed Great Britain in terms of productive capacity, and by 1920 was the world's largest exporter of all products.[20] The steel mills of Pittsburgh, Gary, Steelton, and Youngstown, among others, pioneered improvements in mechanical handling, and the reduction of labour costs and requirements. US firms were also vehemently anti-union, and had ousted unions from major plants by 1900.[21] Some Australian steel managers tried to emulate such policies, but never with the same success.

Pioneering Australian managers argued that US technology and labour management practices were more efficient and suitable for Australia's new industrial economy. Business practice left little room for sentiment, though the economic, political and emotional bonds of Empire unravelled slowly and unevenly. Some US companies invested in Australia before 1945, but they were very much pioneers. Pratt and Whitney won the contract to construct the Lithgow Small Arms Factory in 1911. In 1930 American Smelting and Refining Company invested in the Mount Isa field in north-western Queensland. In the two leading areas of the Australian industrial sector firms such as the Broken Hill Proprietary Company Ltd (BHP), and the Collins House Group, a loose coalition of Broken Hill mining companies, began employing American advisers, purchasing American technology and arranging study tours to American plants. The growth of the US industrial economy, and the development of distinctive labour management strategies, became emblematic of 'new' industrialism; indeed, the contemporary gospel of industrial efficiency was equated, sometimes inaccurately, with 'American practices'. In 1911 the board of BHP, a major mining and smelting company based on the rich Broken Hill mine in western New South Wales, took the momentous decision to establish an iron and steel industry. The board, despite the presence of British investors, naturally looked to the United States for advice, and it engaged David Baker, a steel expert from the commercial and manufacturing city of Philadelphia, Pennsylvania. This began a long tradition of US influence on BHP, which started iron and steel production at Newcastle in 1915 and eventually bought a controlling interest in the Port Kembla steel works in 1935. BHP's only major competitor until the 1935 merger, AI&S also utilised US specialists and equipment, though to a lesser degree.

Other major companies in the Australian mining and manufacturing sector looked to the United States for advice and at times capital investment and personnel. Senior managers from the Collins House Group undertook regular study tours to the United States from 1915. By the beginning of World War I in 1914, the United States was the new benchmark in efficiency and economy for Australian industry.

For the Australian steel industry, and others, Pittsburgh became the quintessential industrial community by which all others were measured. Once itself called the 'Birmingham of America', by the turn of the century Pittsburgh was one of the largest steel-making areas in the world. Its size dwarfed anything in Australia. By 1894, the steel mills in and around Pittsburgh produced one-third of all US steel. From 1880 to 1930 the population of metropolitan Pittsburgh nearly tripled, rising from 235 000 to 670 000.[22] Its products underpinned the making of modern America in the form of new railroads, naval vessels, steel bridges and skyscrapers.[23]

Pittsburgh also had a long history of immigration and ethnic adjustment to American industrial life. The largest groups of migrants following the Iron Age boom of the 1870s to 1890s were Irish, German, Scottish, Welsh, and African-American workers from the southern states. After 1900 migration included increasing numbers of Italians and Yugoslavs. Well before the first wave of continental European migration in the 1950s arrived at Port Kembla, Pittsburgh had already experienced at least two significant waves and the adjustments and difficulties that followed.

The example of Pittsburgh's relative ethnic diversity as compared to Port Kembla holds true at a national level as well. US ethnic diversity became more pronounced from 1880, as European migrant groups travelled across the Atlantic in greater numbers. By 1891 almost 15 per cent of the US population of over 92 million were born outside the United States. Many of them secured employment in manufacturing industries and settled in urban areas. This wave of overseas migrants joined other groups of US citizens and residents on journeys of internal migration; white Americans, African-Americans, and some foreign-born who sought new opportunities in industrial centres.[24]

Australia's patterns of migration, and the exclusion of non-British and non-white migrants, created industrial towns that were overwhelmingly Anglo-Australian in their make-up; a mix of Australian, English and, to a lesser extent, Irish, Scottish and Welsh ethnicities predominated. On the eve of large-scale migration to Australia in 1947 less than 10 per cent of the country's population had been born overseas. More than 70 per cent of those were born in the British Isles, again underlining the numerical and

cultural dominance of British ethnicities. This was one of the principal differences between Australian and US industrial communities. When Port
Kembla's ethnic make-up began to diversify in the 1950s, it was in the
context of an extraordinarily high level of Anglo-Australian dominance in
the local and national population.[25]

The Pittsburgh experience also shows how urban industrial growth
was perceived through the lens of prior experience. With the growth in the
American economy and its manufacturing industry in particular, Pittsburgh
shifted from being compared to Birmingham to becoming the defining city
for steel towns worldwide. As one historian of Pittsburgh remarked, the city
became the 'preeminent and exemplary site of industrialisation in America,
indeed in the whole world'.[26] In the context of these enmeshed British/
American influences, Port Kembla was going to be both the Birmingham of
Australia and the Pittsburgh of Australia, though the British heritage was
undoubtedly stronger until at least the 1940s. In this respect, the town
shared a common experience with Lithgow and Newcastle, which were often
compared, with varying degrees of accuracy, to their British or American
equivalents.

The changeover over from British to US financial dominance did not
happen suddenly; British capital remained influential, even central, in the
1920s and 1930s. In the cultural and political sphere, the British influence
was largely unassailable. Port Kembla residents and Australians generally
did fall for Hollywood in the 1930s, though not without a near-hysterical
reaction from some conservative sectors of Australian society who derided
the growing influence of American popular culture and its characteristic
forms: the western film and the western novel. British financial and cultural dominance, however, was significantly dented in the period following
World War II. After 1945 British decline and US ascendancy were more
clearly marked. The war devastated Britain; the human cost, the damage to
infrastructure and ongoing war debts were crippling. The United States had
channelled resources and soldiers to the Pacific in Australia's darkest hour
in early 1942, and the ANZUS Treaty of 1951 formalised Australian political
re-orientation.

This international context remained fundamental to Port Kembla,
especially as the origins of investment capital shifted from regional to
national, national to international, and British to US. Paradoxically, as outside influences diversified, intensified and internationalised, the local context became sharper and more defined, at least during the formative period.
The development of the town created an aggregation of people, homes,
commercial and industrial premises in a distinct regional and local setting.
The global context, together with an outline of local distinctiveness that
follows, provides a starting point for a deeper understanding of life in this
industrial town.

The 1900 Tour

A party of gentleman autodidacts undertake a tour of Port Kembla in 1900; men on holidays from the City with a keen interest in ports, ships and railways. The Illawarra railway line from Sydney, opened in 1883, would have delivered them easily to Wollongong. Once arrived, their route would have taken them south of the town by horse-drawn coach via the road that ran from the end of Corrimal Street past the Wollongong racetrack to Tom Thumb's Lagoon. Coal trimmers and labourers who worked at Port Kembla and lived in Wollongong had constructed a rough footbridge there in the 1880s, and performed makeshift repairs to keep it serviceable.[27]

The lagoon, located between Wollongong and Port Kembla, was a major obstacle for any traveller to Port Kembla. On Sunday mornings Reverend D'arcy Irvine from Wollongong could be seen wading his horse across the lagoon to attend monthly services for the faithful at Port Kembla.[28] The lagoon was a tidal wetland, surrounded by mangroves and reedy swamps, rich in fish and bird life.[29] Fringing the lagoon was low-lying, marshy land, covered with dense scrub and the occasional golden wattle and tea-tree.[30] The lagoon was usually closed to the sea by banks of white sand that extended around the harbour's foreshores. Although rough seas would sometimes open the lagoon to the ocean, its main source of water was Allan's or Salty Creek.

Another road, Five Islands Road, connected Port Kembla to Unanderra (a small village 6 kilometres to the west) but it was poorly drained and inadequate.[31] Bad roads gave Port Kembla a sense of isolation. In 1900 many of those who lived at Port Kembla, public works employees and cokeworkers camped on crown land, were 'undergoing a kind of semi-imprisonment by being isolated so much from the town of Wollongong and elsewhere by want of roads'.[32]

The travellers would see that off the coast lay the Five Islands—Big Island, Flinder's Island, Bass Island, Martin's Island and Rocky Island. These islands protected Port Kembla from the southerly swell, and gave the region its common name in the early nineteenth century of the Five Islands District.

From the edge of the lagoon looking south, the travellers could see the two private coal jetties of Port Kembla. The Southern Coal Company's jetty was just over 300 metres long. The wharfinger, Thomas Frederick Downie, had lived near there since 1882 with his wife Connie Downie, and their four children. Coke from the Federal Cokeworks at Unanderra was also shipped from the jetty. Further south stood the Mount Kembla Coal Company's jetty, smaller than the other jetty at 230 metres, and more protected thanks to the southern headland and the Five Islands. The Mount Lyell

Cokeworks, constructed in late 1899, shadowed the Mount Kembla jetty, where its sixty-two ovens smouldered away, burning coal from the Mount Kembla mine.[33] The cokeworks were the largest structure in Port Kembla, and the smell and hiss of burning coke and steam predominated. The Mount Lyell company was a Tasmanian-based mine and smelter that had sought coke supplies from Illawarra coal to fuel its new furnaces.

If the travellers turned to the south-west towards the Illawarra escarpment they could see, in the foreground, the higher parts of future Port Kembla. Some of this land was open grassland before European occupation, although considerable clearing and fencing had occurred in the previous seventy-five years. It was dotted with dairy cattle, and had been described by one observer in 1839 as 'fine grazing forest and soil. There are numerous swamp oak and causaurinas'.[34] Since this description, intensive grazing had caused considerable deterioration in the environment. In 1897 witnesses at the Public Works Committee inquiry into the construction of Port Kembla harbour described the land as 'very poor' and 'sour land . . . worth nothing to speak of'.[35]

All of this land was part of the Wentworth estate. Originally an 1817 land grant of approximately 890 hectares to David Allan, it was purchased by W. C. Wentworth—well-known explorer, landowner, author, barrister and politician—in 1828. The estate had been divided into thirty-three small holdings of 8 to 12 hectares in the 1840s and leased to family-run dairies. The land was placed in the hands of trustees upon Wentworth's death in 1872, and became known as the Wentworth estate. The local managers of the estate were the O'Donnell family, who also owned land in the Port Kembla area and had been associated with the estate since the 1840s.[36] In 1900 Frank O'Donnell, who lived on the estate in a large homestead on the north-western side of Port Kembla, was the manager. The Wentworth estate and the O'Donnell family became important players in the development of Port Kembla.

Beyond the Wentworth estate was the Berkeley estate, an 1817 land grant to Robert Jenkins.[37] Before European occupation it was a stand of rainforest outlined by open woodland on the lower, boggy flats.[38] This area would become the site of the first blast furnace of the Hoskins Iron and Steel Company Ltd in 1927, but in 1900 the land was only partly cleared and owned by dairy farmers, the Duncans. In the coming years, trees from here would be utilised as fuel for the furnaces and home fires of Port Kembla. These open woodlands formed a boundary at the western edge of Port Kembla.

The houses and company buildings of Port Kembla clung around the two jetties which had given white settlement its impetus. Near the Mount

Kembla Company's jetty were four houses, a store and the school. Likewise, there was only a handful of houses at the Southern Coal Company's jetty. Both coal companies had leases with the Wentworth estate that limited housing construction. As a result, although the port had been in use since 1883, it remained an isolated collection of scattered houses and dairy farms.

Surveying the houses of Port Kembla, our travellers would have found a small number of company homes, surrounded by makeshift camps and tents. West of the Mount Kembla Company jetty were the four houses built by the company for its permanent employees. While some workers with the Mount Lyell Cokeworks and the Public Works Department travelled daily from Wollongong, others lived in tents and roughly constructed huts in this area. In May 1900 the Council health inspector reported that these 'bag and bark gunyahs' were in an insanitary state.[39]

To the southern side of the Mount Kembla Company jetty stood the wharfinger's house, the flagstaff used for signalling ships, and the school. George Sinclair, the wharfinger, had been with the company since 1887. He lived in a cottage not far from the flagstaff that he controlled with his wife, Catherine Sinclair, and their two teenage daughters. Altogether, there were about twelve wooden houses and a few temporary shacks and tents at Port Kembla with a European population of about a hundred.[40]

The school, built in 1879, was originally a Mount Kembla Company house, and later a rope shed. It was without a ceiling and had a blacksmith's forge in one corner. The company had carried out some improvements (the Department of Public Instruction having refused to pay), but the *Illawarra Mercury* described the atmosphere on a summer day in 1894 as being 'more suitable for Turkish bath purposes'. In this space an average of twenty-four children a day came under the watchful eye of Thomas Collins, the schoolmaster. He was remembered as 'a quiet, steady unassuming young man', who had been in charge since the school opened in 1890.[41]

On Sundays local Anglicans used the school for monthly services given by the Reverend Irvine from Wollongong. In November 1900 twelve local residents, their names not recorded, had taken communion. Early on Sunday mornings the harmonium, kept at Thomas Downie's residence, was carried along the beach between the two jetties to the school. Services continued here until 1903, when a new church was built on land donated by the trustees of the Wentworth estate.[42]

Beyond the homes of the Mount Kembla Company workers and the fence enclosing the property, a Public Works railway line from the tip-face of the eastern breakwater to the quarry was under construction. The kilometre-long line was completed in July 1901, running part of the way over an earthen embankment built using horse and cart. Construction of the breakwater was to commence the following month.[43]

The years around the turn of the century were drought-stricken, and the white inhabitants of Port Kembla suffered constant water shortages.[44] Both coal companies used water from Salty Creek, but the water here lived up to the creek's name. In 1899 the manager of the Southern Coal Company, Walter Evans, had complained that the water was 'scarcely fit for the purposes of household supply at present, although unfortunately, some people have to use it'.[45] The flow of water in Salty Creek had ceased due to the drought, and it now consisted of a series of stagnant pools that leached salt from the coastal soil. The Mount Lyell Cokeworks constructed its own dam in 1899, and enlarged it in April 1901. The company had continuing problems with a lack of fresh water and often had to use salt water in its works, much to the detriment of the machinery.[46]

If our travellers ventured to this southern side of Port Kembla, past the quarry towards the grassy slopes of Red Point, they would have encountered Kooris in an area they knew as Nitoka. There were other Koori camp sites around Port Kembla. One camp was in 'thick scrub' on the southern banks of Salty Creek. Koori families like the Saddlers and the Timberys lived in this area, supporting themselves mainly by fishing.[47]

Tom Thumb's Lagoon was another important place for Kooris. In 1972 Koori elder Jack Cummins unsuccessfully sought compensation from the industries at Port Kembla for the loss of sacred land at Salty Creek and Tom Thumb's Lagoon, saying that 'the area of land served as a sacred tribal ground for the earliest Aboriginal tribes in the Illawarra region'. Likewise, Joan Wakeman, another Koori elder, was told by her mother of a large camp of Kooris near Tom Thumb's Lagoon.[48]

One white resident, Thomas Rieck, in his memoirs written in the early 1940s, recalled that land in between the two jetties 'was covered with Black Huts, made from bark of the ti tree [*sic*]'.[49] After the 1898 *Port Kembla Harbour Act*, this land was resumed, and in 1904 the Public Works Department complained to the Aborigines' Protection Board about the presence 'of a number of half castes on the harbour works reserve at Port Kembla'. On a visit to the area the APB found the inhabitants engaged in permanent employment, probably on the waterfront and as fishers, and unwilling to leave.[50] Other traditional camp sites were at Wonwongorong (the hill above Red Point, renamed Hill 60 after World War I) and Coomaditchie, a freshwater lagoon to the south-west of Port Kembla.

The places seen through the eyes of our white travellers had different meanings for Kooris. In 1969 a single grave was uncovered on the slopes of Wonwongorong. The body was buried facing west on its side, according to local Koori custom, and was interred approximately eighty years ago.[51] Not only was Wonwongorong a burial site, it was also a dreaming place. In 1900 the area behind Coomaditchie consisted of steep sandhills covered with low scrub, and contained other sites of significance.[52] These sandhills were extensively mined, starting in the early 1960s, and the fate of these sites is unknown.[53]

In 1900 our Port Kembla travellers would have seen an undefined and scattered place, and searched in vain for a town centre and definite boundary. The place was understood to be of marginal importance in the Illawarra region; this was evident from the location of the Public Works office at Wollongong harbour, despite the big plans for Port Kembla. The list of harbours and ports of the state for 1900, compiled by New South Wales statistician T. A. Coghlan, excluded Port Kembla, although it listed Wollongong, Kiama, Ulladulla and Lake Illawarra, all smaller and less economically important.[54] As Albert Rieck, who was born in one of the Mount Kembla Company houses in 1894, recalled of his childhood: 'She was a pretty lonely place . . . All the cattle straying around there kicking up of a night . . . Yes she was wild then'.[55]

The 1920 Tour

According to the 1921 Census, the Illawarra region had a population of 33 908. The geographical confines of the coast and the escarpment had largely determined the shape of settlement since 1900. Urban consolidation rather than new developments accounted for the population increase. Illawarra's north/south divide remained prominent. Dairying was still important in the south, though slowly declining as people drifted from rural to urban areas. The Central Illawarra Municipality experienced modest population growth from 4664 in 1901 to 5472 in 1921, while the population of Shellharbour municipality, a rural area just south of Central Illawarra, actually declined from 1929 to 1512 during the same period. The north of the Illawarra grew faster. Population in the Bulli Shire, for example, had almost doubled since 1901 due to the expansion in coalmining, and the growth of the tourist trade to Austinmer and Thirroul, largely the result of increasing numbers of Sydney residents seeking accommodation near the beach. Wollongong's continued economic dominance in the region was highlighted by the location of the majority of professional and commercial occupations in that town. Despite Wollongong's commercial dominance, the major industrial developments from 1900 to 1920 were located at Port Kembla.[56]

In 1920, our travellers may have been Sydney day trippers—a group of middle-class women and men who had resisted the allure of the guest houses to the north at Austinmer and Thirroul and journeyed by train from Sydney to Port Kembla. The line was completed in 1916 for general goods, with passenger services beginning in January 1920. From Wollongong the rail line to Port Kembla afforded many vantage points, and a glance south-east would have revealed Tom Thumb's Lagoon, still largely untouched by the industrial expansion that had occurred in the intervening years. Beyond the lagoon was a section of farming land covered in low scrub. All this land would eventually be drained, filled in and sold to industry. Considerable reclamation work in the harbour area had already been carried out by the Public Works Department using waste stone from the quarries. The government railway skirted Tom Thumb's Lagoon, Salty Creek and the future site of the Hoskins Iron and Steel Company Ltd works. In 1920 this site included a stand of eucalyptus trees, some 30 metres tall, frequented by timber cutters.[57] Some beautiful forested areas still surrounded Port Kembla. Among the eucalypts grew wild orchids, sarsparilla and elkhorns.[58] Further south was the government quarry, in its second location since 1900. In 1920 the quarry was dug into the northern aspect of a hill that backs onto Port Kembla. The quarry remains to this day, fenced off, with discarded and aged crushing equipment still visible.

Looking toward the town from their train, the travellers would have seen that the area around the jetties was abandoned to industry; residential Port Kembla now occupied an undulating, hilly section behind the harbour. Much of the area had been cleared either by the farmers of the nineteenth century or by the copper smelting firm established in 1907, Electrolytic Refining and Smelting Company of Australia Ltd (ER&S), which used the trees on its property as furnace fuel.[59] A few large gums remained, but they suffered from the effects of sulphur dioxide emitted from ER&S, and many were dead or dying.[60]

ER&S was 'practically a branch as it were of the wonderful Mount Morgan Company'.[61] Mount Morgan, in partnership with the German firm Aaron Hirsch und Sohn, established ER&S to treat Australian copper- and gold-bearing ore in Australia rather than shipping it to the United States. Mount Morgan was, at the time, one of the richest gold and copper mines in the country, with its mine in Central Queensland and its head office in Melbourne. It held two-thirds of the share capital of £150 000, while the rest was held by Aaron Hirsch. The German company also signed long-term contracts with ER&S, and acted as ER&S's sole agent outside of Australia.[62] Mount Morgan supplied blister copper (that is, 98.5 to 99.5 per cent pure copper) to Port Kembla for further refining from 1909 until 1927, when the original company went into liquidation.[63] Construction work began at ER&S in early 1908 and production started the following year. The investment by a major Australian and international firm was a significant development for the town that hitherto had attracted mostly regional interest.

Metal Manufactures Ltd (MM) was the other major firm in Port Kembla by 1920. MM was incorporated in March 1916 and construction work began in early 1918.[64] The company was an initiative of two large Australian copper mines, Mount Morgan and the Mount Lyell Mining and Railway Company, together with their English partners, British Insulated and Helsby Cables Ltd. As a subsidiary of Mount Morgan, ER&S was also a shareholding company, and MM used refined copper from ER&S to fashion rod and wire products.[65] MM was some distance from the main part of the town; nevertheless, the rattle and crash of industry, electric motors, steam engines, furnaces and rolling equipment would have greeted the ear of residents and travellers—twenty-four hours a day when there were orders to fill.

The town was now physically dominated by the buildings and chimneys of the major works, ER&S, MM and the Mount Lyell Cokeworks. The larger industries, ER&S and MM, had three stacks each. ER&S's largest towered 64 metres above the town and constantly emanated a wispish white smoke of dubious chemical content—a mix of sulphur dioxide, lead and acid gases.

Port Kembla railway station served as our travellers' introduction to the town itself. Port Kembla was no longer the isolated locality of 1900. Trains and motor omnibuses had increased links with nearby towns. Water-side workers no longer had to ford lagoons or construct their own bridges to get to work. Roads had been constructed, although horses and carriages

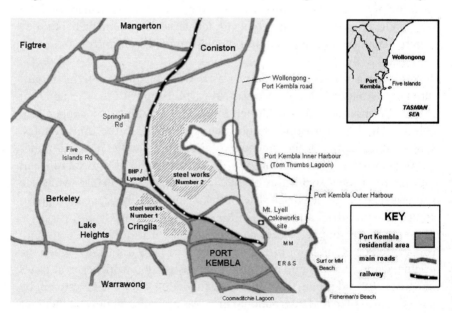

Port Kembla–Wollongong area

tore away at the dirt or base-metal surfaces.[66] Motor cars had made their appearance in the town too, although ownership was confined to wealthy staff from the local industries and local doctors.

The railway station was surrounded by small industry, the South Coast Timber and Trading Company on the harbour side, and the Ulladulla Silica and Firebrick Company on the western side. Across the road were the ER&S company houses, twenty-four in Darcy Road and ten around the corner in Military Road. Their orderly placement in neat rows contrasted with the rest of the town that had developed unplanned, bar the whims of real estate agents and land surveyors. Covering the higher ground and the area around the main street, Wentworth Street, was a ramshackle collection of weatherboard houses and stores. Near the public school were houses constructed by ER&S and MM for senior staff and their families, located in a street tellingly named Private Lane. As we have seen, some locals had other names: 'Pommy Lane' in view of the number of senior staff at the local works who were from England, or 'Rotten Row', an expression of class feeling from residents who found the pretension and privilege of Private Lane too much to bear.[67]

The town's boundaries were now defined by five subdivisions of the Wentworth estate and one government subdivision, all made between 1909 and 1919. The older parts of Port Kembla—Military Road, Wentworth, Kembla, Allan, and O'Donnell Streets—were densely settled, while the fringes of the town, consisting of the most recent fifth subdivision (the Avenues, Bland and Horne Streets), formed a scattered, variously developed edge of town.[68] Nevertheless, it would have been clear to our travellers where Port Kembla finished, for there was a definite sense of a distinct town. By 1921 the town's white population had grown to 1622 people, living in 318 dwellings.[69]

As Port Kembla gained a defined shape, living space for Kooris became more restricted. Gone were the scattered camps of 1900. In fact, our travellers may have overlooked the Kooris completely, for they were now located exclusively on the fringes of town. In 1920 Kooris lived on and nearby Hill 60 and near Coomaditchie Lagoon. In 1915 the APB estimated that there were 60 Kooris at Port Kembla, 22 men, 13 women and 25 children. By 1920 the police census counted 39 Kooris at Port Kembla.[70] This was most probably an underestimation, although the influenza pandemic of 1919 had severely affected the local Koori population.

The water supply problems of 1900 had been alleviated, but still the Water Board did not supply all houses in Port Kembla. Houses in Wentworth Street and Military Road were connected, but the board found it hard to keep pace with residential development. O'Donnell Street and Bass

Street, opened up by the third subdivision in 1916, were not connected until 1920.[71] Likewise, only 101 premises in the town had access to electric power. Approximately half of these were ER&S staff houses, one-quarter belonged to workers from ER&S, and the remainder were local shops and public buildings.[72] There were few streetlights in Port Kembla. Apart from lights near ER&S and those located on the business premises, darkness prevailed in surrounding streets.

Years of unplanned growth and ineffectual councils ensured that the public face of Port Kembla was not pleasant. Conditions at the two hotels, the Great Eastern and the Port Kembla Hotel, were typical of the public health problems plaguing the town. Should the men among our travellers have acquired a thirst, they would have found the bar of the Great Eastern Hotel, in the words of one licensing sub-inspector, 'filthy' or, according to a newspaper man from Bega, 'rather a rough shop'.[73] Both the Great Eastern and the Port Kembla Hotel discharged effluent onto a block of land in Military Road, opposite Allan Street. A Board of Health inspector reported in 1919: 'The surface of the [affected] ground of about 100ft by 30ft was saturated with the effluent. It was discoloured, slimy and smelt offensive, and as the ground was water logged, the offensive matter flowed into the street water table.'[74] The hotels were busiest every fortnight on 'pay Thursday' and after work on Saturdays when men would gather before the day's cricket or football match. The hotels represented a male space and all of the customers and those boarding in the hotels were men. Almost a century later, Port Kembla's hotels still appear to be exclusively male spaces, with the exception of the female bar staff and lingerie-clad waitresses and performers who grace two of the three hotels.

Meanwhile our female travellers, barred from the hotels, may have noticed that the shops were, by contrast, spaces frequented by women, both as customers in the daily task of shopping, and as workers in the family-run stores of the town. The commercial centre of Port Kembla was a busy area and the focus of local life. At the northern end of Wentworth Street, J. G. Fairley's, with the slogan the 'Universal Providers', announced the beginning of commercial Port Kembla. There were two distinct shopping areas, one extending south from Fairley's to the Great Eastern Hotel, and the other at the southern end of Wentworth Street, where the road rose up an incline. In the middle stood the post office, the Bank of New South Wales, and a few vacant lots with cows and horses staring through rickety fences. A small 'green' at the corner of Allan and Wentworth Streets was the venue for Sunday afternoon recitals by the town band. Some shops showed a remarkable degree of diversity in the services they provided. Upon entering A. Hymes & Co. our travellers could have bought a house, land, insurance or used furniture. Mrs Sarah Middleton's newsagency sold newspapers, drapery, clothing, fancy goods and stationery. She counted confectionery and soft drinks as 'a speciality' and ran a lending library.[75]

By 1920 Port Kembla had a commercial centre and possessed distinct boundaries. Its isolation had decreased as roads and railways opened up access to the surrounding towns of Wollongong, Dapto and Unanderra. The town also began to display some of the drawbacks of unplanned urban growth and industrialisation. Port Kembla was still located in a beautiful natural setting, but this environment was increasingly under assault by industrial and urban change.

The 1940 Tour

Illawarra's population had increased to approximately 50 000 by 1940, with considerable growth in the municipalities of Wollongong and the Northern Illawarra. In the Wollongong Municipality the population rose from 6708 in 1921 to 18 116 in 1947. In the Northern Illawarra the population for the same years grew from 6088 to 11 810.[76] Although Wollongong and northern towns like Bulli and Thirroul experienced some industrial growth, industrialisation was still mainly centred on Port Kembla. The size and scale of the Port Kembla's industries, however, had wide-ranging regional effects. The whole region had undergone considerable centralisation and integration. The links between the Illawarra region and Port Kembla strengthened and the boundaries between the locality and the surrounding region blurred.

In 1940 our travellers (perhaps a family visiting relatives in the town) would have motored along the Port Kembla–Wollongong road and negotiated its unsealed surface, and the unmarked train crossings. In peak times scores of men on bicycles rode to work from their Wollongong homes. As in 1920 industry dominated the town, its factories and buildings surrounding it to the north and east. In 1920 Port Kembla's major pollution problems had been caused by an amalgam of industrial, commercial and residential pollution. By 1940 industry was the centre of the problem. Our travellers would have been unable to avoid dust, fumes and acrid smells in their tour of the major works.[77]

Considerable industrial development had occurred in the intervening twenty years. Australian Fertilizers had opened in June 1921, producing superphosphate for the state's wheat farmers. The process of roasting the ore produced sulphuric acid and various fluxes (materials used to remove undesirable substances like sand, ash or dirt from molten mixtures), which ER&S utilised in its refinement processes. ER&S was a joint shareholder in the company, and as with MM, maintained close links with its staff and operations. During the early 1940s Australian Fertilizers emitted significant levels of hydrogen fluoride due to the high fluoride levels in the phosphate ore. In the absence of pollution awareness and control technology, the plant was a major contributor to dust pollution at Port Kembla.[78]

The most important addition to Port Kembla's industrial landscape was Hoskins Iron and Steel Company Ltd. The Hoskins family entered the iron and steel industry in early 1908 when they purchased William Sandford's works at Lithgow.[79] Always conscious of the drawbacks of Lithgow, they had planned to move to Port Kembla since at least 1916, when they purchased a coalmine and coke ovens at Wongawilli near Dapto. In 1920 they acquired 154 hectares of land from the Wentworth estate.[80] This land was situated to the north-west of Port Kembla almost half-way to Wollongong, a location that marked a break with previous industrial expansion, which had closely bordered the town. After prolonged negotiations with the state government, the Hoskins Iron and Steel Company Ltd began construction of its new works in January 1927 and the blast furnace was commissioned in August 1928. The expansion to Port Kembla required considerable capital, and Hoskins had been seeking partners for the formation of a new company since 1924. As we have seen, the result was the formation in May 1928 of a new company, Australian Iron and Steel Pty Ltd (AI&S), with Hoskins in partnership with three British companies: the steelmakers Baldwins, the engineering firm Dorman and Long, and the shipping company Howard Smith.

A drop in steel prices and demand at the onset of the Great Depression financially weakened AI&S. The depression starved the company of capital to invest in new machinery at Port Kembla, and severely disrupted the proper establishment of the new works. Consequently, pig iron produced at Port Kembla had to be railed to Lithgow for rolling, until final closure of the Lithgow works in late 1931. AI&S still recorded profits, but the company was in no state to defend itself against the takeover by BHP in 1935.[81]

By 1940 AI&S had two blast furnaces, an open hearth furnace, a cokeworks and processing mills.[82] Other industries such as John Lysaght (Australia) Pty Ltd, Commonwealth Oil Refineries Ltd and Commonwealth Rolling Mills Pty Ltd (CRM) were established by 1940, usually as subsidiaries of, or joint ventures with, BHP. With the economic power of BHP behind it, AI&S could dominate industrial development at Port Kembla. A turning point was the sale of large amounts of crown land to BHP in 1936. Control of this land gave AI&S major influence over which companies were established at Port Kembla. John Lysaght produced rolled sheets and galvanised iron and opened in 1937. Commonwealth Oil Refineries, which also began production in 1937, was a petrol blending facility which utilised by-products from the BHP coke ovens. CRM officially opened in 1939 and was a division of Lysaght and an American company American Rolling Mill Company

(Australia) Pty Ltd. The company manufactured finished sheet iron for cars, white goods and steel furniture.[83]

In 1940 war-time demand caused AI&S and ER&S to set record levels of production, and consequently pollute more than ever. Steelmaking at AI&S produced particles of iron, nickel and manganese as waste. The coke ovens gave off acid gases and sulphur dioxide. ER&S was estimated to be emitting almost 25 tonnes of sulphur dioxide a day in the early 1950s. A bag house to capture the larger particles from the furnace fume was installed in 1946, but before then the sulphur dioxide plume contained significant amounts of lead and arsenic compounds.[84]

There is little documentary evidence about the extent or effects of such pollution. Respiratory ailments were probably common, and those with asthma and sensitive skin suffered.[85] My grandfather, Hugh Halcrow, worked for ER&S in the bluestone mill in the late 1930s. Although he wore thick flannel shirts, the potent mix of sweat and bluestone gave him irritating red rashes. The smell of sulphur dioxide sent those with vegetable gardens rushing out to water to prevent their plants burning.[86] Houses had to be regularly painted due to the acidic action of the some of the fallout, and clean washing was often soiled. Measurements of pollutants are un-available for 1940, but they were no doubt high. Ann R. M. Young claimed that 'before 1979 lead levels [at Port Kembla] were not markedly different from those in the CBD [central business district] of Sydney'.[87] More gen-erally, in 1960, 10 grams of suspended matter per square metre per month was blanketing the Port Kembla and Wollongong area.[88]

In 1940 the lakes and waterways too were suffering from industrial pollution. From 1937, CRM discharged pollutants into Salty Creek and Tom Thumb's Lagoon. Walter Bailey, a timber cutter and later waterside worker remembers vividly the effects of CRM on Tom Thumb's Lagoon: 'When CRM started that seemed to be the start of it. We then began to see fish, cungi and crabs dying. We were told that this was the sulphuric or pickle acid. This acid also killed all the fish in the little creek behind CRM.'[89] CRM also discharged into the harbour. Frank Gamble fished off the eastern break-water throughout the 1930s: 'We could catch as many [fish] as we wanted. Then CRM would discharge their acid into the harbour. You could see it coming across to where you were fishing. It didn't do much to increase the catch.'[90]

What our travellers found by way of pollution depended on the weather on the day and their exact location in Port Kembla. Waterside workers, steelworkers and those who lived in Wollongong Road and O'Neil Street were subjected to dust pollution from coal loading and emissions from AI&S.[91] The dust was worse the stronger the wind, especially during winter southerlies. At the southern end of the town, ER&S workers and residents in nearby Military Road, Wentworth Street and the Avenues were affected by north-easterly winds, most common in summer. Recent monitoring of lead levels has shown the area adjacent to the ER&S stack (including the former site of the Port Kembla Primary School) had consistently higher readings than Warrawong, only 2 kilometres away, so most of the pollutants dropped quickly in the vicinity of the stack.[92] Whatever the influence of the weather, industrial pollution was a significant factor in the lives of all people at Port Kembla.

Our travellers would have found that residential Port Kembla, with a population of about 5000, possessed what Vance Palmer called the characteristic 'fugitive look' of Australian settlements.[93] A Council report from 1943 stated that there were 380 'sub-normal' homes in the shire, 250 of which were shacks and tents.[94] Most noticeable of these was the Temporary Settlement in Wattle Street, Warrawong. Housing had become a major issue in state politics by the end of the 1930s, and conditions at Port Kembla came under scrutiny from metropolitan newspapers. The *Sydney Morning Herald* and the *Daily Telegraph* published exposés on Flinders Street at Port Kembla, and this public attention, together with pressure from the Council and local politicians, forced the state government to act.[95] The construction of the so-called Temporary Settlement in 1938 was the result. The Department of Works and Local Government spent £24 000 building 150 houses, with one, three or four rooms. The Single Men's Quarters were 1.5 metres by 1.8 metres with weatherboard and canvas walls. The internal walls stopped short of the ceiling (the gap was later covered with chicken wire) and there was no space for food storage.[96] The single men refused to move in (staying in their camps at Flinders Street) until changes were made and the whole settlement earned the bitter unofficial title Spoonerville, after the Minister in charge, E. S. Spooner.[97]

There were other camps around the fringes of town besides Spoonerville. The Official Camp (as it was named in 1932) for the unemployed near Coomaditchie Lagoon consisted of huts and shacks controlled by the Council. A standpipe serviced the area and there were 'conveniences' with bag and linen walls. Mr Khan, who had previously tried to set up shop in Flinders Street, operated a store at the camp. The camp was good enough for people to live in, but not good enough for shops, according to the Council's health inspector: 'The shop was found to be conducted with all due regard to cleanliness. The surrounding environment, however, is one in which food for human consumption should not be permitted to be stored or offered for sale.'[98] Bessie Lockwood came to the Official Camp from the coalmining town of Cessnock in the Hunter Valley of New South Wales in 1937: 'You had to carry your water around in a kerosene tin. You cooked outside on an open grate. You boiled your clothes in a kerosene tin. We had a tent that was very holed and very thin. You could see the stars at night, and the rain came in.'[99]

An inspection of the more settled residential parts of Port Kembla may not have provided a respite for our travellers. They may have also stumbled across the filthy drains in Foster Street, or the 'offensive street water tables' in Cowper Street and Fifth Avenue caused by the 'flat clayey nature of these localities'. A drain running from Fourth to Fifth Avenue was believed to be the source of several cases of infectious disease throughout the 1930s.[1] These problems were caused by a lack of kerbing and guttering and inadequate drainage, though Council had made some progress in cleaning up the public space of Port Kembla. The older, more populated areas like Wentworth Street, Military Road, Allan and Church Streets were all kerbed and guttered by 1940; rest rooms were built in Allan Street in 1939, and nearly 5 hectares of parkland were dedicated in Robertson Street in the same year.[2] The most impressive addition to the town facilities was the Olympic Pool, opened in 1938. It proved very popular with locals, with 6519 people attending in the first two weeks of January 1940.[3]

Our travellers would have found the commercial heart of Port Kembla, Wentworth Street, a busy and vibrant area. There were twenty-six stores that sold foodstuffs including bakers, butchers, grocers, smallgoods, fruit markets and milk bars. In addition there were numerous professional services such as dentists, doctors (in Fitzwilliam Street, just off Wentworth Street), solicitors and estate agents. Clothing retail and repair was the next most common category, including tailors, dressmakers, boot repairers and a shoe store.[4] They would have also seen that the storekeepers lived where they worked. Residences were commonly built above or behind shops. Of the 110 storekeepers in Port Kembla in 1940, 34 lived in Wentworth Street.[5]

This concentration of people and businesses caused some sanitary problems. Behind the clean shop fronts and scrubbed counters, the rear of many shops contained open drains, rubbish bins and jerry-built sheds. In 1939 the Council health inspector reported that 'drastic measures' were necessary to 'clean up and remove dilapidated sheds etc.' in Wentworth Street.[6] One property was found 'to be improperly drained and in a state of disrepair'. The tenant kept four horses in a small yard which was 'covered with a coating of horse manure and offensive odours were causing a nuisance'.[7]

By 1940 the areas of Port Kembla that were considered desirable had changed. New land on the hill overlooking the port was subdivided from the mid-1930s. Bland, Robertson and Donaldson Streets experienced an influx of staff and senior management from the local industries.[8] These new areas of affluence joined the older ER&S and MM housing around Private Lane. This spatial rearrangement of areas of privilege would eventually culminate in the staff moving out of Port Kembla altogether to the affluent suburbs of Mount Keira, Mangerton and West Wollongong after World War II.

Coomaditchie and Hill 60 continued to be the main areas of Koori occupation. Eleven Koori families lived at the Official Camp near Coomaditchie.[9] The Koori section was to the west of Coomaditchie Lagoon and was known as Frogs Hollow. Places like Coomaditchie were not under direct control of the Aborigines' Protection Board, but were monitored by police.[10] Hill 60 offered some protection from white contact, being further from the town and in an area whites generally avoided.[11] The Council health inspector visited in March 1939 and reported that there were no sanitary problems.[12] In late 1939 Hill 60 was taken over by the Department of Defence and this placed pressure on Kooris still living on the hill. They were eventually forced to move in September 1942, some going to Coomaditchie, others to Nowra and Jervis Bay and a few to La Perouse.

War had not left Port Kembla untouched. Almost 200 militia had moved into huts between the beach and MM, and had fortified this area with barbed wire, trenches and two 6-inch guns.[13] Construction work to fortify Hill 60 proceeded throughout the early 1940s. The travellers might have ventured to the Whiteway Theatre in Wentworth Street to attend a 'Win the War' rally. A crowd of 200 was addressed by M. F. Bruxner, Deputy Premier and Minister for Transport:

> Dark stormy days are ahead of us but with that great courage that we always display I feel sure we will come out on the right side . . . The British people had their heads in the scrum to use a football phrase. But they would get the ball and carry it on to victory.[14]

These rallies ended in patriotic singing and sometimes with men enlisting. Afterwards the official party adjourned to the Black Cat, Port Kembla's popular new milk bar, for supper. The people of Port Kembla had responded to the patriotic call and in the first year of war had contributed £20 000 to comfort funds, war bonds and Red Cross collections.[15]

For the white inhabitants, the future of Port Kembla in 1900 seemed promising. The state government was to spend £200 000 on the new harbour, and the Cokeworks was expanding. It was a year of optimism as people looked to a possible iron works and lobbied for a new school; there were predictions of a population centre of tens of thousands. But the town itself was barely established. It was wrongly placed on maps and not even mentioned in T. A. Coghlan's tome on New South Wales. For Koori inhabitants 1900 had different meanings. As Port Kembla grew they were slowly, yet inexorably, forced out of their traditional camp sites and foraging areas. The process of industrialisation which began in earnest that year sped up the forces that were separating Kooris from their land and cutting off their access to abundant food supplies in the area. Eventually industrialisation destroyed the environment which supported that natural fecundity.

Port Kembla in 1920 was more accessible and spatially more defined than in 1900. The town was also more self-consciously an industrial one, with a fading rural past. The dominance of the factories, the sulphur dioxide emissions from ER&S and intensive land clearing had established the town's 'industrial' image, yet this image was moderated by surrounding lagoons and beaches and there were still ample reminders of its dairying background.

By 1940 Port Kembla had assumed a wider significance as the location of the nation's second steel works and third-largest port. BHP, the largest company in Australia, dominated the town as ER&S had done in an earlier period. Port Kembla had become the epitome of a town created by industrial capitalism, though the scale of the new industries was increasingly obscuring its boundaries and distinctiveness. The formative period of industrial society not only changed the physical appearance of Port Kembla. It also had major effects on the formal economy, and that is the subject of the next chapter.

2

The Formal Economy to 1940

IN 1900 GEORGE NEAVES, a dairy farmer at Port Kembla, worked a small 9-hectare farm with his family, and occasionally supplemented the household's income by working for one of his better-off neighbours. In 1940 Morgan Simon had been married one year and earned a weekly wage at Metal Manufactures Ltd (MM) as a leading hand. He had no other income, nor did his wife do any paid work.[1] The formative period of industrial society, corresponding to the first half of the twentieth century, was marked by the transformation of the local labour market. The change from a rural to an industrial economy created new working-class occupations typical of many industrial areas. Despite the growth of industrial wage labour, intermittent work declined only gradually, with notable exceptions such as the recession of 1920–22 and the Great Depression. During the formative period intermittent work patterns remained an important factor informing local politics and culture. This period also witnessed the growth of a viable town-based or local labour market that absorbed regional influences and eventually counterbalanced them by the 1920s. The working class dominated this labour market, but a small though important middle class and petit-bourgeoisie were also established locally.

This chapter covers the economic transformation of the formative period from 1900 to 1940, providing the context for understanding important social and political features of the Port Kembla experience. Industrialisation transformed the rural economy that George Neaves worked in and dominated the industrial economy in which Morgan Simon laboured; it had two decisive effects on society at Port Kembla. The first was the creation of a formal economy based on industrial waged work, and the division of the labour market into three classes: working class, petit-bourgeois and middle class. New industrial workplaces, where working conditions were poor and industrial conflict common, were central to the development of class identity and class politics at Port Kembla. The second effect of indus-trialisation was to facilitate town growth and help establish a town-centred labour market by the 1920s, important foundations for local identity and localist politics. In the 1930s the scale of industrial development over-whelmed this local labour market and produced a more regionalised formal economy, a change that ultimately heralded a political and administrative shift from locality to region. These two contradictory effects of industrialis-ation were fundamental to political life in the town.

The analysis of class and class structure generally has a national focus, but local expressions of an overarching class structure contain complications that need to be examined.[2] Thrift and Williams, for example, argue that:

> Classes can no longer be thought of as unified and uniquely determined objects set in an abstract space-less realm. Given the fact that classes are geographical objects, they can never be anything but fragmented and overdetermined . . . In other words, the relations of production (and reproduction) do not float above places. They are constituted within them.[3]

At Port Kembla this 'fragment' included a 'working class', defined as those who sell their labour power for income or resources.[4] A 'bourgeoisie' or 'ruling class' as such was not present, and their local representatives—managers, engineers, foremen and clerks—almost never owned shares and seldom had a controlling influence on the production processes. These workers in supervisory positions or with technical qualifications are defined as 'middle class', sandwiched between the working class and the bour-geoisie.[5] The local experience of class also indicates the need for a separate class grouping for those who laboured in the stores and small businesses of Port Kembla, the 'petit-bourgeoisie', or at times 'storekeepers' for brevity.[6]

There are no Commonwealth census figures that cover Port Kembla exclusively, so this chapter utilises occupational data from electoral rolls. Occupation is only one measure of class, but by collating this information from selected electoral rolls from 1900 to 1940 the economic dimensions of Port Kembla's transformation can be outlined. The principal weakness of electoral roll data is its coverage of women's work. From 1900 to 1940 only 3 to 4 per cent of all enrolled women recorded occupations on the electoral rolls other than 'domestic duties'. Evidence beyond the gaze of state officials and census takers suggests that some women were active in the formal econ-omy, but still registered their occupations as 'domestic duties'. For example, Alexander Pascoe, a blacksmith at the Public Works Department quarry, stated before the Licensing Court in 1914 that 'his wife kept a boarding house at Port Kembla and has done for about 11 years'.[7] At that time she housed twenty-five boarders who paid eighteen shillings each a week, yet her occupation is recorded on the 1912 Electoral Roll as 'domestic duties'.

Electoral rolls also overlooked itinerant male workers. Their constant movement in and out of the town often disqualified them because of the six-
month residential clause for voter enrolment. Similarly, workers under
twenty-one were excluded from this picture of the formal economy given
by the electoral rolls. A combination of sources is required to fill in the
picture of working life at Port Kembla. While it is clear that the electoral
rolls underestimate women and children's participation in the formal economy, industrialising Port Kembla offered few jobs to these workers, in what
was an overwhelmingly male-dominated formal economy.

The Beginnings of Industrialisation at Port Kembla

The character of the Port Kembla labour market was initially fluid and
indistinct, as men moved in and out according to fluctuating demand. The
labour market that developed from 1900 to 1907 was ever-changing and
open to outside influence, particularly from the surrounding towns of the
Illawarra region. In this early period, the importance of regional labour
mirrored the importance of regional capital.

In 1900 the Public Works Department opened a quarry, built a railway
between the quarry and the site of the eastern breakwater, and began
reclamation work on swampy land around the harbour. The quarry was
exhausted by 1906, and a new site was developed at Reid's Hill, which was
used until 1928. Another quarry at Gillian's Hill, 2 kilometres west of Port
Kembla, was then opened. Work on the eastern breakwater continued intermittently until 1937. Vulnerability to storm damage and settling of stone
required continuous maintenance.[8] The Public Works Department also
initiated major projects such as the construction of the low-level jetty
(1911), the northern breakwater (1912), the Port Kembla Power House
(1914) and new coal loading facilities (1915).[9] Along with the harbour
works, the Mount Lyell Cokeworks (which our travellers had seen at the
base of the Mount Kembla company's jetty), was at least initially successful
and was prospering to the extent that it had produced more than company
requirements and coke was sold to 'outside sources'.[10]

The labour market developing around Port Kembla was characterised
by uncertainty. Harbour maintenance and quarry work employed 80 to 100
men, and itinerant workers supplemented this workforce in times of peak
demand. However, work at the Public Works Department was highly susceptible to the climate of New South Wales politics. During 1903 and 1904
the alleged excessive expenditure on public works undertaken by the state
government under Premier John See was a major issue, and this ultimately

resulted in cutbacks in the Port Kembla workforce. In May 1903, thirty-two men were dismissed from the workforce of 100. Another thirty were discharged in August 1903.[11] The election of the Liberal–Reform state government in August 1904 led to a more cautious approach to expenditure and lower employment levels.[12]

After some initial success, the Mount Lyell Cokeworks also endured setbacks in the 1900s that threw the future of the plant into doubt. The Mount Kembla mine disaster of July 1902, in which ninety-six miners were killed, closed the mine, and the Cokeworks was forced to find other sources of coal.[13] These setbacks occurred in the context of decreasing demand for coke from Mount Lyell in Tasmania, where new smelting techniques adopted in late 1902 more than halved coke consumption in 1903.[14]

The uncertain future of local industries limited Port Kembla's development. Between 1900 and 1907 it was a town where paid work came and went, where labour flowed in and out according to the rhythms of production. Consequently, few workers settled locally and those from nearby regional towns were well placed to fill jobs not taken by itinerants. Many Wollongong waterfront workers, for example, found work at Port Kembla as the harbour at Wollongong declined in importance and the Port Kembla coal trade boomed. In 1891, 79 692 tonnes of coal were shipped through Port Kembla. By 1895 this figure had risen to 192 171 tonnes.[15] By 1908, 90 per cent of the 50 to 60 coal trimmers employed at the harbour were from Wollongong.[16]

John Cronan was typical of workers from regional towns who found employment at Port Kembla. Cronan was foreman at the Public Works quarry from 1900 to 1908, and had a reputation as 'a true disciplinarian'. A man in his forties, he lived in Corrimal, a coalmining town 15 kilometres north of Port Kembla, with his wife and ten children, until his death in a quarry accident. Many of the labourers in the quarry were also from nearby towns. Patrick Mulligan was a Public Works labourer and travelled to work daily from his Dapto home, 13 kilometres away. He too died in an accident in 1909.[17]

The regional influence on the Port Kembla labour market was strengthened in 1907 when the Dapto-based smelter, Australian Smelting Corporation Ltd, purchased approximately 26 hectares of land at Port Kembla from the state government, and began relocating its works to the port.[18] The Smelting Company of Australia Ltd had originally established the smelter at Dapto in 1895 for the smelting of lead, silver, gold and copper. After various changes in management and ownership, the works abruptly closed in March 1905. The Dapto company's failure related to its poor access to a seaport, an expensive sulphuric acid plant constructed in 1903, and increasing competition from German firms.[19]

In 1907 a re-capitalised company with a new board of directors began moving the Dapto works to its new Port Kembla site. Many of the Dapto employees transferred with the works, and itinerant labourers were also attracted to the area, so that by March 1907 Australian Smelting Corporation Ltd employed 150 men and had thirty drays engaged in construction work. 'Hundreds of people are camped here' reported the *Illawarra Mercury*, and later that month noted that 'the place was a hive of activity and new arrivals are daily reported'.[20] However, a lack of capital and a drop in world base metal prices led to a sudden halt in October 1907, and the company went into liquidation in January 1908.[21] As late as November 1908 there was still hope of re-forming the company, and its agents searched Queensland mines looking for suitable ores.

The failure of Australian Smelting Corporation Ltd left scores of men waiting for work as rumours and reports suggested that the company would re-form or find the necessary capital. However, they waited in vain: production never began.[22] The only visible reminder of the Dapto company's attempt to relocate to Port Kembla was a caretaker's hut, the foundations of a furnace and a cleared and levelled factory site.

From 1900 to 1907, then, the beginnings of industrialisation provided paid work for increasing numbers of mostly unskilled male labourers. The result of the fluctuating and unpredictable demand for industrial workers, however, was domination of the labour market by non-locals—itinerant workers or men from nearby towns. It would take the arrival of a new large employer at Port Kembla to help build a local economy, break down the regional basis of the labour market, and provide the economic context for the development of the town.

Consolidation of the Local Labour Market

The establishment of a new copper smelter at Port Kembla, the Electrolytic Refining and Smelting Company of Australia Ltd (ER&S), provided the basis for a viable local labour market. This labour market centred on Port Kembla, though it had regional influence as well. The eventual success of ER&S solidified the emerging patterns of an industrial class structure at Port Kembla, and initiated the expansion of the town-centred labour market during the formative period.

In its first few years, however, ER&S came close to failure. The Port Kembla site was announced in January 1908, and production began the following year. By mid-1909 the directors were considering closure 'till copper market recovery', but the company's prospects brightened in 1910 when it secured a large contract to refine blister copper from the Mount

Lyell Mining and Railway Company. This helped ER&S through the early years, and led to the first small profit of £757 in 1912.[23]

The scale of ER&S and its provision of fairly regular paid work attracted workers to settle locally, and the outlines of a local class structure became more established. Construction work at ER&S, started in 1908, employed 250 men, and when the smelter was officially opened in February 1909, 300 were engaged.[24] From 1908 the future of Port Kembla was increasingly linked to the economic fortunes of ER&S, and the make-up of Port Kembla's paid workforce was increasingly dominated by the industrial working class. By 1912 the working class made up 90 per cent of all paid workers living in Port Kembla (461 altogether), with ER&S workers forming 65 per cent of the town's workforce.[25]

ER&S improved its economic position from 1912, but there was a major hurdle for the company to overcome before its future was assured—the economic effects of World War I. Among other things, the war led to a major reorganisation of the Australian copper market.[26] German firms, which had dominated the market, lost their position through a political campaign carried out in state and federal parliaments to eject 'enemy' firms. The Commonwealth *Trading with the Enemy Act*, passed in November 1914, required companies to register their contracts with German firms with the Comptroller-General.[27] In 1915 both the Commonwealth and New South Wales governments introduced legislation cancelling contracts with German companies.

This legislation and its economic consequences threatened ER&S's major customer and sole overseas agent, the large German cartel Aaron Hirsch und Sohn. Rumours that ER&S would close circulated immediately after the declaration of war, and were officially denied in the local press.[28]

From the beginning of 1915 increasing political pressure forced ER&S to distance itself from its German contacts. In January the Superintendent reported that three Germans employed at ER&S had been 'paid off'. In July 1915 the Commonwealth Attorney-General, William Morris Hughes, threatened to declare ER&S an enemy company. Consequently, in August changes were made to the company's Articles of Association to allow for the removal of a parcel of shares held by the estate of the late Siegfried Hirsch, a former principal of Aaron Hirsch und Sohn.[29]

Once this issue had been dealt with, ER&S benefited enormously from the war. War-time demand for copper and the beginning of imperial preference signalled a period of prosperity and expansion. There was a profit of £10 742 for the year ending October 1915, a dividend was paid to shareholders, and additions to the factory costing £45 000 were planned.[30] This success was a turning point for Port Kembla. After 1914, with ER&S booming, the industrial future of Port Kembla was assured, and the initial period of uncertainty ended. While occasional downturns produced some unemployment or underemployment, the directors of the company never considered complete closure again until the downturn of the late 1920s. The viability of ER&S became the foundation for the growth of the town.

In 1916 ER&S's position was consolidated with the formation of a new firm, to be situated at Port Kembla, that would be a major consumer of the company's refined copper, Metal Manufactures Ltd (MM). The formation of MM was the result of the movement of Anglo-Australian capital into the gap left by ousted German firms. With ER&S's major German customer lost, the Collins House Group, with the encouragement of the Commonwealth government, moved to secure a domestic market for refined copper.[31] MM was a vital part of this plan. Together, ER&S and MM formed the major industries at Port Kembla until the late 1920s, and dominated the local labour market.

MM had three distinct parts: the Wire Factory, the Telephone Cable Factory (or the TCF as it was more commonly known) and the Tube Factory. The Wire Factory began operations in 1919 and was the most productive part of MM before 1939, producing 60 to 80 per cent of the company's total output.[32] The Tube Factory began operations in 1921, initially employing about 90 men. This factory produced copper tubes and piping for boilers, locomotives and other general purposes. The TCF was constructed in 1922 and commenced operations in 1923, producing cotton and paper-covered conductors, mostly for the expanding telephone, tram and household electrical market.

The establishment of MM underlined the developing industrial character of Port Kembla, and further centred the labour market on the town. The workforce at MM soon outnumbered ER&S. By 1924, 815 were employed by MM and 350 by ER&S, with another smaller firm, Australian Fertilizers Ltd, employing between 60 and 100 men.[33] The expansion of the number of industrial jobs available at Port Kembla encouraged local settlement and town development, vital preconditions for the growth of local loyalty, and ultimately vital for the development of the localist politics.

Conditions in the new industrial workplaces also fostered the growth of unions at Port Kembla, and helped forge an industrial class consciousness vital for class politics. At the Reid's Hill quarry in the late 1900s, where average wages were between eight and nine shillings a day, brittle stone made working conditions difficult and dangerous. Steam-powered drills were used to bore deep holes in the rock face into which explosive charges were placed. Large rocks would collapse with the explosion or remain precariously balanced on the rock face. These pieces had to be broken into 27-tonne blocks and loaded onto railway trucks to be sent off to the breakwater for tipping. After a series of accidents in 1908 and 1909, some fatal, quarrymen at Port Kembla, under the leadership of officials from the United Labourers' Protective Society, stopped work and sought a one shilling per day wage increase because of the dangerous conditions.[34]

ER&S workers too suffered hot, dusty, dangerous, and sometimes deadly working conditions. Molten copper fatally burned Joseph Warrington, who was operating an overhead crane when a pot of molten copper exploded below him. Most such explosions occurred when molten material contacted water. Thomas Wellings was killed when the head of a hammer being used by a workmate flew off and struck him in the head. Frank Le Gros was run over by an electric trolley.[35]

Once through the furnaces, copper ingots were transferred to the tank-house, where highly refined copper was produced. The tankhouse contained none of the extreme heat of the furnaces, but had its own nasty features. The tanks contained an electrically charged solution of hydrogen sulphide and copper sulphide at a temperature of 74 degrees Celsius. Every twenty-four hours plates were removed and stripped with a chisel.[36] At both the Public Works quarry and at ER&S, workers became more organised and militant from 1909, not only because of the similar developments in the nation-wide labour movement during this period, but also because of the local experiences of paid work.

Other aspects of the industrial workplace also influenced local politics. While the long-term future of Port Kembla's industries seemed secure by the 1920s, intermittent employment remained an important feature of the formative period. Irregular work patterns were pronounced on the waterfront. Industrial action, bad weather or a shortage of loading and unloading facilities could stop waterside work. Slack periods were followed by back-breaking 24-hour shifts, a consequence of the unpredictable nature of the shipping industry, and oppressive working conditions.[37] Long shifts took a tremendous physical toll on workers and the situation was not alleviated until industrial action in the late 1930s, and then only partially.[38]

Other industries at Port Kembla were susceptible to stoppages in the industries that supplied or transported raw materials. During the General Strike of 1917, for example, ER&S wrote to customers informing them that the company was 'unable to take delivery of any ore or copper bearing material until further notice'.[39] Finally, if nothing else stopped work at Port Kembla, then the weather could. In July 1910 a fierce storm swept away 150 metres of the northern breakwater and those tipping stone were idle for a week awaiting repairs.[40]

The experience of intermittent work engendered varying political responses. Intermittent employment was one of the forces behind the strategy of lobbying the state government to improve the town's infrastructure. Throughout the 1920s the local branch of the Australian Workers' Union

(AWU), for example, called on the government to improve the port and construct better jetties, loading facilities and railway links.[41] Such demands must be seen in light of the frustration and economic hardship that workers experienced during stoppages at work, but calls for government intervention and government solutions were demands that the AWU shared with other non-working-class organisations like the Port Kembla Traders' Association and the Port Kembla Chamber of Commerce—ultimately common political ground upon which to base localist politics.

Other groups of workers developed quite different responses to irregular work. The waterside workers, plagued by the most oppressive working conditions and irregular work patterns at Port Kembla, eventually developed a strong union organisation by the mid-1930s. Increasing militancy and strike action targeted at local stevedoring companies constituted their major political response. The branch regularly elected communist leaders from 1937 and was at the leading edge of class politics at Port Kembla.

In contrast, Public Works Department labourers developed collectivist traditions to deal with irregular employment. If half the workforce was retrenched, for example, a 'five days on/five days off' system was introduced. Workers adopted such a roster in 1903 after a severe storm had ripped 30 metres of rail line from the eastern breakwater, effectively stopping quarry work until repairs were completed.[42] These workers introduced a similar roster in 1929 because of government cost-cutting.[43] Such experiences of union organisation, solidarity, and collective action were important forces behind the development of working-class identity. Whatever its political effects, intermittent work would not substantially disappear until wartime economic mobilisation in the 1940s, and the longer, more stable post-war boom.

By the beginning of the 1920s the industrial working class overwhelmingly dominated the paid workforce at Port Kembla. There were 484 unskilled workers living at Port Kembla, mostly labourers, firemen, greasers and fitter's labourers at ER&S and MM, and they represented 69 per cent of the town's paid workforce. Labourers made up the vast majority of the unskilled working class, numbering 361, or 75 per cent of all unskilled workers.[44]

Industrialisation brought new skilled positions to the workforce, but still the numbers of skilled workers were small at fifty-six, or 8 per cent of the paid workforce in 1924. Many of these jobs required precise judgement and dexterity, often in the face of harsh working conditions.[45] The ladler in the anode furnace at ER&S, positioned only 6 metres from the spout of the furnace, had to judge amounts of molten copper in the furnace and the moulds and 'act as a reservoir between the furnace and the moulds, thus permitting the flow of metal from the furnace to be continuous and to avoid overflow'.[46] In May 1920 ladlers earned 14s a day, as compared to 10s 6d per day for labourers.[47] Control of machinery such as ladles, lugging machines and cranes, as well as the supervision of other workers, also meant higher wages for some workers.[48]

The Middle Class

During the formative period of industrial society the local labour market diversified to include a local middle class. Port Kembla industries required a number of supervisory, technical and management positions in the production process—clerks, foremen, accountants, engineers and metallurgists—who formed the basis of a local middle class.[49]

ER&S and MM 'staff' were the main source of this middle-class growth. Employees seen as being part of the 'staff' included those in management positions and the more technically qualified workers. While staff also included a few in working-class occupations such as nightwatchmen, cleaners and typists, it was essentially a middle-class category. At the beginning of the 1920s ER&S staff numbered ninety and were divided into junior staff, who were employed on weekly contracts, and senior staff, who were employed on monthly contracts. Staff at MM in the early 1920s numbered fifty, many of whom were migrants from MM's English partner. Their task was to train workers in techniques new to the nascent Australian electrical manufacturing industry. In 1928 at ER&S junior clerks and junior assayers, and the nightwatchmen, earned slightly over £4 a week. Salaries rose from here through foreman, inspectors and engineers (£5 to £7) to the company accountant at £9 a week. The chief engineer, works superintendent and general manager were employed on yearly contracts paying from £700 to £1500 (£13 to £29 per week).[50]

In contrast to the experiences of the local working class, the defining feature of the paid work of middle-class men was their immunity from unemployment or underemployment. Intermittency, as an essential feature of the working-class experience during the formative period, did not extend to middle-class occupations. When work slowed at ER&S staff took holidays they had accrued, while workers survived as best they could by picking up odd jobs, fishing and tending vegetable gardens, or relying on credit at local stores.[51] At MM the TCF shut down in September 1926 owing to the delay in orders from the Postmaster-General's Office, and did not re-open until January 1927. As was typical of Port Kembla's industries, staff at the TCF processed a few small orders and worked on improvements to machinery.[52]

These very different conditions of work show that the class structure, as revealed by the electoral rolls, is not a statistical sleight of hand, but indicative of major differences in the working lives of different classes.

Many of the 150 MM and ER&S staff lived in Port Kembla. In 1924 there were ninety residents with middle-class occupations at Port Kembla, or 14 per cent of the paid workforce. Poor roads in and out of the town, and company housing for staff, were effective incentives for staff to live locally. Compared to some other towns, however, the middle class at Port Kembla was a small minority. According to the 1921 Census, at Wollongong 25 per cent of the workforce of 2622 was from the 'professional', 'commercial', or 'independent' categories—a reasonable approximation of the local middle class. Similarly, the figure for the Sydney metropolitan area was 20 per cent.[53]

Some of the few places in the Illawarra region that had a comparatively smaller middle class were the mining towns of the Northern Illawarra municipality—Bellambi, Balgownie, Mount Pleasant and Mount Keira. There only 11 per cent of the paid workforce of 2180 was in professional, commercial or independent occupations in 1921.[54] Although the Central Illawarra, of which Port Kembla was a large part, did have a comparatively small middle class, it was nonetheless a significant and observable social group. The middle class were important actors on the local political stage. They implemented and interpreted company policies, and busied themselves in political matters outside the industrial arena.

With the significant presence at Port Kembla of both the middle class and working class by the 1920s, the labour market centred more on the town. The establishment and success of ER&S and MM were crucial factors in undermining the regional basis of the labour market apparent from 1900 to 1907. Both companies needed a stable supply of workers, conversant with industrial production. Despite irregular employment, jobs would not disappear, as was the case with government work, which tended to rely on periodic public works. Consequently, many ER&S and MM employees settled locally and were the basis of the town's early population growth. By 1920, 500 of the 800 workers at ER&S and MM lived in Port Kembla.[55] A significant local population also gave the town a greater capacity to deal with any further labour demand. Well-placed local workers filled daily gaps in the Port Kembla workforce.

The town-centred labour market was further reinforced by the industrial strategies pursued by ER&S. The company attempted to turn Port Kembla into a company town. The company built houses for staff and workers, set up a co-operative store in 1916, and sponsored a range of local initiatives such as a Recreation Club and a Provident Fund.[56] This strategy was partly a response to the need to make Port Kembla more attractive to skilled labour, but it also related to the company's bid to control the social and political development of the town. The provision of local infrastructure and the company's focus on local services further established the town as the centre of the labour market.

The attempt to create a company town had ramifications beyond the creation of a more localised labour market. At ER&S especially, the company became the centre of the staff's social, as well as working lives. A staff Recreation Club was set up in Military Road where young engineers and metallurgists could play billiards or use the company's library. A staff tennis club was built near the works and became known as 'Terascoa' (The ER And S Company Of Australia).[57] Senior members of staff became active in the politics of Port Kembla. Control of the labour market spilled over into a considerable influence on local society itself, as ER&S staff became prominent in the social and political life of the town in the 1910s and early 1920s.

The paternalism of ER&S facilitated contact between the staff and the local working class. Through the provision of company housing, a company store and company-initiated sporting and social organisations, workers were considered not just as part of the labour process, but in their communal and family context. Although there was a hidden industrial and political agenda behind this engagement (which workers sometimes reacted against), industrial paternalism was one of the important forces that built cross-class links. Such links were the foundations of a cross-class local identity.

The Petit-bourgeoisie

Industrial development facilitated commercial growth at Port Kembla, and this attracted a petit-bourgeoisie to the town. By 1917 seventeen store-keepers were living and working in the town, or 4 per cent of the paid workforce.[58] By 1924 this figure had grown to sixty-one, or 9 per cent of the paid workforce. The petit-bourgeoisie had a key role in the creation of a local commercial centre that was both a site for interaction between classes at Port Kembla, and a symbol of local unity.

In 1906 the Middleton brothers, John and Harry, opened the first general store and newsagency at Port Kembla, on the western side of the newly constructed Military Road.[59] Middletons' was a small family-based store, typical of the early stores at Port Kembla. Harry died in late 1908, and Sarah Middleton, his widow, and brother-in-law John Middleton took over operations. Sarah Middleton handled the postal duties and their only employee was a boy who delivered telegrams.[60] Their business expanded along with the town, and in 1913 they opened 'the most up to date of any building in Port Kembla' with 'large ventilated rooms' and ceilings 'nicely finished off with artistic designs in cement'.[61]

J. T. Philpot's, a medium-sized general store in Wentworth Street, opened in 1921. John Philpot (junior) started work in the shop aged fifteen in 1927. He remembers work as 'strained, but not hard'. Deliveries were completed twice a week by motor car, and the family lived in rooms above the shop until 1950. Since there was no separation of work and home, the hours of work were long: 'Well, we lived in the shop, we'd work while there was work to be done'.[62] As with Middletons', Philpot's relied for the most part on family labour.

It was not long, however, before wealthier storekeepers, many of them from surrounding towns, became aware of Port Kembla's commercial opportunities. From the 1920s stores requiring more capital and often more workers joined the family-based businesses in Wentworth Street. In the 1910s Robert Shipp, a Keiraville-based storekeeper, owned and operated one store in Port Kembla and one in Keiraville. He moved to Port Kembla to live in 1920 and by this time employed four people in his Wentworth Street store. That year he also purchased the Empire Theatre in Wentworth Street (renaming it the Amusu Theatre), and in 1923 bought land in Port Kembla for speculative purposes. Shipp clearly had more capital available to him than smaller storekeepers like the Middletons and Philpots.

Hotels, another area of potential commercial investment in the expanding town, also became larger and more capital-intensive. The McCaffery brothers, experienced hoteliers from Kiama, opened a large two-storey hotel in Wentworth Street costing £4000 in June 1912.[63] Charles McCaffery, who managed the hotel, was forced to leave in 1913 because of illness. The Port Kembla Land and Building Company, a public company with £10 000 of share capital, purchased the hotel. From its salubrious beginnings, it soon became a working-class hotel and boarding house run by resident managers.[64]

The change in ownership of the hotel was an early indicator of the increasing size and capitalisation of commercial operations at Port Kembla. Regardless of whether businesses were family-run or larger operations, the workplaces of the petit-bourgeoisie were sites of economic and social interaction between all classes at Port Kembla. Economic relationships between the petit-bourgeoisie and the working class were particularly close. Storekeepers' incomes were closely linked to working-class employment. Edith Neaves's father worked as a furnaceman at ER&S in the 1920s: 'If he came off work sick [it was] too bad, we would have to rely on the trader people to stand by us'.[65] Credit offered the working class some breathing space in the scramble to survive on meagre wages, and for the storekeepers it secured the loyalty and trade of customers that would pay off when conditions were better. Such economic links with other classes at Port Kembla highlight the petit-bourgeoisie's important role in creating the economic context for the emergence of town identity and the development of political alliances between classes.

The small businesses in the town were also a common site for women's paid work. In 1924 twenty-two women, or 3 per cent of the paid workforce, recorded occupations other than 'domestic duties' on the Electoral Roll, with thirteen of them in petit-bourgeois occupations like boarding house keeper, shopkeeper and tailoress.[66] Women mostly ran the town's boarding houses. Sarah Watson established the first boarding house in 1903. This large two-storey building was located on the corner of what became Darcy and Military Roads and catered for sixty men. Watson employed her three daughters and her granddaughter, Sarah Drury, in what was very much a family business. Drury worked at the boarding house between 1923 and 1925, making beds and serving tables in the kitchen for ten shillings a week.[67] The 1924 Electoral Roll recorded six official boarding houses in Port Kembla, concentrated in Wentworth Street and Military Road. In running boarding houses women brought apparently 'private sphere' skills of cooking, cleaning and household management into the formal economy.

Among enrolled working-class women, only seven listed occupations on the 1924 Electoral Roll; three housemaids, two typists, one shop-assistant and one waitress. There is one workplace excluded from these figures that highlights the limitations of the electoral rolls as evidence of labour market activity. The TCF at MM was one of the few areas of industrial work open to women at Port Kembla, but is not reflected in the electoral roll figures because they were not old enough to vote. There were 60 to 100 women between sixteen and twenty years of age employed at the TCF. They worked from 7.30 a.m to 4.00 p.m overseeing the operations of twelve to sixteen cotton braiding machines. The first award rate was set in April 1923 at £2, which was (typical for such rulings), half the adult male basic wage. By 1933 depression conditions had reduced the adult female rate to £1 7s.[68]

These women worked in that period of their lives between leaving school and getting married. After working in her grandmother's boarding house, Sarah Drury worked at the TCF from 1925 until her marriage in 1927.[69] Edith Neaves 'loved' her job at MM and stayed two years until her marriage in 1929. The idea of continuing work after marriage was never considered, as Neaves recalled: 'Oh no, no I left. When you were married you had to leave. You don't work after when you were married. That's silly. [laughter] No you get married to be a housewife and look after your husband.'[70]

Middle-class women also had limited access to the formal economy, although the local school presented some opportunities. Agnes McCaulry became a pupil teacher at Port Kembla Primary School in March 1905. The headmaster, Thomas Collins, wrote an assessment of her performance that provides some idea of what was expected of young women students. In assessing her 'Conduct out of School', he wrote: 'Her character out of school is of the highest moral worth; her choice of associates wise and well-considered and her leisure time at Port Kembla has been principally spent in the interests of education and morality'.[71] An image of a hard-working, ambitious young woman emerges from this report, but the extent to which her private life was up for assessment is also graphically demonstrated. Collins was assessing McCaulry's moral worth as much as her value as a teacher, and this moral scrutiny was an important element in responses to women's paid employment.

While teaching offered some opportunities, working conditions could also be very poor. Sanitary arrangements at the Port Kembla Primary School were less than adequate. In 1908 the mayor of Central Illawarra Municipality wrote to the Department of Public Instruction complaining of the school cesspits and the smell that emanated from them.[72] Overcrowding was also a problem. The Port Kembla Progress Association complained in August 1913 that because of a lack of space 'a number of them [children] receive their instruction on the open verandah, exposed to the heavy wind and dust'.[73] That year 137 children were enrolled with three teachers in charge: the headmaster and two female assistant teachers.

The opening of the new school in Military Road in 1916 relieved the overcrowding, but even so, the formal economy presented other difficulties for women workers. The school employed three assistant women teachers: Miss Flynn, who boarded at Wollongong; Miss Bovard, who lived with her parents at Port Kembla; and Mrs Bourke, whose husband worked at Port Kembla where they resided. If women could not find accommodation at Port Kembla, they were forced to board at Wollongong because, as a departmental inspector noted: 'The boarding houses at Port Kembla are for men only, and a woman cannot obtain suitable accommodation, so must live in Wollongong'.[74] Such male-oriented services made the formal economy even less accessible to women.

As for working-class women, the paid work of middle-class women often ended upon marriage. In early 1919 Mrs Bourke wrote to the Department of Public Instruction applying for a permanent position. Both the headmaster and the senior inspector recommended the appointment to alleviate overcrowding, but the department replied that it was practice 'not to appoint married women to permanent positions'.[75] The department continued to police the gendered boundaries of the formal economy, regardless of the advice from local officials and the extensive overcrowding at the school.[76]

Despite the numbers of women in paid work who escape the official records, the formal economy remained overwhelmingly male-dominated. Women workers at the TCF or in the town's stores may have added to women's share of 3 to 4 per cent of the formal economy (as recorded by the electoral rolls), but certainly to no more than 10 per cent of the total workforce. This male domination distinguished the formal economy at Port Kembla from that of many other towns. According to the 1933 Census, 21 per cent of the Wollongong Municipality's workforce of 5113 were women. The figure for the whole of New South Wales was similar, at almost 20 per cent.[77] Even allowing for electoral roll and census figures that are not entirely comparable, the differences are still significant.

The effect of this gender-segmented formal economy was to expose men and women to separate workplaces and different influences on their identities and politics. While working-class and middle-class men were concentrated in industrial workplaces with harsh working conditions, noticeable class divisions and occasional class conflict, the few areas of the formal economy occupied by women were workplaces less infused with class difference and class conflict. Indeed, workplaces like the town's stores, where women found some paid work, actively encouraged cross-class interaction. The masculinised and male-dominated industries of Port Kembla became the typical sites of class politics, while the town centre, with less clear-cut gendered meanings and more women present as both workers and customers, became a crucial symbol and rallying point for localist politics.

Downturn and Depression

Periodic downturns, and the Great Depression, punctuated the inexorable growth of industrial society at Port Kembla. After 1925 especially, Port Kembla industries began shedding jobs, and this downturn had major implications for the labour market and the town. Even as employment prospects dimmed, itinerant workers increasingly looked to Port Kembla for work, undermining the localised labour market and re-establishing strong outside links. The overwhelming scale of industrial development at Port Kembla compounded this challenge to the boundaries of the locality. Nevertheless, with the effective recovery of the industrial economy by the late 1930s, it was well placed to meet increased demand associated with war-time mobilisation in the 1940s.

The late 1920s were marked by expressions of regional optimism that were, in hindsight, unfounded. The new arrival on the industrial front, the Hoskins Iron and Steel Company Ltd from Lithgow, created great excitement in the Illawarra. The *Illawarra Mercury* began 1927 with this editorial:

The prospects for 1927, so far as this district is concerned, are very bright. It is pleasing to note that its attractions as a tourist resort are now fully established ... In addition, we have the assurance that Hoskins' big works are definitely established ... [This] will mean work for the unemployed, and added prosperity for the district.[78]

Despite the projected size of the steel works, and the hopes for the tourist industry, employment at Port Kembla was already contracting. In September 1925 the Mount Lyell Cokeworks closed, putting sixty men out of work.[79] In 1928, fifty-two men were dismissed from the Government Power House at Port Kembla.[80]

For the larger industries the picture was no brighter. By the late 1920s ER&S was no longer the premier industry in Port Kembla and the 'largest copper smelter in the British Empire', but a 'ghost refinery', starved of both orders and raw material.[81] Copper prices, never buoyant after the war, dropped further after 1925. Mount Morgan went into liquidation in late 1927, cutting off one of ER&S's largest suppliers of blister copper.[82] The Queensland mine's shares in ER&S were purchased by Broken Hill Associated Smelters in 1928, a major company of the Collins House Group.[83] The new owners of ER&S believed the company's future was a bleak one, more a matter of survival than expansion.[84] In 1928 the Mount Lyell Company in Tasmania built its own smelting works, partly cutting off another major source of ore for the Port Kembla smelter. The ER&S workforce, numbering 450 in 1925, dropped to 150 by 1929, and remained at that level throughout the depression.[85]

MM, also taken over by Broken Hill Associated Smelters, fared rather better than ER&S through the late 1920s and the 1930s, but the company was not immune to the effects of the depression. After record levels of production and employment in 1925, the situation deteriorated by 1929 and a 'reduction of hands in certain sections [was] unavoidable'.[86] In 1930 the Rod and Wire Factory and the TCF closed and orders for the Tube Factory declined. The worst year for MM was 1932, as it was for the manufacturing industry throughout Australia. The highest number of workers employed at MM that year was 200, compared to 787 in 1925.[87] Postmaster-General orders, which virtually kept the TCF running, were only 7 per cent of the pre-depression levels. Only the Tube Factory remained in continuous (albeit limited) production.

Throughout the region the economic situation was no better. Unemployment in the coalmines of the Illawarra was chronic in the 1920s, and by July 1930, 1300 miners, or one in every three, were unemployed. Many of these men, as well as itinerant labourers from outside the region, looked to Port Kembla for some hope of work, regardless of the poor prospects there, because of the interest, excitement and hope generated by the Hoskins venture and the state government's plans for a cross-country railway from Port Kembla to Moss Vale.[88] In June 1927 over one-half of the 521 men registered at the Wollongong Labour Exchange were from outside the Illawarra, and only 106 could be placed in employment.[89]

Hoskins Iron and Steel Company Ltd began construction work at Port Kembla in early 1927.[90] The following year Australian Iron and Steel Pty Ltd (AI&S) formed and a new type of employer had arrived at Port Kembla. The AI&S blast furnace, completed in August 1928, was not significantly different from furnaces at ER&S and MM, but it represented industrial production on a scale that was new to Port Kembla. AI&S had British investment partners and to a limited extent sought advice from US experts. It was a decisive change from the earlier regional interests that had located to Port Kembla. AI&S also brought new management practices and a new generation of technology. Cecil Hoskins, managing director, noted that 'efficiency and economy of operation were one of the prime objects sought and the programme included the installation of the best labour saving machinery and equipment obtainable'. One hundred men operated the blast furnace at Lithgow constructed in 1907 by William Sandford's Ltd, while the new Port Kembla furnace required only thirty.[91]

But 'efficiency and economy of operation' only went so far at AI&S. The company developed a reputation for inefficiency, disorganisation and heavy-handedness in industrial relations. On one occasion, bags of concrete were left uncovered in a rainstorm and set concrete had to be torn out of the ground.[92] Horse and cart carried out much of the initial construction work of the blast furnace and rolling mills, with only one steam-powered crane available. M. Finch started work in August 1933 as a mill hand at the 10-inch mill at AI&S. Finch, like many other steelworkers, had transferred from Lithgow where he performed the same job.[93] He recalled the hard physical labour required, despite the technical sophistication of some of the equipment:

> We used to work at a furnace that was about six feet by ten feet that they used to put the billets into. They had four furnaces in the mill. You had to pull the door open with a pair of tongs, grab hold of the billet and pull it out . . . We had to drag it about forty feet to the mill to be rolled. Everything was done manually. They even moved the billets on wheelbarrows.[94]

While the blast furnace was the latest US design, the rolling mills transferred from Lithgow were of British origin. In contrast, the Broken Hill Proprietary Company Ltd (BHP) at Newcastle relied on more sophisticated US technology.[95] Despite the fact that AI&S had 'one of largest blast furnaces in the Empire' which could produce 660 tonnes of pig iron per day, the steelmaking furnaces were not properly suited to the mills that were eventually constructed to work the iron.[96] These mills were all steam-driven (often production had to be stopped to wait for pressure to build in the furnaces), while BHP in Newcastle had electrically driven mills from 1927.[97]

The success story of AI&S was, however, the spun pipe plant that turned the copious amounts of Port Kembla iron into pipes from August 1929 until its closure in 1963.[98] The large demand for iron pipes was in part due to the state government relief work programme that used considerable amounts of this material. On the eve of the depression, the spun pipe plant was one of the few profitable parts of 'the steel works', as AI&S was commonly known.

Despite the gap between the rhetoric of AI&S management practices and the reality of disorganisation at the workplace, the company's approach was a decisive change from the paternalism of ER&S. AI&S had no interest in where and how workers lived. It viewed its workforce instead as labour power mobilised for the company ends. In conditions where there was an established industrial workforce with such an oversupply of labour, AI&S had no reason to be concerned about strategies for attracting labour or ensuring company loyalty. During the depression the reality that there were hundreds of men ready to fill the shoes of any recalcitrant worker was effective enough discipline.[99] The breakdown of links between industry and local society helped clear the way for the regionalisation of the labour market, and the decline of industrial paternalism removed one important force behind the mobilisation of local identity.

The effects on the labour market of the economic slump, and AI&S's half-finished integrated steel works, were catastrophic. The establishment of AI&S attracted nation-wide attention and the new works for many unemployed men represented a chance to find employment. In 1928 the organiser for the newly formed Illawarra Trades and Labour Council, Steve Best, reported that 'men continue to pour in from other districts'.[1] Ces Catterel, who lived on the main road from Wollongong to Port Kembla in the 1920s and early 1930s, recalled seeing numerous men arriving in the town alone and on foot during the depression.[2] Although itinerant male workers had long been a presence in Port Kembla, the depression brought them in as never before. Their presence in the town, and their hessian bag and kerosene tin shacks on its outskirts, increased markedly from 1930.

This influx of outside labour led to a major rearrangement of the labour market. Itinerant male workers, sometimes with their families, lived in two main unemployed camps on the margins of the town: the Official Camp near Coomaditchie Lagoon, and the Flinders Street camp near AI&S. Other areas where the unemployed lived included a small camp near the mouth of Tom Thumb's Lagoon, shacks behind Fisherman's Beach and Perkin's Beach, and the town's hotels or boarding houses, where a few of the better-off stayed. Altogether, the *Illawarra Mercury* noted that there were over one thousand

A poster advertising the first subdivision of the Wentworth estate in 1909.
This subdivision defined the central area of the future township.

The fourth subdivision of the Wentworth estate in 1916 opened up blocks in the Avenues, as well as in Keira and Bland Streets. The sections covered by the first, second and third subdivisions are clearly marked.

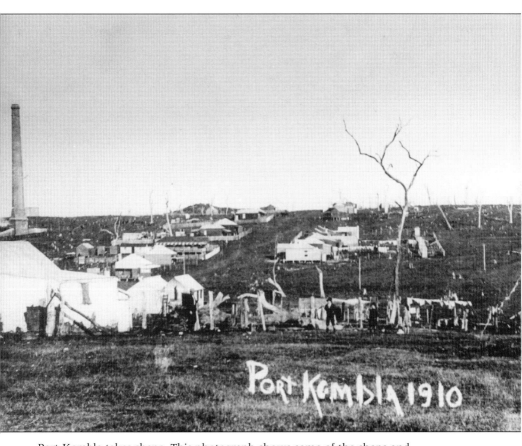

Port Kembla takes shape. This photograph shows some of the shops and houses in Wentworth Street in 1910. The dead trees are the result of the sulphur dioxide emanating from ER&S, whose stack can be seen on the far left.

Port Kembla in 1914 photographed by G. Oyston, showing some of the new cottages in Wentworth and Horne Streets. The grazing horses and cattle are a telling reminder of Port Kembla's not-so-distant rural past.

men camped around the Port Kembla area in early 1932. Movement in and out of the town was constant. In January 1932 the *South Coast Times* reported that as many as fifty men per week were arriving at Port Kembla.[3]

The influx of itinerants during the depression reflected a broadening of the boundaries of the labour market at Port Kembla. Workers from throughout the Illawarra region were also asserting their presence at Port Kembla. By counting occupations on the 1933 Electoral Roll that can be definitely traced to Port Kembla (such as 'steelworker' or 'smelter') the extent of this regionalisation of the labour market can be gauged. By 1933 there were 41 'steelworkers' living in Wollongong, 34 in Corrimal and 25 living as far away as Dapto and Bulli. This regionalisation was part of a broader structural and political challenge to the locality upon which later chapters will expand. The decline in the close correlation between the boundaries of the labour market and the town was the economic foundation of these challenges.

The presence of itinerants at Port Kembla, and their living conditions, highlighted emerging divisions in the local social structure between locals and non-locals. The great advances in industrial production and productivity failed to provide essential requirements for many. The detritus of the industrial age housed some of the unfortunates. At Perkin's Beach a family of six was living in a shack of scavenged material, mostly hessian bags and galvanised iron. By late 1933 they had been there for a year. When Council officers visited they found a woman sick and bed-ridden. The eldest school-age child cared for the children while the husband was at work. The moral pressure and anxiety that surrounded these living conditions were significant. A few with enough energy and resources, together with a core of dignity and resistance, turned their hovels into palaces. An MM company survey in 1933 found many of the shacks on Perkin's Beach 'tidy', and one had even maintained 'a good garden'.[4] Such strategies were a way to normalise the crisis, and a desperate attempt to gain respectability in the eyes of a world that was quick to judge.

The apparent division between locals and non-locals was an important context for the revival of localist politics at the onset of the depression. Calls to isolate the town from outsiders or often-inaccurate claims that campers were not 'locals' were among the first reactions to this crisis. Yet a more powerful effect of the depression was to underline class differences and precipitate class conflict. The politics of the local working class, embittered by oppression and unemployment, eventually shifted to the left, just as the politics of the local middle class shifted to the right in search of ways to deal with what they understood to be a crisis that threatened private property and private affluence.

Intermittent employment had declined at Port Kembla during the early 1920s, but from 1925 irregular work resumed as ER&S and MM began suffering from the economic downturn. By the time the depression had arrived, as Richardson notes, for many workers it was like 'a depression within a depression', exacerbating conditions that were already common in the late 1920s.[5] For many workers at Port Kembla, especially the unskilled, intermittent no longer accurately described what were long stretches of unemployment. Worsening periods of underemployment and finally unemployment were experiences that eventually informed more militant and radical union organisation at Port Kembla from the mid-1930s.

Although there are no specific unemployment figures for Port Kembla, the 1933 Census indicates that 767 men in the Central Illawarra, or 24 per cent of the municipality's male breadwinners, were unemployed on the day of the Census. This was higher than the rate for Wollongong (22 per cent), but well below that for Bulli (35 per cent) and the Northern Illawarra (38 per cent). This reveals the more severe situation on the northern coalfields, although the figure for the Central Illawarra is misleadingly low. Many of the 767 unemployed were concentrated in or around Port Kembla itself, and those in the town's unemployed camps with no permanent addresses may have been overlooked by the Census. Using Census information on income in the previous year reveals the financial effects of movements in and out of employment. In the year before the Census 1777 men, or 37 per cent of male breadwinners in the Central Illawarra, earned less than £103.[6]

These figures reflected the depressed state of the Port Kembla manufacturing industries. The temporary interruptions to production in the 1920s became lengthy closures during the depression. In April 1930 the AI&S blast furnace was shut down due to a lack of orders, and 1600 men laid off.[7] In June 1930 Colin Fraser, managing director of ER&S, lamented that the supply of ore for ER&S from Queensland (Mount Morgan and Cloncurry) 'had practically ceased and we are thrown back on scrap copper to paddle along in a small way'. Most of the furnaces at ER&S operated in rotation; men were employed only when orders were received and 'let go' once they were filled.[8] The TCF at MM was closed down in December 1930, affecting 100 women employees. The TCF did not resume continuous production until late 1933.[9]

Public works projects, the traditional state government response to unemployment, were also cut back at the beginning of depression. In June 1932, however, the government moved to place some men on food relief into an emergency work relief programme.[10] The Central Illawarra Council adopted the scheme in May 1933, and the municipality employed 581 men, 307 of them from the Port Kembla area. Jobs included cleaning out water tables, bridge repairs, road maintenance, tree planting and footpath construction. Single men were paid 9s 4d for six hours' work a week, and married men were paid on a scale depending on the number of children, starting at 15s 7d for ten hours' work a week for men with one child.[11]

Relief work successfully absorbed some of the long-term unemployed. By the end of 1935 there were 341 men in the Central Illawarra employed in emergency relief.[12] Such work helped sustain some workers during the worst of the depression, and from 1936 ordinary relief work projects paying award wages were re-established.

Some men, usually those with industrial experience and skills, found work at the local industries, which began re-employing in 1933. Yet continuous paid work was still uncommon. For example, between May 1934 and May 1935, sixty-nine men, mostly labourers and wharf labourers, were employed in the permanent construction gang at AI&S. Despite being paid similar hourly rates, their average weekly earnings varied from £2 18s to £5 5s and yearly earnings ranged from £92 6s to £273 17s. Even for a group of workers who were apparently 'permanent employees', wages could vary considerably due to sickness, wet weather, overtime or temporary stand-downs.[13]

Mirroring the increasing size of industry, stores at Port Kembla in the 1930s were growing larger and employing more waged workers. Fairley's, Port Kembla's largest store in the 1930s, employed ten staff by the end of the decade. Increased land values in Wentworth Street also restricted entry into small business ownership. Only those with capital, high turnover and high profit margins could afford these prices. Cecil Messiter opened his men's clothing store in late 1937, after purchasing the land in June 1937. He grossed £114 a week with a profit of £34 before overheads.[14]

The Great Depression, together with the increasing size and capitalisation of stores, had a particular impact on smaller storekeepers. In 1922 Jean Payne's grandmother had opened a mixed business in Wentworth Street selling drinks, cakes, fruit and vegetables and serving counter meals, but, as Payne recalls: 'Then my Gran started to fail and the depression hit us very hard. It hit the town very hard; my grandmother went bankrupt and lost everything'.[15] The divisions in the class structure were reinforced and the possibility of class mobility reduced as it became harder to set up a small store and 'go into business'. The high turnover of licensees at Port Kembla's hotels demonstrates the precarious nature of petit-bourgeois occupations. Between 1929 and 1932 the Commercial Hotel (formerly the Grand) had six different licensees. The Port Kembla Hotel had five different licensees from 1931 to 1935.[16]

The decline of the family store adversely affected women's participation in the formal economy. By 1940 women held only 6 per cent of petit-bourgeois occupations, as compared to 21 per cent in 1924. Such work was either gendered male, with women replaced by male shop assistants, or de-skilled to female working-class occupations such as 'cashier' or 'shop assistant'.[17] What was occurring in the town's stores reflected the changes in Port

Kembla's industries, with increasing size and capitalisation of business, the growth of wage labour, and the increasing male domination of the formal economy.

Despite the improvement in employment prospects by the mid-1930s, the labour market still attracted scores of men seeking work, and for some the crisis hardly abated with the beginning of the 'economic recovery'. Even by October 1937 there were still 566 people in the Official Camp near Coomaditchie, the vast majority unemployed.[18] With such an oversupply of labour, local industries were in a strong position to dictate working conditions and resist union demands for wage increases, but this recalcitrance, along with better employment prospects in the late 1930s, pushed the labour movement towards a wide-ranging industrial mobilisation.

Regionalisation and Wage Labour

Industrial growth and expansion at Port Kembla in the late 1930s reinforced the regional basis of the labour market. Despite some lingering unemployment and underemployment, more men secured work as major companies began employing again. ER&S and MM recovered financially, reaching pre-depression production levels by the late 1930s. The ER&S workforce increased to 343 by November 1940.[19] At MM the recovery was quicker. By 1935 its workforce was back to 520, and by the end of the 1930s it had increased to 1000.[20]

These industries, however, were no longer at the centre of Port Kembla's industrial employment. At AI&S recovery and expansion occurred at a far greater pace than either ER&S or MM, and after the BHP takeover of AI&S in 1935, large amounts of capital were spent upgrading and enlarging the plant. A second blast furnace was completed in May 1937. In 1938 some of the larger mills were upgraded, the original blast furnace was reconditioned and new coke ovens were built. Other industries, such as John Lysaght Pty Ltd and Commonwealth Rolling Mills Pty Ltd (CRM), also expanded rapidly in the 1930s. John Lysaght took over a BHP sheet rolling mill at Port Kembla in 1936, and built its own mill in 1938, shutting down the older operation. From the late 1930s the focus of industrial development had moved from ER&S and MM to AI&S and its near neighbours. By 1940 Lysaght and CRM employed over 1000 workers.[21]

With a growing industrial labour market, the working class at Port Kembla increased both numerically and as a percentage of the total paid workforce. In 1930 the working class numbered 795 on the joint State–Commonwealth Electoral Roll, or 67 per cent of the paid workforce. By 1940 this figure had increased to 1970 or 73 per cent of the paid workforce. This figure is likely an underestimation for it excludes working-class men camped around the town, or moving in and out in search of work. The skilled working class too had increased numerically from 168 in 1930 to 297 in 1940, but relative to the population growth in the town their share of the paid workforce had decreased from 14 per cent to 11 per cent.[22] The large-scale industrial expansion at AI&S required a mostly unskilled workforce. While there were many new skilled positions available at the steel works, these were partially offset by the decline in workforce numbers at ER&S, which formerly had employed a number of skilled workers. Changes in the production process at AI&S also eradicated some skilled positions.

A major change to the paid work of working-class men in this decade was the growth of regular wage labour. The working day was increasingly marked by clocking on and off, the regulation of time via the factory whistle, and the control of work by company foremen. At ER&S in the late 1930s, as orders flowed in and reliable supplies of copper ore were secured, dramatic fluctuations in workforce numbers became less common. Information on the daily movement in the workforce shows that the vast majority of ER&S workers maintained their jobs throughout the week, and this was indicative of month-to-month employment numbers as well. In the first week of November 1937, for example, the size of the workforce hovered at around 340 to 380 throughout the week, with smaller numbers on Saturday (300) and Sunday (85).[23]

At AI&S there was a growing permanent workforce from the mid-1930s who, like the workers at ER&S, could expect regular work. AI&S management had recognised that many workers developed useful skills during their stints on construction gangs, and made an effort to keep more of these men.[24] Large retrenchments did not cease—when the construction of Number 2 blast furnace was finished in May 1937, 600 men were laid off, and throughout the works construction projects or production itself was continually stopping and starting—but by 1938 AI&S employed almost 3000 men who could reasonably expect paid work every week.[25] In fact, many of these men endured long hours of enforced overtime, the subject of considerable industrial action in the late 1930s. Unions were incensed that AI&S worked men overtime when there were still large numbers of unemployed in the region.[26]

New forms of company surveillance were the downside to more regular work. Erratic and uncertain periods of paid work resulted in uneven and insufficient wages, but did free workers from the discipline and monotony of the workplace. In 1936 AI&S established an 'Industrial Department' in an effort to manage the workforce more effectively. This department maintained extensive personal information on workers, closely scrutinised union affairs, and made a concerted effort to encourage workers to seek redress for any grievances through the department individually, rather than via their union.[27]

At the same time, more regular employment was one of the springboards for the reconstruction of the union movement. Regular employees were easier to organise and their pay packets replenished union coffers, making funds available to organise and support workers during industrial action. Moreover, in conditions of close control and scrutiny of their work, local workers reacted with increasing militancy and engaged in industrial strategies to increase their own 'job control' over the workplace. A more permanent and increasingly unionised workforce, embittered by the depression and experiencing new invasive management strategies, was a volatile mix that culminated in widespread industrial class conflict from the mid-1930s.

Where ER&S and MM once pursued industrial strategies that attempted to blur the boundaries between staff and workers under the guise of a town-centred paternalism, in the late 1930s AI&S worked to maintain these divisions in the labour market, and introduced some aspects of scientific management to the workplace. The question of the role and impact of scientific management on the Australian manufacturing industry is beyond the scope of this study, but the new AI&S strategies did have implications for the local middle class, who were now more commonly seen as representatives of a company, rather than members of local society. The AI&S approach focused exclusively on the worker in the context of the workplace, thus severing the links forged by industrial paternalism between locality and industry.[28]

AI&S encouraged divisions in local society by reinforcing differences in the workplace through the creation of a dual labour market. Close attention was paid to staff wages at AI&S, ensuring that they were higher than the wages of labourers working with them, and prospective staff had to officially resign from their unions before their new status could be confirmed.[29] The practice of using staff to cover for day labour during industrial action reinforced divisions in the workforce and often soured industrial relations. The bricklayers' strike from July to August 1934, for example, was precipitated by a wage decrease under a new Industrial Commission award, but the use of staff labour to replace the men hardened the strikers' resolve and led to the involvement of other unions at the steel works.[30]

AI&S pursued a policy of widening staff membership to create a core of reliable non-unionised workers. In strategic parts of the works it was important to have staff labour to cover during industrial action. At the AI&S power house, stoppages could affect the whole works and the head of the Industrial Department, V. R. Petney, closely monitored the situation so 'that in the event of an emergency sufficient staff men are available'.[31] During the late 1930s, however, the policy was met with increasing resistance from unions who saw it as a way to undermine union numbers and the effectiveness of strikes. Petney recognised this and recommended that new staff appointments be suspended in December 1938 'because of industrial matters'.[32] Even so, this policy, along with the continued expansion of the works, meant that by 1941 there were 363 staff at AI&S.[33] Such an approach reinforced class divisions in the formal economy and, at times, exacerbated tensions between management and unions.

By 1940 the scale of industrial development had expanded well beyond the confines of the town. In that year the *Sydney Morning Herald* estimated that 5000 workers commuted to Port Kembla daily by train, car or bus. By 1947 one in seven male jobs in the paid workforce were in steel or related industries in the Illawarra region.[34] The industrial labour market was now more regional than local.

This was also the case for the local middle class and petit-bourgeoisie. By the late 1930s Wollongong had re-established itself as the commercial and suburban centre of the Illawarra. Improvements in roads and the increasing availability of motor cars for the better-off made it possible to commute to Port Kembla. The growth of suburbs surrounding Port Kembla also had an influence in widening the spatial boundaries of the labour market. While there were 137 storekeepers on the 1940 Electoral Roll for Port Kembla, 27 of them were from the nearby suburbs of Warrawong, Cringila, Windang and Lake Heights. Suburban growth had spilled over into surrounding areas and presented new opportunities similar to those that Port Kembla had offered in the 1910s and 1920s.

The middle class too was moving into these new suburbs around Port Kembla. On the 1940 Electoral Roll they numbered 298, of which 47 were from Warrawong, Windang, Cringila and Lake Heights. This reduced the size of the middle class actually living at Port Kembla in 1940 to 251. The scale of industrial and commercial development could not be contained within the locality. The formal economy moved through a cycle of being tied to the regional in the 1900s, becoming more localised in the 1920s, and finally regionalising again in the 1930s.

Industrialisation dramatically changed Port Kembla's social structure, creating a shifting set of influences on the experiences and allegiances of local residents. The division of the industrial workforce between staff and labour reflected and reinforced the class divisions in local society between working class and middle class, and provided the context for the development of class identity and class conflict. At the same time, local economic and commercial development created a labour market based on the town— an important foundation for cross-class local identity—and facilitated the growth of the petit-bourgeoisie, a class with a vital role to play in local cross-class interaction.

3

The Informal Economy to 1940

IN 1916 A COAL TRAIN from Mount Kembla sped down the track towards Port Kembla. A bull belonging to farmer Alfred Duncan had strayed onto the line, but engine driver William Purcell did not attempt to stop and knocked the bull aside, killing it instantly. 'Hell Fire Jack', as he was known locally, was heard to cheer and shout 'hooray'. Purcell had killed seven other animals in the previous three years.[1]

Purcell's wild driving is symbolic of the pace and destructive force of industrial development. Those in its path were swept aside, especially rural interests who had other plans for the land at Port Kembla. New powerful economic forces descended upon the Illawarra from the beginning of the century, but even the all-embracing nature of industrialisation was unable to obliterate signs of the town's rural heritage. In the 1910s, when paid work at Port Kembla harbour was scarce, some waterside workers fished from the jetties, while others headed off to Lake Illawarra or Coomaditchie to catch fish or prawns.[2] The natural resources of Port Kembla, especially those given up by the sea, helped local workers deal with intermittent paid work. As late as the 1970s the persistent Duncan family, distant relatives of Alfred Duncan, still ran cattle on a small property at nearby Lake Heights. Some rural practices were obliterated by industrialisation, while others adapted to become central to the survival of working-class households during the formative period of industrial society.

Beyond the formal economy, and its dominance by heavy industry and male workers, was the equally significant household economy. If we follow many working-class men home, and describe the household economy and its distinctive features; then a fuller picture of the economy emerges. While the vast majority of wages were earned in the formal workplace, the decisions regarding expenditure were made in the household. Parts of the informal rural economy merged and adapted to the new formal economy of industrial society. This distinctive blending was the hallmark of work experience and family life in the formative period.

Rural Life and the Informal Economy

In the 1900s, the informal economy was a central part of production and an important means of survival at Port Kembla for the white inhabitants of the area. In 1903 there were sixteen farmers at Port Kembla. A few of these, such as the O'Donnells and the Barretts, ran large dairies on land that they owned, but the majority were leaseholders on 8- to 12-hectare sections of the Wentworth estate.[3] These small farmers relied on home-based production rather than wage labour for survival. Women had central roles as milkers and butter makers, and children were important since there was little surplus or profit to employ outside labour.[4] In 1948, Arthur Cousins, an early regional historian, described life on a dairy farm in the Illawarra:

> The man, his wife, and his children from about eight years old, generally assisted in the milking. This meant very long hours for school children, as well as for the others. Besides milking, pigs and calves had to be fed, land to be cultivated and fodder grown, cattle had to be fed, weeds to be destroyed.[5]

In these households links with the formal economy were minimal. Men sometimes took paid work outside the farm, working for a better-off neighbour clearing paddocks or erecting fences, but family members usually worked together in the production of milk and other home-made products, and the maintenance of the farm.[6]

Other workers at Port Kembla such as waterside workers and labourers were more reliant on wage labour than dairy farmers, but they often had more than one source of income. John Patterson, a labourer for the Southern Coal Company, also ran the unofficial post office from his home from 1900 to 1907, earning £52 a year for providing this service.[7] Peter Rieck, a labourer for the Mount Kembla Coal Company, shared the mail contract with local dairy farmer Michael O'Donnell, worth a total of £62 a year in the early 1900s.[8] Local waterside workers were well-placed to supplement their wages through fishing from the harbour or nearby beaches.[9]

Universal education removed children from household work, though this did not stop them working before and after school, or missing school altogether to carry out essential work for the family. Large families were often the basis of successful home-based production. The average number of people per occupied dwelling in the Central Illawarra was 5.08 in 1901, and 4.79 in 1911.[10] At Port Kembla families as large as seven, eight or more were common early in the century. Bob Rees, born in 1904, had six brothers and two sisters. Ursula Lindsay, born in 1907, grew up in a family of nine children. This active and rurally based informal economy, well-supplied with labour by large families, was an important context for the large-scale industrialisation that would follow. Some of its features persisted, and were adapted to the demands of industrial society.

Industrialisation and the Informal Economy

In the 1910s and 1920s the informal economy at Port Kembla was still a major component of a household's survival. Rural traditions were maintained. Keeping cows, chickens and geese, and tending vegetable gardens were common practices. The increasingly industrialised society, and the growth of male wage labour, however, was not without its effects on the informal economy.

Because of the male domination of the industrialising formal economy, the informal economy was of special importance to women. Taking in lodgers was an important source of income, especially since the periodic demand for male labour at Port Kembla's industries created a large floating population of men looking for accommodation. In 1912 Anne Chesher had at least two full-time boarders living in her front room.[11] Gordon Rodwell's widowed mother had two boarders in the early 1920s, distant male relatives who worked at ER&S and whose board helped the family survive without a 'male breadwinner'.

This type of work was closely linked to the state of the male labour market. In 1907, when the labour market at Port Kembla was swamped by Australian Smelting Corporation labourers, the *Illawarra Mercury* reported that 'almost every second house at the Port has been converted into a Restaurant. Mrs Jackson daily feeds about 70, Mrs Pascoe over 50 and others from 2 or 3 to a dozen'.[12] In late 1912, a generally poor period for Port Kembla's industries, Elizabeth Johnson had three lodgers. Only three months earlier she had had fourteen, but 'they left because they were out of work'.[13]

Other home-based production such as cooking, jam-making and sewing were also common, but are too numerous to deal with extensively. When Albert Rieck married in 1920, his wife resigned from her job as a tailoress in Wollongong. She purchased a sewing machine and continued work at home. As Rieck recalls, 'She bought a sewing machine, and she used to do all her own [clothes], and all the kid's clothes'. In the 1920s Avis Bright's mother had fruit trees in her backyard from which she made jam. The frequency of these activities is impossible to gauge, but home-based production was important for a family's survival, as it helped balance tight budgets and stretch scarce resources.

Women's work also extended away from the household to include irregular forays into the labour market. This work was characterised by the lack of defined rules or procedures of work, and the expectation that such labour market participation was only temporary. Gordon Rodwell's mother took casual jobs such as cleaning, washing and ironing, which supplemented her income from two boarders. Some local petit-bourgeois and middle-class women employed domestic help. In 1913 Mrs H. R. Lee, wife of the prominent ER&S accountant, advertised for a 'competent general servant', offering fifteen shillings a week. In 1915 Sarah Middleton advertised for an 'experienced girl for household duties', but if the small number of advertisements is any guide, then numbers of domestic servants were very small.[14]

In the 1910s and 1920s men had their own niches in the informal economy, primarily outdoor activities such as fishing, prawning, shooting, and blackberry picking. The irregularity of waged work provided opportunity for such activities, but these extra resources were sometimes necessary to cover for insufficient wages. Working as a waterside worker from 1926, William Bailey experienced considerable breaks between employment. During this time he would fish in the harbour, gather mushrooms west of Port Kembla (in an area that became Cringila) or go shooting for quail near Lake Illawarra.[15] Fishing trips to Lake Illawarra, Coomaditchie or the beaches around Port Kembla were common. Men rowed to Big Island—the largest and closest of the area's five offshore islands—hoping to benefit from its resources of fish, birds and birds' eggs. The shoals and reefs around the island were prolific, if dangerous, fishing spots.[16] The demand for rowboats in the 1920s supported a small boat-hire business in Port Kembla harbour.[17]

The informal economy helped some men at Port Kembla through periods of unemployment, but this was not the 'positive culture of poverty' that historian David Potts found among oral recollections of Victorians in the Great Depression.[18] Not all men had the opportunities to survive long periods without paid work, especially itinerant labourers, who sometimes lacked the knowledge of local resources and the skills to exploit them. For these men often the only means of survival was gambling or theft. In February 1928 William H., who was camped at Port Kembla and had not worked for the last six months, lived off a £174 win at the races, and frequented two-up games at Corrimal.[19] That same year Lionel H., an itinerant labourer camped at Port Kembla, was charged with stealing from Frost Brothers, a general store in Wentworth Street. He told the Wollongong Police Court:

> [We] camped in the bush at Port Kembla. We were having a rough spin. My Uncle was giving us a few shillings but it wasn't enough to keep us in food, so we all decided the only way to get some money was to break into some place.[20]

Even for men with the skills and resources to exploit the informal economy, its resources were seasonal, its harvest unpredictable. Fishing and prawning were primarily summer activities, and there was competition from commercial white fisherman at Lake Illawarra and Koori fisherman at Port Kembla.

In the 1910s and 1920s children collected bottles, firewood, and loose coal from beside railway lines, picked blackberries or helped in the family business. Many, such as Gordon Rodwell and Sarah Drury, left school at the minimum legal age of fourteen to find jobs. For girls, especially the eldest in large families, the demands of housework led to their early departure from school. Ursula Lindsay, the eldest of nine children, left school on her fourteenth birthday in 1921 to 'help out with the family'.

Children still at school were required to undertake chores or part-time work. Ethel Combes and her older brother helped their widowed mother before and after school at her cleaning job in the ER&S offices. In the mid-1920s they also trapped rabbits and birds and collected mushrooms in the bush at Lake Illawarra (near what later became Warrawong). The rabbits were skinned and sold for 1s 6d a pair, while the fish and mushrooms were used by the household: 'Anything we made like that we always gave to mum, but it was only fun to us'. This kind of work was often understood by children to be leisure—especially fishing, which was a popular childhood pastime—but there was also an illicit side to their activities. Local children carried out theft on a small scale. During the 1920s young thieves constantly raided the best gardens in Port Kembla, as Colin Warrington remembers: 'During the appropriate period we would jump over other people's fences at night and pinch food from them—grapes and what have you . . . we would have to go and find food just to keep the family going'.[21]

There were plenty of gardens to target. In the 1920s vegetable gardens were a major component of household production and labour, and they filled the backyards and spare blocks of the town. As Ethel Combes recalled, 'everybody had their gardens those days'. The minimum block size at Port Kembla of 43 by 12 metres ensured that most households had the necessary space.[22] Both the Simons and the Drurys had vegetable gardens on the spare block next door during the 1920s. Suburbanisation also offered more space for lemon, apple, and apricot trees and choko vines; cows, chickens and ducks were also a common sight in the backyards and spare blocks of the town. Because vegetable gardens provided food, women had considerable claim to their upkeep. Sarah Drury's grandmother and mother both tended large vegetable gardens. While women cultivated and harvested gardens, men sometimes carried more out 'physical' labour such as weeding and digging.[23] These patterns of home-based production represented the skills and practices of a rural economy transplanted into an urban context.

In the formative period of industrial expansion, large areas of vacant land surrounding Port Kembla provided space for cows, or were useful foraging areas for mushrooms and blackberries. Industrialisation had not yet degraded the resource-rich areas around Port Kembla—beaches and headlands, Lake Illawarra, Tom Thumb's Lagoon, Coomaditchie Lagoon and scattered patches of vacant crown land—which offered fish, prawns, birds, birds' eggs, mushrooms and blackberries. Port Kembla residents could readily access these kinds of resources, unlike their counterparts in the inner suburbs of Sydney or Melbourne.[24] The barren environs of other industrial towns like Broken Hill or Mount Isa also offered no such possibilities. The rich coastal environment at Port Kembla created an unusual amalgam of industrial and rural methods of survival during the formative period. Port Kembla was similar to towns like Wonthaggi and Newcastle in this respect. These industrial towns also had easy access to relatively resource-rich natural environments. Historian Peter Cochrane found that in the Victorian mining town of Wonthaggi, 'idle time facilitated a growing dependence on local game and fish from the nearby coast'. At Newcastle, labour historian John Merritt noted how unemployed ironworkers, who built shacks on the banks of the Hunter River during the depression, fished and caught rabbits.[25]

The economic importance of the informal economy was not lost on either the local unions or companies. In 1920 at the New South Wales Board of Trade case to determine the living wage on the south coast, ER&S pointed to the prevalence of vegetable gardens and lodgers as an argument for lowering the basic wage.[26] The Australian Workers' Union (AWU) and the Federated Engine Drivers' and Firemen's Association (FEDFA) resisted moves to have the informal economy form part of the basic wage determination. They attacked the company's evidence, claiming it had been given mostly by male clerks, 'whose living in the first place is substantially different to the average manual worker and who in the second place are not able to speak of home expenditure as well as their womenfolk'.[27] The company was unsuccessful in this case, but attempts to appropriate the informal economy and the depth of resistance to such moves demonstrate its importance to the working class.

Each household member applied their skills and abilities in the prevailing conditions of the informal and formal economies, but different members of a household had differing claims on its resources.[28] Eleanor Allan, a music teacher, told the Board of Trade in 1920 that her husband, a ladler at ER&S, received a wage bonus, 'but it is no good to me. It is his property; I do not know what he does with it'. Her own income as a teacher went into 'a common fund for housekeeping and trying to get a home together'.[29] In other households, husbands gave their pay packets to their wives, who were responsible for expenditure and budgeting. Edith Neaves recalled that her father gave his pay packet to her mother, but not before he tried to obscure the exact amount:

> Of course he'd get hold of the end of the envelope and he'd do this some-
> times [rubbing the envelope] so she couldn't see what was on it.
> Q: He tried to keep a little for himself?
> Yes a little bit for his grog. [laughter]

In contrast, Morgan Simon remembered that his father was in control of budgeting, although it was still a consultative process: 'I think Dad was the one that handled the purse strings. He brought his pay home and they'd [mother and father] sit down together and they'd budget things out and that was the way that he did it.' A range of negotiations over money and resources occurred within Port Kembla households, but generally the extensive informal economy present during the formative period gave women and children some independence from male wages, while men could also deal more effectively with lengthy interruptions to waged work.

The town and its surrounds were more than just a context for paid work, family and social life. The rich environmental context came to be appreciated for the resources it offered and the quality of life it ensured. The decline in the informal economy, beginning in the early 1920s, slowly undermined this important local economic relationship.

The Decline of the Informal Economy

In the 1920s and 1930s land and land use came under increasing control and surveillance by state and local government authorities, and this began to restrict opportunities in the informal economy. In 1921 three 'Port Kembla residents' were charged with stealing oysters from the lagoon: 'Constable McLaughlin noted that there had been several complaints to the Fisheries Department of such action'.[30] For many years this had been a commonly accepted practice, but the Fisheries Department began leasing the oyster beds in 1914, and taking oysters from the lagoon became 'illegal harvesting'. From the 1920s the Council became increasingly concerned about the preservation of the Port Kembla Reserve (situated between MM and Hill 60), and prohibited cutting trees in the area.[31] In 1928 the Council resolved to fence off the Department of Defence land near the eastern breakwater in an effort to stop its 'unwanted exploitation'.[32] Government and Council action was motivated by a number of different factors. Crown land around Port Kembla was becoming increasingly valuable to the state government and a source of potential revenue from new industries, while decisions to set aside and protect reserves were attempts by a rural-dominated Council to control and regulate large-scale urban growth at Port Kembla.[33]

Such moves gave rise to conflict with the local working class, who understood the areas around Port Kembla to be a legitimate public storehouse of valuable resources—an attitude akin to the idea of a 'village common'. In a letter to the *Illawarra Mercury* in 1921, a correspondent using the name 'Enthusiast' objected to the restriction of private fishing at Tom Thumb's Lagoon: 'Hitherto this was a place where a working man and his family could enjoy one of the luxuries provided by nature . . . insult has been added to injury by leasing the best oyster beds to a private individual'.[34] An incident at a Council meeting in 1935 demonstrated different class-based understandings of the environment. Alderman William Gorrell, a dairy farmer from Unanderra, moved that blackberries be declared a noxious weed in the municipality. For farmers, these introduced bushes took over valuable grazing land and injured cattle. Alderman Jack Mathews, a labourer from Port Kembla, disagreed: 'I like blackberries. I'm not going to vote for it'.[35] Other aldermen were ambivalent and the motion lapsed, but the Council officially declared blackberries a noxious weed in 1939. Families were still taking trips to the Illawarra escarpment in the 1970s to pick blackberries, but eradication campaigns and spraying finally saw an end to the practice in the 1980s.

Not only government authorities and councils were tightening control on land. In the 1930s the industries of Port Kembla also stepped up security measures. This was partly in response to the theft by the unemployed of industrial and construction material that littered the works to build temporary homes. In February 1935, during Cyril R'.s court appearance for allegedly stealing copper pipe from AI&S, Sergeant Pye from Port Kembla claimed that 'the AI&S coy [company] was losing property worth thousands of pounds every year'.[36] Those who had gathered coal that had fallen from waggons in the 1910s and 1920s ran the risk of prosecution in the 1930s. The state government's role in this process was a more rigid policing of industrial property from 1930. This led to numerous charges of stealing coal, corrugated iron, piping and other materials from the local industries coming to court during the early 1930s.[37] There is no direct evidence, but the responses of government and local companies may have been motivated by the concern to protect industry and private property in the worsening economic and political crisis which engulfed New South Wales in the early 1930s.[38]

Regulatory moves regarding land and land use occurred in the context of the increasing environmental degradation of the areas around Port Kembla. Industrialisation, through land clearance and the pollution of air and water, slowly destroyed the resources that had supported an active informal economy, while at the same time it cemented male wage labour as the dominant means of making a living. Urbanisation, too, led to a decrease in the amount of vacant land in and around Port Kembla and produced environment-destroying pollution.

There were other setbacks for the informal economy. As average family sizes fell, the labour available for household production decreased. Edith Neaves, growing up in Port Kembla in the 1910s and early 1920s, had two sisters and two brothers. An ER&S survey of its workers in 1920 found that the average number of children under fourteen per family was two.[39] At the 1921 Census there were an average of 4.64 people per occupied dwelling in the Central Illawarra, declining further to 4.16 by the 1933 Census.[40] Birth rates in the municipality fell from 46 children born per 1000 people in 1917 to 34 per 1000 in 1928. By 1934 the birth rate in the Central Illawarra had fallen to 18 children per 1000 people, slightly above the state average of 17.[41]

Falling family sizes robbed the informal economy of potential labour, and sped its decline. As a consequence the dependence on and knowledge of the local environment also declined, undermining economic links residents traditionally had to their locality. The onset of the depression, however, revived some of these traditions.

The Great Depression

In the absence of paid work during the Great Depression, men relied heavily on traditional male responses to unemployment—fishing, rabbiting and shooting. Ces Catterel, whose father worked as a tally clerk for the Public Works Department, recalled the effects of the depression:

> It got to the stage where they had to put half the workers off. So they [the workers] decided they wanted to work week on week off, and that's what they did. Then on the week off they'd go out and either catch rabbits or catch fish and give them to their mates, grow vegies and try and help one another. Everybody got in and helped and it was quite good really.

The mention of vegetable gardens, usually women's work, is significant, for many men moved into tending gardens during long periods of unemployment. My mother, Heather Eklund, recalls leaving for school in the morning in the mid-1930s, and she knew that if her father was in the garden then he had no paid work that day. We can only speculate what kind of domestic tension this re-negotiation of roles in the household economy produced.[42]

Families were often the centre of strategies to deal with poverty caused by the depression. Scarce resources were shared along family and kinship lines. Vegetable gardens became an important area where reciprocal relations of family and neighbourhood support played out. As Edith Neaves remembers, 'If you had any surplus you'd give it away. You didn't sell things them days—more friendly'. These cultural strategies were built on a long tradition of activity in the informal economy and were vital to many people's survival through the depression. As Edith Neaves commented, 'Oh yes we had to have our gardens. That kept us going'. Itinerant workers, who lived on the edges of the town isolated from this form of support, tended to be marginalised from these strategies developed by more established working-class households.

For women at the head of such households the task of turning reduced male wages into a subsistence living was difficult. Ces Catterel remembers the great amount of work that his mother did during the depression:

> Yes my mother was wonderful; she coped all right, she used to work pretty hard. We had eight in the family and she was working all the time. She did everything she possibly could for us and of course we appreciated that, more so in later life.

Pressure to survive on impossibly tight budgets took an emotional toll on some women. One of my mother's enduring images of my grandmother, Eva Halcrow, was that 'she always seemed to be cooking, with a worried look on her face'. The burden of managing scarce money and resources also reduced the time and energy women had available for informal economic activities. At the same time, widespread male unemployment gave men more time for such activities, and their participation became more common. The depression decreased the range and frequency of married women's informal economic pursuits, and centred their lives more firmly on home and the domestic sphere.

For single women the depression sometimes had the opposite result, bringing them into paid work. During the depression Jean Payne worked as a cleaner and child minder for a local woman. Her wage of ten shillings was based on piece work, rather than hours worked: 'I would do housework, ironing, preparing vegies for tea. I had to work till I was finished, maybe [till] 2 or 3 or 5 o'clock'.[43]

During the depression children worked to support struggling households. All of the children in Ces Catterel's family had to leave school. Ces found work in a garage selling petrol. Ursula Lindsay's two younger brothers 'left here and went off to Queensland to get jobs'. Bill King left school aged fourteen in 1933 and began working on a milk run, earning 7s 6d a week.

Children of the skilled working class were also affected. Len Ewart stayed at school till he was eighteen, including a year's technical education. He too was forced to leave in 1932 because of the cost of textbooks and fares to Wollongong, and was subsequently unemployed for four years.[44]

If a job was unavailable locally, another option was to send children to board with relatives. Gordon Rodwell found work at MM in 1926 aged sixteen, but he was laid off in 1929. He was sent to his uncle's property near Crookwell: 'He sent word "You better send Gordon up to me. That would be one less you've got to look after there." So I went up there for eight months'. Edith Neaves went to Sydney for two years to live with her grand-mother because 'you couldn't get work here'. The resources of the extended family in some cases helped share the burdens of the depression, and the dependence on those beyond the geographical boundaries of the locality brought new outside influences on the informal economy.

For the local middle class the impact of the depression on family life was less significant. Staff at the local works were not retrenched, but carried out maintenance work or processed the few orders that did arrive. Albert Rieck, in charge of the weighbridge at ER&S, recalled that the depression 'didn't hurt us very much. You were knocked a certain amount [10 per cent] off your pay. It did [affect] a lot of people I suppose but it didn't affect us'. Rieck did recall, however, a reduction in money available for leisure: 'You wouldn't be able to go to places like you used to go. You might have to cut that down'.

Building on traditions established in the 1910s and 1920s, the local working class relied heavily on the resources of the informal economy during the depression. While recollections of coping and 'getting by' have to be approached with caution because such narratives minimise conflict and hardship, these memories do highlight the reciprocity that developed between working-class households. These experiences were an influential cultural background to the later political mobilisation of the working class.

The Formal Economy Recovers

The Great Depression halted the decline in the informal economy, but from the mid-1930s it suffered further setbacks precipitated by economic re-covery and continued industrialisation. From late 1933 male employment picked up steadily, if not dramatically. By November 1940 only 556 men in the Illawarra region were registered as unemployed.[45] Households again became more reliant on male wage labour for survival.

In these conditions women's work was increasingly centred on the care of house, children and husband, as the production of resources for the household declined. Household chores, such as washing, took considerable time because of the dirt, soot and dust of industrial work at Port Kembla. Women scrubbed men's work clothes daily and hung them out overnight to dry, while wash days for the rest of the family were usually at the beginning of the week. Consumption was also an integral part of this home-centred work. Before the widespread availability of refrigeration in the 1950s, a visit to the town's stores was a daily task, although home deliveries of items such as milk and bread lessened the burden.[46]

While the informal economy declined, it did not disappear. Fishing remained an important activity for men and there were often other sources of occasional income—a win at the races or casual work. Women still took in lodgers or did other odd jobs. After marrying in 1934, Bertha Rodwell lost her job at MM, but occasionally worked at the local hotels as a kitchen-hand. As her husband Gordon Rodwell recalled, his wife would work 'whenever she got a chance, she was well known. Somebody would ring her up and she would do odd jobs'. Income from such work often was spent on a special purchase, as Rodwell adds: 'That's when we bought the car, and we borrowed the money off mother to buy the car and we wanted to pay her back quick'.

The decline in the informal economy decreased options for the local working class. Wage labour came to dominate a labour market that was overwhelmingly industrial and male. By the 1940s, households were increasingly distant from production and the experience of earning. The highly localised informal economy had been both restricted in scope and to some extent opened to outside influence. The informal economic activities that survived in the period after World War II became more male preserves, and benefited from fewer natural resources, as industrial and urban pollution damaged the rich natural environment around Port Kembla. The informal economy would have one major revival after World War II as migrants tapped its resources in new ways. Before moving to this later period, however, it is necessary to outline the social and political developments during the formative era.

4

The Structures of Locality, 1900 to 1920

Iₙ 1914 Pᴀᴛʀɪᴄᴋ Tᴜʀɴᴇʀ, an ER&S nightwatchman of 'temperate habits', was killed in a bicycle accident on his way to a meeting of the Wollongong branch of the Manchester Unity Independent Order of Oddfellows. Turner was unfortunate for by the end of the year a branch had opened at Port Kembla that would have made his journey unnecessary.[1] This new branch was indicative of the growing number of locally based organisations, established in the 1900s and 1910s, which created a relatively self-sufficient town society for Port Kembla's white inhabitants by the 1920s.[2]

During the formative period of industrial society at Port Kembla, industrial, commercial, residential and social development focused attention on one particular place, the town itself. This chapter charts the material conditions of the town's development and outlines its characteristic social relations and cultural practices. Aspects of the town's development, such as the emergence of a class-based understanding of different areas of the town, fostered a class-based identity. Yet the overwhelming effect of the infrastructure and social development of the town from 1900 to the late 1920s was to reinforce local identity, and underpin a strong localist politics. The following account will concentrate on the period up until the 1920s, since it was in this period that the most important material changes occurred.

As Table 4.1 demonstrates, the population of Port Kembla in 1901 was small, but in the following years it steadily increased with commercial, industrial and residential expansion.

The overwhelming majority of males in 1901 highlights the status of the locality as a centre of new employment. Many of these men camped in tents or shacks on crown land while the work on the government breakwater was proceeding. As employment became more regular and the town developed residential and commercial infrastructure, a more gender-balanced community appeared, though there was still a preponderance of males by 1921.

Table 4.1 Population and housing at Port Kembla, 1901–21

	1901	*1911*	*1921*
Population	123	844	1 622
Males	115	550	910
Females	8	294	712
Occupied dwellings	34	181	318

Source: *Census of the Commonwealth of Australia*, 1901, 1911, 1921.

Commercial Port Kembla

Port Kembla came to life as a town in the first twenty years of the twentieth century, though early developments were modest. In December 1900 John Patterson was appointed the unofficial postmaster, a service he ran from his house near the Southern Coal Company's jetty.[3] A new full-time primary school was built in 1902, as fate would have it, on the future site of ER&S.[4] St Stephen's Church of England opened in August 1903 on land purchased from the Wentworth estate.[5] Father Walsh performed the first Catholic Mass and Holy Communion in 1905 at the home of Martin Fitzpatrick, a ganger with the Public Works Department.[6]

These changes represent the beginning of a trend that situated important facilities and services at a local level, yet at this early stage the town was still without an identifiable centre. The locality appeared formless and indistinct to visitors. In August 1907 an inspector from the Postmaster-General's Office visited Port Kembla and noted that the present location of the post office near the Southern Coal Company's jetty was 'not central but no objection had been taken to its present position as owing to the very unsettled state of the place it cannot be determined what would be the most suitable position for any length of time'.[7]

Township subdivision and development was delayed throughout 1907 by negotiations between ER&S and the state government over land and wharfage rates, and legal action between the government and the Wentworth estate. These matters were resolved in January 1908 and ER&S began construction work immediately.[8] Twenty temporary houses built by Public Works employees were removed from the new ER&S site, some of them being transferred north of Salty Creek where the primary school was also relocated.[9] North of Salty Creek, in an area now occupied by the BHP steel works, appeared to be a possible town centre, and a site for future commercial development. In 1908 the *Mercury* noted that 'new structures are being built north of Salty Creek and there is quite a respectable population there'.[10]

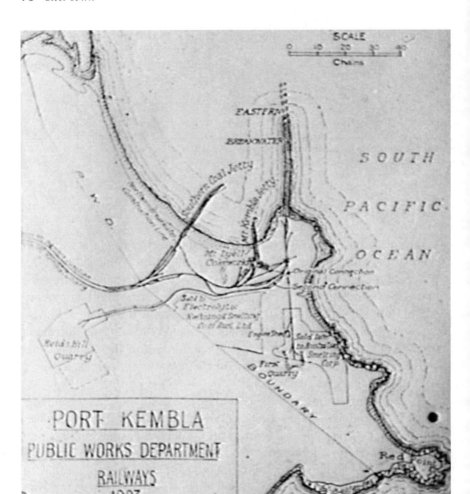

A Public Works Department map of Port Kembla from 1907

The establishment of ER&S, the survey of the Wentworth estate for subdivision, and the creation of two major streets, Wentworth Street and Military Road, gave the town a more definite location and shape. The rival site north of Salty Creek quickly faded as this area was taken up by industry. Once ER&S officially confirmed its choice of Port Kembla in January 1908, there was more certainty regarding the site of future town development, and residential and commercial development located west of the new ER&S industrial site. In April 1908 the Wollongong postmaster found the location of Patterson's unofficial post office near the Southern Coal Company's jetty 'ridiculous and certainly inconvenient' since 'the township's position is clearly defined'.[11]

While industry led the way in defining the shape of Port Kembla, commercial activity soon followed. Port Kembla's growing population and cheap land, first auctioned in June 1909, attracted storekeepers. The 43- by 12-metre blocks varied considerably in price. The best sites in Wentworth Street fetched up to £3 10s per foot, while some low-lying blocks were as cheap as £1 per foot. At the first auction J. G. Fairley, storekeeper, and W. P. Laughlin, a barber, both from Dapto, bought land and the following year opened stores at Port Kembla. A Wollongong-based builder and business-man, William Waters, also bought four blocks in the first subdivision.[12] Along with storekeepers and builders, the Christian churches were quick to purchase land and establish themselves in the new town, providing local forums for religious and social life. The Methodists opened a church in Wentworth Street in 1912, while the Presbyterians had an active presence in the town from 1914 and opened their church in 1923. In February 1915 Catholic authorities purchased two blocks of land in O'Donnell Street, and a combined Catholic church and primary school was opened in 1919. In December 1923 the school was taken over by the Sisters of St Joseph.[13]

Projects that required large-scale commercial investment became more common and these helped change the face of the town centre. In 1911 the Licensing Court approved the licence for the Port Kembla Hotel, and the hotel was completed in June 1912 at a cost of £4000. In 1915 senior staff from ER&S, including H. R. Lee and E. A. White, along with a local publican Dan Murphy, formed the Port Kembla Hall and Amusement Company. The company, supported by capital of £1200, constructed the Empire Hall in Wentworth Street, opposite Middleton's newsagency, with the aim of showing moving pictures twice weekly.[14]

New halls and meeting rooms built in the late 1900s and 1910s pro-vided local forums for political, religious and sporting groups. By 1915 there were three halls in Port Kembla: Murray's Hall (1909), Simon's Hall (1911) and the Empire Hall (1915).[15] Murray's Hall (formerly Jackson's) was also the dining room of Sarah Murray's boarding house in Military Road, which could be converted for special occasions. Another boarding house at Port Kembla, Pascoe's, also had 'rooms' available for meetings.

Halls also offered respectable mixed-sex venues for dances, balls, and showing moving pictures. The 1914 Annual Ball of the Political Labor League, held in Simon's Hall, attracted sixty couples, including a number of visitors from Wollongong and Mount Kembla.[16] During winter Simon's Hall was also used for roller skating. As an indication of their role in supporting local organisations, Pascoe's Rooms and Murray's Hall both waived their fees for Progress Association fund-raising evenings.

The Port Kembla Hotel (renamed the Great Eastern Hotel in 1914) also provided a venue for meetings, including those of new male sporting organisations. The Port Kembla Cricket Club, the Surf Club (both formed in 1912), the British Soccer Association (1913) and the Port Kembla Rugby League Club (1914) all held regular meetings and 'smoke socials' at the hotel. The Progress Association used the hotel as a venue for annual dinners and banquets.[17] More importantly the establishment of the hotel allowed informal male recreation and socialising to be carried out locally. Before the hotel's opening, an enterprising Wollongong hotelier had canvassed orders for drinks in the town and then delivered them to a pre-arranged place by coach.[18] A second hotel opened in March 1917, highlighting the popularity of these hotels as social venues and meeting places for local men.[19] Hotels, halls and meeting rooms provided the necessary venues for the development of local social and political organisations. They helped situate social life within the town.

The town's continued commercial prosperity in the 1910s was ensured by population growth and the economic survival of ER&S. Rees, a baker from Woonona, opened a bakery in Military Road in February 1914.[20] The ES&A (English, Scottish and Australian) Bank established a branch in the town in 1915, supplementing the services of the government savings bank at the post office, which had been operating since 1911. Indicative of the extent of commercial development, the first issue of a town-based newspaper, the *Port Kembla Pilot*, was published by Robert Shipp in September 1920.[21] Political action by local residents enhanced the town's civic development. In 1915 the local Progress Association, a broadly based organisation of locals formed in 1908, successfully lobbied the state government to move the primary school back from Salty Creek to Military Road. When the new school opened in 1916, many children who had previously commuted to Wollongong because of the poor conditions at Salty Creek returned to their town's school.

By the beginning of the 1920s the location of Port Kembla west of ER&S and MM was firmly established by subdivisions of the Wentworth estate and one government subdivision.[22] The development of a bustling commercial area further underlined the town's location and helped define its centre. In 1920 commercial Port Kembla boasted four boarding houses, two butchers, two milk vendors, two bootmakers, two carriers, a baker, a blacksmith and other specialised services such as doctors and banks, located mostly in Wentworth Street, Military Road and Fitzwilliam Street (just off Wentworth Street).[23] This busy commercial centre catered for a population of 1622 people, living in 318 dwellings, and contained the stores and services necessary for the development of a relatively self-sufficient locality.[24] Port Kembla people still travelled to Wollongong for specialised services, such as hospitals and secondary education, but the change from 1900 was profound. By 1920 the essential requirements for everyday life were met by the town itself.

Residential Port Kembla

Residential growth accompanied industrial and commercial expansion. From the initial subdivision of the Wentworth estate in 1909, the Wentworth trustees (the administrators of the estate) were the major landowners and agents at Port Kembla. This gave them a decisive influence on the form of residential Port Kembla.[25] The Wentworth trustees had controlled 890 hectares of land around Port Kembla since the death of W. C. Wentworth in 1872. In 1900 most of the estate was leased to dairy farmers for five shillings an acre per year. As part of the state government's plans for the Port Kembla harbour in the late 1890s, the Public Works Department initially considered resuming the whole parcel of land, but this move was challenged in the New South Wales Supreme Court in 1907. The estate's trustees successfully argued that 'it was outside the functions of Government to go in for [the] trafficking of land'.[26] Subsequently, the size of the resumption was reduced to 226 hectares, giving the state government only limited control over the development of the town.

The Wentworth trustees owned most of the land adjacent to an area where the government was about to spend over £200 000 on the new harbour. As one parliamentary critic argued during debate on the Port Kembla Harbour Bill in 1898: 'The Government are to spend thousands of pounds in making a harbour and in resuming land, and when the work is completed the holders of the adjoining land will be able to scrape in thousands of pounds from the public'.[27] Later events proved this prediction accurate. By 1915 the trustees were able to dispose of parts of the estate for prices ranging from £150 per acre for less desirable sections of the estate, to £600 per acre for prime sites in Wentworth Street.[28]

However, the development of Port Kembla could have progressed very differently. During 1907 and 1908 it was unclear how the creation of a township would proceed. Workers suffered from poor living conditions because of a lack of freehold land, and the local Progress Association called on the state government to plan the township. In January 1909 a deputation from Port Kembla presented to the Minister for Lands a petition with 400 signatures calling for the subdivision of a government township to alleviate the housing shortage.[29] However, the Progress Association lacked significant support from those who controlled Port Kembla's development. The local Council, controlled by representatives from the surrounding rural towns of the Central Illawarra, feared having to pay the costs of forming and metalling the roads of a government subdivision. The state government had indicated its approach to the matter in 1907 when the Minister for Public Works, C. A. Lee, told the *Illawarra Mercury* that 'he did not intend to cut up the land for sale in building allotments, as he considered Wollongong as the residential area for the men working at the Port'.[30] In a feature on the development of Port Kembla in 1908, the *Sydney Morning Herald* observed: 'it is understood in well-informed circles that Port Kembla would become the industrial centre of the South Coast, and Wollongong the residential portion of the district'.[31]

Government reluctance to subdivide partly related to the failure of its initial 890-hectare resumption, but it also reflected government attitudes to Port Kembla. Port Kembla was seen as not so much a future 'town' with stores, services and houses, but as an 'industrial centre', with workers commuting daily. In 1916 the state Labor government, led by Premier W. A. Holman, was more sympathetic to criticism of land companies reaping profit on rising land values, and released 100 lots in the area of Reservoir, Marne and Gallipoli Streets.[32] The delay in government action, however, allowed the Wentworth trustees to dominate and benefit enormously from Port Kembla's growth.

Because of the lack of government involvement, Port Kembla was not a planned town. In the early stages of industrialisation hundreds of hopeful workers, sometimes with their families, simply camped on crown land in temporary houses or tents. Living conditions for these workers were very poor as industrial growth outpaced the provision of housing, roads and basic services such as sanitation and water. In March 1907 the *Illawarra Mercury* noted the 'absorbing topic here just now is the water supply' as Port Kembla's dams were drained by hundreds of workers and sixty horses. 'From a health point of view', continued the *Mercury*, 'there is some cause for anxiety about overcrowding of tents and stables'.[33] A continuing theme in the history of the town was a lack of adequate housing, yet people were determined to live locally and the residential areas of Port Kembla soon developed, despite C. A. Lee's vision of Port Kembla as purely an industrial area.

Together with the Wentworth estate, the local industries had a major influence on the residential space of the town. By the early 1920s local companies had built 10 to 15 per cent of Port Kembla's housing stock. ER&S owned sixty-three houses in Port Kembla by 1920. The Mount Lyell Cokeworks built sixteen homes for its employees, and in 1921 MM bought an entire section of the government subdivision consisting of nine lots in Somme and Reservoir Streets.[34]

The social geography of residential Port Kembla is revealed by an analysis of the 1917 Electoral Roll. Wentworth Street was the most populated street, with 220 residents enrolled to vote. These were mostly working-class householders (113 residents), but also included the shopkeepers in the central area of the main street (10). Military Road, where 81 electors were enrolled, had a similar ratio of working class (52) to storekeepers (5). Darcy Road (61 residents), with its company housing, also contained a large number of working-class households (28). The Avenues were part of the successful second subdivision of the Wentworth estate, first opened in 1913, and had 44 people enrolled. The remainder of Port Kembla consisted of smaller, more middle-class streets, such as O'Donnell Street (11 residents), Marne Street (7), Allan Street (6), Reservoir Street (5), Bass Street (4) and Church Street (2). There were also a number of houses behind Surf or Fisherman's Beach (22), and Perkin's Beach (31). In addition, there were some Public Works homes on Port Kembla-Wollongong Road (10) and some remaining in the Salty Creek area (4).[35]

The ER&S cottages in Darcy and Military Roads were typical of the working-class homes at Port Kembla. They were four-room weatherboard houses, consisting of three bedrooms and a kitchen. Ted Livermore, a labourer from ER&S, lived with his family in a four-room cottage at a cost of ten shillings a week. He and his wife slept in one room, and his two children had a room each.[36] Eleanor Allan worked as a music teacher and her husband was a ladler at ER&S. Their two incomes allowed them to add a front and back verandah and a washroom onto their basic Darcy Road home. The Allans' home cost £375 in 1917, and they paid sixteen shillings a week as part of a rent purchase scheme operated by ER&S.[37]

ER&S cottages were atypical in one sense. Rent purchase schemes were not common at Port Kembla, and only ER&S workers in company houses had this option. Using state-wide provincial figures as a guide, about 60 per cent of all Port Kembla households lived in rental accommodation.[38] Prices in the local rental market reflected the variable cycles of demand for labour at the local industries. A 1912 report noted an 'outcry here against excessive rents' of twelve shillings per week for a four-bedroom cottage.[39] At the beginning of the wartime boom at ER&S, single rooms were advertised at Port Kembla for as much as £1 2s per week.[40]

Home additions were one way of expanding small four-room houses, and their popularity reflected not only the inadequate size of many Port Kembla homes for growing families, but also the energy and commitment that people invested in improving their homes and thereby staying in Port Kembla. Verandahs were modified or rooms added to provide more space as families grew. Iris Jenks' father enlarged their small Public Works home during the 1920s:

> There was only three rooms . . . and then he eventually more or less built two more rooms, two bedrooms onto that for my sisters and I. He built two more rooms out of iron and some of it used to be built of bags, and we'd paint them with whitewash!

Gordon Rodwell's family lived in a two-bedroom weatherboard cottage in Third Avenue. During the mid-1920s one bedroom was for his mother and three sisters and one for two boarders, while the verandah was turned into a 'sleep-out' for Gordon. Sleep-outs were a common addition and were usually reserved for the eldest male child in working-class households.

The well-off petit-bourgeoisie had more spacious homes than those of the working class, as evident from real estate advertisements. A year after the death of his wife, H. F. Banfield, manager of Fairley's, decided to sell his house in Wentworth Street:

> Port Kembla—For sale. W.B [weatherboard] residence 'Nirvana' . . . possessing unsurpassed outlook and containing 3 bedrooms, dining room, breakfast room, kitchen, laundry. Land 40 × 140 [feet]. Apply H. F. Banfield.[41]

The homes of the local middle class were obviously more spacious than working-class homes, and often had better services and facilities. Albert Rieck, engine driver and later weighbridge foreman at ER&S, married in January 1920. Upon returning from their honeymoon, the couple moved into a new home in O'Donnell Street. To do this immediately after marriage was unusual at Port Kembla, as most couples lived with parents for a few years to save money for a deposit. Rieck purchased the land from his father for £80 and this was one of the first houses in O'Donnell Street. It was a two-bedroom weatherboard home built by a Wollongong builder, Parsons. Water and electricity were available from the mid-1920s.[42]

Even more salubrious were the company houses for the staff. The first house constructed by ER&S was for the general manager, Bernard Magnus, in 1908. This house formed a clear contrast with the working-class houses in Darcy Road. As the *Illawarra Mercury* reported:

> On Tuesday Mr Magnus took possession of his residence. It is a splendid building of the Queen Anne style of architecture. It is built of brick with a tiled roof. The walls are plastered inside and out. The length of the building is 80ft, and it contains 13 rooms, all of which are tastefully furnished. The building is lighted with 35 electric lights, and electricity is used for every conceivable purpose throughout the house.[43]

These staff houses were located in Private Lane near the Port Kembla Primary School. Port Kembla contained few wealthy areas, but Private Lane was one exception until the mid-1920s. Thereafter, both ER&S and MM purchased staff houses throughout Port Kembla.

By the 1920s Port Kembla possessed a thriving commercial centre surrounded by a distinctive residential area. This commercial and residential landscape formed a crucial part of the structures of locality, and facilitated the town's social development. Alongside such changes to the built environment, the town's residents began to perceive their locality in more optimistic terms, and these two factors together were powerful forces for the development of local identity.

Changing Perceptions of the Locality

Before 1900 Port Kembla did not excite the imagination of non-Aboriginal residents the way it would in later years. In 1890 George Sinclair, wharfinger for the Mount Kembla Coal Company, was chosen by residents to answer a Department of Public Instruction questionnaire regarding the application for a new school. Answering the question 'Is the locality likely to be permanently inhabited?' Sinclair wrote: 'There will always be some inhabitants, but the number will depend very largely upon the number of persons employed by the Port Kembla [Mount Kembla] coal company at their jetties at Port Kembla'.[44] This modest answer lacked the self-assurance typical of later communications with government departments. Industrialisation changed this, and unleashed a great optimism among Port Kembla residents. In February 1902 the Port Kembla correspondent for the *Illawarra Mercury* reported that 'new buildings were springing up all over the place' and that 'Altogether our little town has an air of prosperity'.[45] ER&S preference for Port Kembla in 1907, despite the delays, engendered confident predictions of a bright future. One correspondent wrote to the *Mercury*: 'I picture in my mind's eye, on account of the security of the works, hundreds of beautiful model cottages with their garden plots and families like olive branches around their table all brought about by the establishment of industries'.[46]

This confidence was becoming more widespread, but not common to all sections of society. In 1907 a carpenter from Sydney, who was camped at Port Kembla waiting for work, told the *Illawarra Mercury* that he was returning home because 'from what he can see, [Port] Kembla will remain a canvas town for some time to come'.[47] This was a view common to itinerant male workers who often experienced the downside of rapid industrialisation. These men led lonely, isolated lives in tents or roughly constructed houses on the fringes of Port Kembla, and the image of a 'canvas town' suggests poor living conditions and an uncertain future. The currency of this image increased during the Great Depression, as one of the characters in Kylie Tennant's *The Battlers* remarks, 'If it's anything like Port Kembla . . . I'd sooner stay away. Men waiting around the steelworks, so that when a chap is killed they could get his job'.[48] The divergence between the views of itinerant labourers and those of established residents reflected not only their different perceptions of the locality, but also the social distance between these two groups.

An understanding of Port Kembla divided into class-based streets was another perception which contradicted the image of a confident, thriving industrial town. This perception was based on the class differences in housing described previously, and it is most clearly revealed in the oral recollections of working-class residents who lived in Darcy Road. Many identified themselves as 'Darcy Roaders', a group of families who shared the experience of living in ER&S houses and working for ER&S. Colin Warrington grew up in Darcy Road. He remembers:

> Well they were always a close community in Darcy Road and Military Road which surrounded the football ground, and we grew up together as one huge family, and if you lived in Darcy Road you most certainly didn't take any cheek from anyone else living in Port Kembla. They were a pretty wild mob, but I don't think we were really bad.

In this close-knit street community an important focus was on informal economy activities and outdoor recreation: 'We always had something to do, fishing or anything we could do . . . [to] find food to keep the family going, but mainly we specialised in any sport and in Darcy Road the girls were generally as good as the boys too'.[49] As we have seen, residents from Darcy Road were more likely to identify the staff houses in Private Lane as 'Rotten Row' or 'Pommy Lane', indicating their awareness of class divisions within the town.[50] Others from Port Kembla were also aware of the specific identity of 'Darcy Roaders'. My mother, Heather Eklund, spent her childhood years in Reservoir Street not far from Darcy Road, and she recalls their toughness and their ability to 'look after themselves'. Experiences as ER&S tenants may have sharpened the class feeling in Darcy Road. Whatever its origin, this alternative perception of Port Kembla was cultural capital which both reflected and facilitated working-class identity and class politics.

These voices of dissent were no match for the range of interests promoting Port Kembla's boom town image. Press and industry leaders were some of the first to encourage this image. In 1907 the editor of the *Illawarra Mercury* wrote that 'there is every reason to believe that Port Kembla is destined to become an important industrial as well as shipping centre'.[51] In 1910 a *Sydney Morning Herald* correspondent claimed that at ER&S 'quite a thousand men will be employed by the end of the year'.[52] Employment levels, in fact, never went above 400 in 1910. Land companies joined in with claims that the town may become bigger than Wollongong, and exaggerated predictions of the size of the future workforce.[53]

As was common with Australian industrial towns in the first half of the century, contemporaries tried to make sense of Port Kembla's industrialisation by a comparison with the English experience.[54] In 1921 federal Treasurer and former Liberal Prime Minister Sir Joseph Cook visited Port Kembla and claimed that 'there was nothing to stop the district forging ahead and becoming the Birmingham or Manchester of Australia'.[55] Parallels were also drawn between Port Kembla and the Australian town of Newcastle. In 1923 the manager of ER&S, E. A. White, told a party of visiting farmers 'that he was confident that people now living would see Port

Kembla as big as Newcastle'.[56] These large industrial centres were seen as blueprints for future Port Kembla. The town's future did not have to be creatively imagined; it was already embodied in the industrial towns of England and Australia. Port Kembla was destined to become 'the next Newcastle', or even 'the Birmingham of the South Coast'.

The logical extension of this growth narrative was the idea that Port Kembla had matured, and this idea became common in the early 1920s. In 1924 George Simon, a foreman at ER&S, spoke out against his town's ambulance services being run by the Wollongong Ambulance Committee: 'We are of age. Residents here think the time has come that Port Kembla should have a district of their own . . . Port Kembla people say: We want an Ambulance in Port Kembla and we don't want any dictation from Wollongong.'[57] The 'maturity' stage was characterised by increasing calls for municipal reorganisation and autonomy. In recognition of the town's development, local businessman and storekeeper Robert Shipp was elected mayor of the Central Illawarra Council in 1922. In 1927 the Port Kembla Progress Association debated the idea of new municipal boundaries based on the town.[58] Appeals for municipal autonomy remained on the agenda until 1947. Simon's claim of maturity was the culmination of a birth/growth/maturity narrative that dominated interpretations of the spatial changes at Port Kembla. In the 1890s Port Kembla was understood to be a suburb of Wollongong, a 'backwater' with an uncertain future. Industrialisation initially led to optimistic, sometimes utopian visions of Port Kembla's future. By the 1920s the realities of economic and social change gave most people a new sense of confidence and pride in Port Kembla. Rather than looking ahead, residents celebrated the town's 'coming of age', and passionately argued for its recognition and respect.

Town Life

The confluence of these spatial and social changes gave Port Kembla society a distinctive shape and quality in the 1920s. The establishment of commercial and residential Port Kembla, the shared dependence on local services and positive expectations for the town's future turned social life inward and helped create a distinctive town-based society and fostered local identity. A particular 'structure of feeling' developed that revolved around the political and cultural importance of town life. This powerful industrial, commercial, residential and cultural context had profound effects on the generation of residents who were born in the 1910s and 1920s. The memories of this generation, extensively recorded by historians since the early 1970s, reveal the importance of this locally centred structure of feeling.

It was during the formative period of industrialisation that the cultural and social effects provided the greatest opportunities for town-based development and pride. The achieved and mooted industrial changes were promising but not so large-scale as to overwhelm an essentially localist interpretation of their meaning and importance.

The meanings conferred on the main street, Wentworth Street, were central to the construction of an apparently united locality. Commercial Port Kembla was a focus for friendly social interaction between residents of all classes, and the petit-bourgeoisie had an important role in fostering local identity. Apart from the provision of credit and the cross-class contact engendered by their workplace, as already mentioned, the petit-bourgeoisie mobilised local identity through the Traders' Association and the local Council. The Traders' Association was formed in 1911, and was concerned with the promotion of local stores, the organisation of street-based entertainment, and the scrutiny of the commercial space of Port Kembla to ensure that it was attractive and appealing.[59] Throughout the 1920s the Traders' Association organised competitions, bazaars and shopping weeks.

The storekeepers also tried to protect their economic interests through the local Council. In 1929 moves by Alderman Shipp to reduce bus services to Wollongong gained the attention of one *Mercury* reader from Coniston, a small settlement located approximately halfway between Wollongong and Port Kembla. A. Fairfield wrote that Shipp was representing 'the interests of the storekeepers at Port Kembla' in trying to reduce bus services to Wollongong: 'He [Alderman Shipp] would no doubt have liked a compound built around Port Kembla so that the people would be forced to spend their earnings and lives within for the benefit of a few storekeepers and himself'.[60] The control of bus timetables and the condition of roads were important issues for the storekeepers, whose economic survival depended on local customers. The political and economic interests of the storekeepers were influential in building local loyalty, and this commerce bound residents into local economic relationships. Such relationships were the material context for the cultural importance of the main street.

Another factor that encouraged patronage of local stores was the relative lack of mobility of the customers. The compound image that A. Fairfield referred to was already present—the result of poor roads and a lack of affordable transport options. In 1899 a storekeeper from Wollongong was given three hours to supply a coastal steamer at Port Kembla. He had such trouble negotiating the road and Tom Thumb's Lagoon that he arrived at Port Kembla only to see the ship leaving.[61] Improvements to the road occurred over the years, but initial isolation helped the Port Kembla-based petit-bourgeoisie establish themselves in the face of competition with stores from nearby towns.

The staff of J. G. Fairley's outside the store in Wentworth Street in 1937.

Children outside a billiard saloon in Military Road, c. 1914. Across the road
the ER&S workmen's cottages stand in a neat row, while behind them dust
and fumes are whipped up by a strong north-easterly breeze.

Looking south-east down Wentworth Street in 1961. A range of stores are evident including Cakebread's Electrical Store, the CBC bank, Ford's Sports Store, and across the road, Woolworths.

Another view of Wentworth Street in 1961 that captures the busy nature of this commercial centre before a significant decline from the late 1960s.

A view of Allan's Creek and Tom Thumb's Lagoon with the new steel works in the background. Within ten years much of this land was drained, filled in, and sold off to industry.

An aerial view of the Port Kembla–Wollongong Road showing the new inner harbour shortly before the road was cut in 1960.

Work begins on the site of the Hoskins blast furnace in early 1927 with loads of fill being dumped by horse and cart. The main building seen in the photo became the time office.

New transport services, such as buses or trains, became available, but often the costs were prohibitive or the timetables were not suitable for a quick shopping trip to Wollongong. In 1913 a motor bus joined coach services running between Port Kembla and adjoining centres such as Wollongong, Unanderra and Dapto.[62] Yet in 1918 one Port Kembla resident at a meeting in Wollongong to lobby for a rail service complained that 'he had known them [residents] to have to wait two hours for a car or bus, and then the fares are not too reasonable. A good many people in Port Kembla could not afford to pay 3s return too often.'[63] In 1918 three shillings bought two pounds of butter or one pound of coffee. Many working-class households survived on such slim margins that a shopping trip to Wollongong was an unaffordable luxury.

The recurring image of a united and valued town centre in oral and written evidence suggests that the storekeepers were highly successful in their efforts to encourage local loyalty. In the 1920s Wentworth Street became a powerful symbol of local identity and unity. Edith Neaves, who came to Port Kembla only 'a few weeks old' in 1909, recalled of her childhood: 'We used to go down the street of a Saturday morning and we go down purposely to have a chat. Everybody gathered in the main street in Port Kembla them days . . . and you'd see groups having a little chat and it was lovely. It was happy days.' Shopping was more than just consumption, it was an occasion that expressed attachment to locality. Ursula Lindsay, who also arrived at Port Kembla as a young child in 1909, remembered that her parents did shop in Wollongong but shopping in Port Kembla was altogether different:

> it was a nice little town, everyone knew one another. When we were children, by the time we left the top of the street [she lived at the top of Wentworth Street] to go down, the shops closed at nine, we'd be lucky to get down the shop before they'd closed because you'd walk a little way and you'd meet someone you knew and it was a nice little town then.

Even during the Great Depression Wentworth Street was alive with energy and excitement, as this report from the *South Coast Times* demonstrates:

> The main street presented a brilliant spectacle during the holidays, hundreds of people were busily engaged looking at the window displays, while all the storekeepers reported good business. Many competitions were held the winning numbers being announced by loud speaker outside the General Agency.[64]

The local commerce of Wentworth Street reinforced the connection people had to their locality. This was particularly the case for women who shopped daily in the main street. Edith Neaves recalled: 'You'd go and you'd sit down and there would be a seat for you to sit on behind the counter and talk while they were serving you'. Home deliveries also meant sociable though business-like contact between delivery men and female customers. Avis Bright remembered that 'relations with the tradespeople in town were very friendly', and during their delivery rounds 'they'd come in and have a cup of tea if they had time'.[65]

Wentworth Street was also a major venue for various local organisations. To raise money for the local churches Ladies' Guilds held 'bazaars', where decorated stalls selling home-made and donated goods lined Wentworth Street. In 1929 the Roman Catholic Bazaar, which sold home-made sweets, refreshments, cakes, and arts and crafts, raised £350 for the church funds after expenses were met.[66] The town band held monthly recitals on 'The Green', a vacant block diagonally opposite the Great Eastern Hotel. The use of Wentworth Street by such groups extended the symbolic meaning of the main street beyond shopping and socialising, to include religious and recreational aspects of local life.

Despite this evidence of unity and togetherness, the oral record does reveal other allegiances and reflects the conflicts and divisions of Port Kembla in the 1920s and 1930s. Respondents who spoke of people being more friendly and helping one another also related stories of stealing fruit and vegetables or identified particular social groups within the town. Edith Neaves, for example, recalled that one of the local storekeepers used the depression to sell old stock and also labelled the staff houses in Private Lane 'Rotten Row'. The oral recollections of the local waterside workers most clearly reveal competing class allegiances, and memories of harsh working conditions dominate.[67] When asked about politics, many respondents identify Port Kembla as a 'Labor area', a place where working people generally saw their interests as best served by the Labor Party. As Gordon Rodwell recalls: 'politics here has been very laborised, and I presume if you were to be real brutal about it if you were a worker most of the good things of a worker's life has come from the Labor Party so, and it's always been a Labor area'.

There were distinct though muted ethnic divisions at Port Kembla during the formative period that tended to reinforce and reflect class divisions. Some ethnic divisions were revealed through religious affiliation, though there was an overarching Anglo-Australian culture. An Anglican community formed around St Stephen's church and included many of the senior management and their families from the local companies. Some of these were English migrants, such as the English foreman imported by MM. This importation of English managers and skilled technicians gave the Anglican community and middle-class circles generally a significant boost in the 1920s. While many families of humble background were involved in St Stephen's church life, the well-known manager families gave the church its public profile, standing, and access to financial and other resources. Such resources were effectively employed to build a solid and imposing church for the otherwise struggling industrial town. Meanwhile the 'Darcy Roaders' were predominantly Catholic and working-class. Their social networks, based on the Catholic Church that opened in 1919, their workplace, their street, and a shared passion for rugby league, were quite different to their Anglican bethren.

A careful reading of the oral record reveals a range of representations of local society, indicating the complexity of identities and the existence of allegiances other than local loyalty. Both oral and written evidence, however, supports the view that local identity was generally more important, especially in the 1920s, and this had wide-ranging effects on town life. In the 1920s Port Kembla society turned in on itself, and this can be seen through the personal relationships, cultural practices and patterns of leisure of this decade.

Port Kembla men and women overwhelmingly married each other. From April 1920 to April 1931, 57 marriages were recorded at St Stephen's. At the time of marriage only 10 of the 114 newly-weds lived outside Port Kembla.[68] Typical was Edith Neaves who, in January 1929, married a man she had known since childhood. Gordon Rodwell met his future wife 'on the dance floor' at the Port Kembla Soldiers' Memorial Club, where popular dances were held every week. They married in 1934.

Friendship networks also centred on Port Kembla, although there were gender differences. Ethel Combes recalled that most of her friends were from the town because 'those days you really couldn't get out of Port Kembla'. For women, the requirements of childcare and participation in the more locally based informal economy limited their mobility. This limited mobility, combined with their daily local shopping, deeply embedded women's lives within the locality.

Men shared many of these experiences. Gordon Rodwell remembers 'all the friends were from Port Kembla I think, all from Port Kembla. Well you didn't get much chance to get away anywhere. See you had no transport'. However, men's relationship to locality was complicated by wage labour. With the regionalisation of the labour market from the late 1920s, the pool of friends, acquaintances and contacts from beyond the locality grew. As Morgan Simon recalled:

> When you work in a factory like that [MM] a lot of your workmates came from other parts of Greater Wollongong [the current Wollongong City Council boundaries from Helensburgh in the north to Windang and Dapto in the south] and I made some very very close friends and friends that I still have that worked with me all those years.

Yet the oral record of men from Port Kembla still emphasises attachment to the locality, if for different reasons. Men valued their town in terms of male friends and outdoor leisure activities. Port Kembla was 'a great town' because it offered access to surf beaches, fishing, Lake Illawarra and the relatively secluded bush around the lake.[69] Men's memories of outdoor recreation contrast to women's memories of shopping and the emotional work of 'gossip' in the main street, but in both cases the oral record emphasises attachment to locality.

Local cultural practices also played a role in reinforcing attachment to locality. The ritual of 'the farewell', for example, had special meaning not just for those leaving the town, but for those staying behind as well. The farewell was usually held in a local hotel and was for men who were about to leave the town:

> On the eve of his departure for Sydney, Mr J. Fitzpatrick [a public works labourer] was tendered a send-off by his fellow workers in the private smoke room of the Port Kembla hotel on Monday. The guest was presented with a silver mounted pipe as a token of esteem by his comrades.[70]

Doctors, bank managers, storekeepers and aldermen received larger farewells akin to civic functions. Dr Noel Kirkwood, on his move to Wollongong in April 1924, was farewelled by both the Port Kembla Cricket Club at their 'Annual Smoke Social', and by the town at a general civic farewell held at the Amusu Theatre with newsagent T. J. McCann presiding. Kirkwood was presented with a gold watch and Mrs Kirkwood with an etching of the University of Sydney. Women were rarely farewelled personally, but were sometimes included as wives or daughters. After speeches from prominent citizens, the music programme included 'Auld Lang Syne' and 'Jolly Good Fellow'.[71] These social events enabled townspeople to express their appreciation of a valued local citizen, but they also symbolised the unity of those staying behind. The act of gift giving reminded locals of the small-town values that they felt resided in their 'community', and helped affirm their act of staying while their comrade set out for a new place.

The corollary of 'the farewell' was 'the welcome', an important way for newcomers to be introduced to local society. As with farewells, welcomes were for prominent male newcomers. Local organisations such as friendly societies, the Returned Sailors' and Soldiers' Imperial League, unions and political parties were active in staging welcomes for newly arrived men. In the latter years of World War I the 'welcome home' was common for soldiers returning from France.[72] Friendly societies also prided themselves on welcoming members from other areas or recruiting new members. In August 1926 Sister Stewart from the Grand United Order of Oddfellows at Port Kembla (Five Islands Lodge) received a gold medal for her recruitment of twelve new members.[73] Later that year the lodge gained a special mention for initiating seventy-one new members, the largest number throughout the state for the year.[74]

Friendly societies and Ladies' Guilds from the local churches performed similar roles for women, but generally women's welcomes were informal greetings from neighbours. Evidence is scant, but some women were welcomed by neighbours with either a short visit or a gift of food to help 'settle in'.[75] Kin migration was often an important reason for movement to Port Kembla, and many newly arrived women received help and support from relatives already living in the town. These links were the beginning of relationships between women played out in the street or over the back fence, and were carried over to, and reinforced by, the interaction and shopping of the main street.

These points of entry into local society were crucial because in the 1920s population growth came mostly from immigrants—new arrivals out to try their luck in the industrial boom town of the Illawarra. Explanations for the strength of local identity often concentrate on birthplace or long-term residence[76], but an analysis of marriage registers at Port Kembla show a large percentage of people were not locally born. Out of the forty-five weddings performed at St Stephen's between 1920 and 1927, only five of the newly-weds were born in the town. Similarly, from 1927 to 1931 of the twenty-one weddings at St Stephen's only two people were born in Port Kembla.[77] That there was such strong local identity in a population where many were not locally born attests to the successful operation of the processes and cultural practices that introduced and bound people into local society.

By the 1920s Port Kembla had acquired sporting, leisure and hobby clubs that catered for all tastes. The town had a number of halls and two picture theatres. Sporting teams, especially the Port Kembla first-grade rugby league side, the Blacks, were a focus of local loyalty. Throughout the 1920s the first-grade team was a spectacular success. In its debut in Illawarra first-grade football it was narrowly defeated by the Wollongong team in the grand final. The team, formed in 1914, were Premiers in 1922, 1923, 1924, 1927 and 1928 and reached the semi-finals every year until 1931.[78] Trips to nearby towns were often undertaken to watch the Blacks play, so even when residents left their town they often were reaffirming their identity as Port Kembla people.

Port Kembla, however, lacked a race track where the important male pastime of gambling could be centred. Wollongong, Unanderra, Bulli and Dapto had race tracks for horses and dogs and some men did travel to these tracks. However, the prevalence of 'SP', or starting-price betting, and two-up in the town's hotels, billiard rooms and back lanes enabled some local gambling.[79]

For the youth of Port Kembla, organised leisure activities ranged from church youth groups to Cubs, Scouts and Guides. By the beginning of the 1930s Port Kembla had the biggest scouting group on the South Coast with a membership of 78, and an attendance rate of 82 per cent. This included 31 cubs, 41 scouts and 6 scout masters.[80] The Girl Guides formed in December 1926 and were never as successful as the Scouts. By 1931 they numbered only 31.[81] All the major churches had youth groups, and these were important social networks for young people, with many meeting their future spouses in these forums.[82] Morgan Simon recalled: 'We had a young people's organisation in the [Methodist] church in those days and a lot of them married in the clubs, like I mean in the church clubs, and they are still very close friends to us now'.

Leisure of a less formal nature was more common. Oral history respondents remember the harbour, beaches, Lake Illawarra and Tom Thumb's Lagoon as places where they played as children, whether it was sliding down the sandhills at the back of Perkin's Beach or catching fish in the harbour. Disused industrial buildings, like the old shacks that belonged to the Mount Kembla Coal Company or the abandoned Public Works quarries, were popular haunts. In the mid-1930s, one Sunday afternoon, my mother, her brother and elder sister found themselves marooned on Big Island. An adventurous cousin had rowed them out and promptly forgot about them until late evening. These childhood experiences provided a common fund of nostalgic memories that were drawn upon in later life to reaffirm the importance of one's locality.

The distinguishing 'structure of feeling' of Port Kembla society in the 1910s and 1920s was its town-centredness; a feature which had its origins in the material conditions of Port Kembla's development, and the cultural practices of everyday life. Industrial development closely bordered the town, had not yet overwhelmed the locality, and was serviced by a town-based labour market. The commercial and residential development of the town encouraged a growing perception of Port Kembla as a boom town, and formed a unique context for local society. The social relations and cultural practices that came with town growth led to an inward-looking society. This experience was not always shared by itinerant labourers and some of the working class who developed a class-based understanding of the town, but most residents shopped locally, married each other, had locally based friendship networks and energetically participated in town-centred social and cultural life. These conditions were fertile ground for a politics based on the centrality of local interests above all others, including class interests, and these competing political allegiances are the subject of the next chapter.

5

Class, Locality and Politics, 1900 to 1930

DURING THE FORMATIVE PERIOD of industrial society at Port Kembla two principal types of politics dominated the political landscape. The first was localist politics, based on assertions of local unity and calls for development and progress through town-based organisations. Its origins were in the material conditions of local society, and a powerful ideology of localism. The second type was class politics, based on tensions arising out of the class divisions in local society, and most clearly revealed during industrial conflict. This chapter focuses on these modes of political mobilisation till 1930, and argues that localist politics predominated. Two periods when class politics did challenge the general dominance of localist politics are identified—1917 to 1920 and the late 1920s to the beginning of the depression in 1930. The depression marked such a fundamental change to local political patterns that political developments after that date will be dealt with separately.

Localist politics prevailed for a host of reasons. Industrial development had not yet overwhelmed the boundaries of the locality, and its so far modest scale was amenable to town-based politics. Structural, social and cultural factors were also relevant, as the previous chapter showed. Localist politics was fuelled by intermittent work patterns characteristic of the formative period of the formal economy. Intermittent work patterns suggested remedies such as better loading facilities or more public works expenditure to even out the ebb and flow of labour demand. Such remedies gave local industries and storekeepers better facilities and infrastructure, and answered working men's need for wage labour. There were common interests across many different social groups. These demands were always more credible when backed by a broad coalition of groups. In the 1920s the practical demands of defending and enhancing a common space threw local classes and their organisations together in what was often a whirlwind ride of lobbying, public campaigns and activism.

Localist Politics

Localist politics made its first tentative appearance at Port Kembla as the town's infrastructure failed to meet the demands of a growing population. In 1906 locals complained of the inadequate water supply. A petition signed by ninety residents was forwarded to the Minster for Public Works, and a public meeting was held in June, the first of its kind at Port Kembla.[1] The lobbying was successful and a reservoir was built the following year, in an area that was later subdivided and named Reservoir Street.[2]

This new town-based politics solidified with the formation of the Port Kembla Progress Association in 1908. The association took the form of many similar organisations throughout the Illawarra, as town-based Progress Associations became more common around the turn of the century. These organisations arose out of the growing urbanisation of the region and the increasing responsibilities of local government. Organised groups of rate-payers found they could more effectively and persuasively present their grievances to councils. There was also a broader ideological context. Enthusiasm for decentralisation (which led to a Royal Commission into Railway Decentralisation in 1911), and the identification of 'the city' as a parasitical and pernicious influence on the whole country's development, also informed many of the demands for progress and development at a regional or town level.

The immediate origin of the Port Kembla Progress Association was a public meeting where it was agreed that 'the time has arrived when a Progress Association should be formed'. Both residents and those employed at Port Kembla who lived elsewhere were eligible to join, although only residents were eligible for office. As there were nineteen nominations for a committee of twelve, a ballot was held at Middletons' General Store which resulted in an executive dominated by the local middle class and petit-bourgeoisie.[3] These men had many of the skills and resources for leadership and public speaking, but the executive also contained two labourers from Electrolytic Refining and Smelting Company of Australia Ltd (ER&S), and two untraceable names who were also probably labourers who had not registered on the electoral roll.

The mix of men from different classes highlights an important aspect of localist politics. For the association to represent the legitimate political voice of the town it had to appear representative. This can be seen in constant references by the *Illawarra Mercury* and the *South Coast Times* to a 'representative number' or a 'cross-section' of local residents being present at meetings.[4] In this sense, then, the Progress Association represented a political coalition of different classes in the town, its success or otherwise a barometer of the state of class relations at Port Kembla.

The Port Kembla Progress Association lobbied the Central Illawarra Council and the state government for services and public investment at Port Kembla. Throughout its history a core of twelve male executive members conducted the association's affairs. Many grievances arose out of what was seen as municipal neglect and mismanagement, and issues such as the sanitary service, the state of local roads, bridges and footpaths and the subdivision of the Wentworth estate dominated proceedings.[5] In 1908 the Progress Association was even performing some of the actions of a council, collecting donations from tradespeople and others at Port Kembla for road maintenance.

The association arose out of the common problems facing residents in a new town with few services or amenities, and the increasingly powerful feelings of local identity that accompanied Port Kembla's development. But locals also shared common political adversaries in Wollongong-based interests, the local Council and the Wentworth estate. Conflict and competition with these adversaries helped unite the town politically, and fuelled localist politics in the 1900s, 1910s and 1920s.

In 1908 before a Hotel Licensing inquiry, E. A. White, general superintendent of ER&S, claimed that Port Kembla residents 'did not want to remain an offshoot of Wollongong, but [wanted] to be better than Wollongong'.[6] White's comment highlights the political implications for Port Kembla of the proximity of the large commercial centre of Wollongong. Influential political organisations there—the Wollongong Council, the Wollongong Chamber of Commerce and the Wollongong Traders' Association—had different political agendas, but all shared a concern to capture for themselves the benefits of Port Kembla's industrial development.

Wollongong interests dominated the early political debates surrounding Port Kembla's future. From 1897 representatives and officials from Wollongong enthusiastically supported the proposal to construct a deepwater harbour at Port Kembla. While many from Wollongong had hoped Wollongong harbour would be the centre of any new development, the failure of the Wollongong Harbour Trust in 1895 cleared the way for Wollongong representatives to support the Port Kembla proposal. In 1897 the Parliamentary Committee investigating the construction of the harbour at Port Kembla found that 'local feelings and interests have merged in a general agreement that all further expenditure should be incurred in giving effect to the Departmental proposal in connection with Port Kembla'.[7]

The representatives from Wollongong were confident that the town's regional dominance would continue, despite the location of the harbour at Port Kembla. This confidence came from a particular understanding of the new harbour. The mayor of Wollongong, Henry McCabe, was asked by the 1897 Parliamentary Committee about the effects of Port Kembla's future growth. He replied:

> When we get the Port Kembla harbour, I think I am quite right in saying that the mines will be kept going certainly half as much again as they are now. The increased wages which are paid will be distributed in the town and that of itself will make a great difference. I dare say a large population will gather around Port Kembla, but the providing for ships and that kind of thing will go on from here [Wollongong]. In my opinion Port Kembla will be to Wollongong as Port Adelaide is to Adelaide.[8]

Such views continued into the twentieth century. In 1912 Alderman R. M. Krippner of Wollongong Council wrote to the *Illawarra Mercury*: 'It is because I take the broad outlook I can see in the not very distant future a large manufacturing centre at Port Kembla with Wollongong as the business and residential centre'.[9] Thus, the Port Kembla harbour was seen to be of direct benefit to Wollongong's economic development, and Wollongong representatives pursued this vision of a wholly industrial Port Kembla, serviced by a commercial and residential centre at Wollongong. Political conflict between representatives of the two towns was in part motivated by different visions for the future of Port Kembla.

Tension and conflict with Wollongong interests continued throughout the ensuing decades, adding to Port Kembla's insularity. The maintenance of the road from Wollongong to Port Kembla was one contentious issue, and in 1927 the *Illawarra Mercury* reported these comments by Alderman T. Kiernan of Wollongong Council:

> Despite the natural advantages of Port Kembla he did not think anyone would prefer to live there than Wollongong, provided Wollongong was equally as accessible. The present Port Kembla Road was a disgrace to the Municipality and hundreds of people were kept from shopping in Wollongong every week.[10]

For Kiernan the road represented both a link to Port Kembla so that workers could live in Wollongong and work in Port Kembla, and a way of siphoning trade to Wollongong. The case of Kiernan demonstrates the economic as well as the political dimension to relations between the two towns. Kiernan himself was a building contractor who undertook considerable work at Port Kembla, and the state of the road had a direct bearing on his ability to access the Port Kembla market. These moves by Wollongong interests provided the residents of Port Kembla with a readily identifiable opponent. At a Progress Association meeting in 1925 a state government plan to unite Wollongong and Port Kembla brought shouts of 'We don't want anything to do with Wollongong'.[11]

Wollongong interests were not the only ones opposed to the idea of a viable town at Port Kembla. The farmers of the Central Illawarra were uneasy about the plans and hopes for an industrial Port Kembla, and through their domination of the local Council, they came to represent major opponents to Port Kembla's growth and development, further uniting disparate political groups in the industrial town.

The Central Illawarra Council was established by a group of well-to-do dairy farmers and land owners in 1859. By 1900 the municipality was divided into three wards with three aldermen each, covering the towns of Dapto, Marshall Mount, Yallah, Mount Kembla, Figtree, Port Kembla and Unanderra, the site of the council chambers. In 1900 the mayor was James O'Donnell, dairy farmer and landowner at Port Kembla and Unanderra. Franchise and eligibility for local government elections were limited. Under the *Local Government Act* of 1906 only male ratepayers could stand for office, and only male ratepayers, lessees of crown land and owners of companies occupying rateable land could vote in local government elections.[12] At the 1901 Council elections, 670 electors were enrolled, but only 126 voted.[13] This municipal electoral apathy, combined with the paternalistic dominance of wealthy local dairy farmers and storekeepers, ensured that the Council was dominated by rural interests well into the twentieth century.

Farmers reacted uneasily to the coming of industrialisation to their municipality. James and Michael O'Donnell, farmers who held land at Port Kembla and Unanderra, objected to the proposed smelting works at Port Kembla in April 1907, fearing that pollution from the works would 'create a nuisance'.[14] However, economic change also presented opportunities that the O'Donnells soon recognised. Within two years James O'Donnell was acting as local agent for the Wentworth estate, and Michael O'Donnell had sold his farm and opened an auction firm with H. N. Stumbles.[15]

Gentlemen farmers like the O'Donnells readily adapted since subdividing and land speculation was only a step away from the experience of subletting to small leaseholders, but others remained ambivalent and sometimes hostile to Port Kembla's ensuing growth and industrialisation. The farmers on the Council hindered the subdivision of Port Kembla, and were slow in providing metalled and formed roads and an effective sanitary service.

The reaction at Port Kembla was to identify farming interests on the Council as opponents of Port Kembla's development. In 1913 Thomas Downie, wharfinger at Port Kembla and former president of the Progress Association, told a meeting that 'his opinion was that the present members of the Council only know how to make roads and bail yards'.[16] At a public meeting called at Port Kembla to discuss 'Municipal grievances' in May

1918 H. R. Lee, alderman since 1912 and accountant at ER&S, claimed that the council had 'no right to take rates at Port Kembla and spend it on farmers' roads'. His comments met with applause, and Lee backed his claim, saying that the Council collected £800 in rates at Port Kembla and only spent £200 on the town.[17]

In the 1920s the farmer-dominated Council was also the focus of political struggles at Port Kembla for municipal reform by groups such as the Progress Association. The demographic changes that had occurred in the Central Illawarra since 1900 had left the Council with an anachronistic ward structure. A fourth ward had been added in 1908, but municipal representation had very little to do with population density. By the 1920s Port Kembla made up the bulk of Ward No. 1 and its population had increased rapidly to almost 3000, while Ward No. 4 (the rural areas of West Dapto, Brownsville and Yallah) had decreased to 300. Alderman Shipp expressed the Progress Association's view of the matter to the Council: 'It was not fair that 3000 ratepayers that provided three-fifths of the revenue should only have the same representation as 300 ratepayers that provided one-eighth of the revenue'.[18] Municipal representatives such as Shipp, who had moved away from the Labor League towards the Progress Association, had been advocating civic autonomy since the early 1920s.[19] In February 1927 a separate municipality attracted the attention of the association.[20] In June representatives from the Port Kembla Traders' Association, the Progress Association, the Australian Workers' Union (AWU) and the Tourist Association approached the Minister for Local Government, M. F. Bruxner, with a plan to create a separate municipality.[21] The Minister suggested altering ward boundaries, a compromise the Progress Association was willing to accept. The rural representatives on Council, however, successfully stalled the proposal, arguing that the viability of the Council would be undermined with a significant part of its revenue base removed. From the point of view of the Port Kembla representatives, the Council was using the revenue generated by Port Kembla ratepayers to subsidise less-populated rural areas that were the farmers' traditional electorates.

The trustees of the Wentworth estate were another 'outside' influence identified as pernicious by Port Kembla-based interests. In 1915, when the trustees asked the Department of Education for £1800 for just under one hectare of land for a new school, they attracted considerable criticism. The Minster for Education, A. C. Carmichael, had criticised the Wentworth trustees after meeting with the 1915 deputation of Port Kembla organisations seeking a new school. The Minister called the trustees an 'unpatriotic body of citizens [without] the soul or instincts of citizens . . . If they had had any of the bounden instincts of citizens, they would have given the land to the Government'.[22] His comments were reported in the local press, and a correspondent identified as 'Taxpayer' wrote to the *South Coast Times* in support of his sentiments:

> The local bodies have done excellent work in attending to the wants and welfare of the township and for its general advancement, but who has ever heard of the Wentworth Estate or family doing a hand-stand or giving a single shilling to anything in the district . . . Their main object appears to be dodging expenses in forming roads on the various subdivisions . . . Mr Carmichael was fully justified in using the language reported, and I for one hope that he will see 'these soulless people damned' before paying them any fancy price for land to be used for educational purposes.[23]

'Taxpayer's' anger was directed at the trustees' uninterest and lack of support for local development, and the letter explicitly contrasts this disinterest with the actions of 'local bodies'. Characteristic of the ideology of localism that underpinned localist politics, the political sphere was divided into locals versus outsiders. The former were seen to be motivated by genuine local 'needs', the latter by monetary gain only. Tense and conflict-ridden relations between the representatives of Port Kembla, Wollongong-based interests, the farmers of the Central Illawarra and the Wentworth trustees helped forge links between diverse political groups at Port Kembla. This political map seemed to confirm the role of 'outsiders' as the main threat to local development and reinforced the dominant perception of local politics as a united town struggling against 'outsiders'. With political problems and threats located beyond the boundaries of Port Kembla, the mirage of a united town could remain largely unchallenged.

While outside forces promoted localism at Port Kembla, there were also powerful local political interests behind the formation of the Progress Association and the mobilisation of local identity. The role of ER&S was crucial and, as part of its wider agenda to secure control over the town, it attempted to control the Progress Association. Three of the original twelve executive members of the association were staff from ER&S, while the first president, Bernard Magnus, was manager of ER&S, and company accountant, H. R. Lee, was one of the two vice-presidents. The first issue which the Progress Association concerned itself with, the provision of classes in engineering, assaying and surveying in co-operation with the Department of Public Instruction at the local primary school, clearly demonstrated the self-interest of ER&S.[24]

ER&S had a strong paternalistic interest in Port Kembla and endeavoured to control the town's development and create an image of unity that belied class difference. Influencing the Progress Association was only one strategy. ER&S also tried to construct a residential environment owned and managed by the company through a vigorous housing policy, as previous chapters have shown. ER&S also opened a company store, the Port Kembla Industries' Co-operative Store, better known as 'the Co-op', in Military Road in 1916.[25]

The creation of an appropriately skilled yet pliant local workforce was another important priority for ER&S. To this end the company focused on the technical and industrial education of local children. In October 1917 the copper smelter agreed to provide an instructor in woodwork one afternoon a week free to the sixth-grade boys at Port Kembla Primary School.[26] In November 1918, after the company complained of the 'deplorable lack of efficiency' shown by its typists, it donated six typewriters to the school and provided a trained typist to instruct the children.[27]

ER&S's influence extended beyond the industrial and political sphere. Senior staff such as H. R. Lee were active in local society in a range of political, cultural and sporting groups. Lee's activity was never as official representative of the company, but the board of directors of ER&S was aware of his invaluable work, covertly looking after the company's interests in local politics. In 1912 he was granted an 'honourarium' of £52 for 'services in connection with the public institutions of Port Kembla'.[28] During the 1919 influenza pandemic ER&S stepped in to organise public health and welfare measures. Inoculation depots were set up at the Co-op Store and at the company's ambulance room.[29] In April that year employees at ER&S began contributing three shillings per week to the families of those affected.[30] This was soon formalised into the Staff and Employee Provident Fund (which included MM), with the staff each contributing 2s 6d per week.[31]

Localism's rhetoric of unity and consensus merged neatly with the company's own agenda, and ER&S attempted to harness localist politics for its own industrial and political gains. Company management had correctly gauged the strength of local concern about the town and its future, and through judicious influence in the political and social life of the town hoped to endear the company to residents and ensure future development suited its interests.

Attempting to draw on the power of localism, many of the ER&S's policies presented the image of a united, classless locality. Joint picnics between employees and staff began in 1913 and were organised by a Picnic Committee. These committees were forums where staff and workers could mix in a co-operative atmosphere. On picnic day conciliatory speeches from both management and unions usually finished off a day of sports and prize giving. In March 1919 an official luncheon was held at the Port Kembla Hotel, where E. Johnson, local secretary of the AWU, proposed a toast to ER&S and claimed that 'the men always got a fair crack of the whip at the hands of the company'. The state secretary of the AWU, George Buckland, in proposing 'the day we celebrate', stated that picnic day was a day when 'they should unite for the purpose of social reunion. They were always fighting the other side and the other side were always resisting, but the electrolytic employees, in normal times, were as a rule met by the company in a very fair spirit'.[32]

The 1910s were years of increasing union activity and class conflict both throughout the nation and at Port Kembla (detailed below), but localist politics remained influential despite the rise of class politics. This was possible because the town-based coalition extended beyond the uneasy truce embodied in the Progress Association to include other local organisations acting in concert over specific issues. In February 1915, for example, the deputation that met the Minister for Education, A. C. Carmichael, over the new school consisted of representatives from the Progress Association, the Labor League and the Parents' and Citizens' Association. The deputation presented a united case for a new school at Port Kembla. All of the speakers supported the opening comments by H. R. Lee, representing the Parents' and Citizens' Association. Mr Farrar told the Minister, 'I am instructed by the Political Labor League to fully endorse the remarks of Mr Lee in connection with the school'. Likewise, other speakers 'endorsed' Lee's opening remarks in what was an impressive demonstration of town solidarity, influential in securing a new primary school for Port Kembla which was built the following year.[33]

Along with increasing working-class activism, World War I also had a deleterious effect on the Progress Association, as active members left and money was redirected to the Port Kembla Red Cross League and other war-related fund raising. By June 1915 Port Kembla-based organisations had raised over £700 for the war effort.[34] Many of the former leaders of the Progress Association, such as H. R. Lee, Thomas Downie and Percy Laughlin, focused their energies on the work of the Port Kembla Recruitment Committee or the Port Kembla Rifle Club.[35] While World War I sapped the strength of the Progress Association, localist politics was not necessarily the antithesis of the nationalist and patriotic work that war brought. Nationalism and localism were not mutually exclusive. Indeed, during the war, the affirmation of nationalism, patriotism and fund-raising for the war was carried out by town-based organisations, and this had the effect of reinforcing local bonds, at least until heightened industrial conflict dating from 1917.

Class Politics

The origins of the industrial conflict of the late 1910s at Port Kembla can be traced to the increasing organisation and activism of local working-class organisations from 1910. An important forum for the development of class politics was the industrial and political struggle between staff and workers at ER&S. The company's management wielded a significant amount of power in Port Kembla, but an increasingly active local working class responded to this management agenda.

The workers at ER&S formed the Electrolytic Employees' Association (EEA) in December 1910 and submitted a list of claims to the company.[36] The EEA's use of the name 'association' instead of 'union' suggests its moderation in industrial affairs. Although it did not have radical or militant intentions, it embarked on a successful campaign of industrial action in 1911. In July the first serious stoppage occurred at the works, precipitated by the removal of a labourer, William Fargood, from the tank house to the yard and his consequent loss of a bonus payment.[37] As the *Australian Mining Standard* reported, 'a state of irritation prevail[ed] in some parts of the establishment'.[38] The strike lasted twenty-two days and the dispute was then submitted to arbitration. The EEA also went to the Wages Board for a general increase. 'If the Board makes any important amendments' noted the pro-company *Australian Mining Standard*, 'it will be an admission that it is not beyond the influence of vigorous appeal'.[39] The EEA was successful in arbitration and a more favourable award was handed down in December 1911.[40]

ER&S management was keenly aware of working-class political activity, and new paternalistic strategies were in part reactions to union activity. For example, company picnics and garden competitions were established in 1913, a few years after the strike action of 1911. In November 1916 E. A. White, general superintendent of ER&S, cabled one of the directors of the company, R. G. Casey, at that time in London. He asked Casey to inquire about insurance 'against damage caused through riots or civil commotions'.[41] Casey replied that the insurance market in London was 'congested with similar business for Australia'. Clearly managers and company directors across Australia were fearful of working-class mobilisation. In 1917 ER&S also tried to attract more police to the town by offering a house on the corner of Military and Darcy Roads 'to be rented to the police department for an extra constable'.[42] The rhetoric of local unity evoked by the company through industrial paternalism was linked to the rise in class politics at Port Kembla. In this case ER&S attempted to draw on the localist rhetoric of unity to counter increasing class mobilisation.

Working-class resistance not through organisations but through more informal means was also an important context for ER&S's industrial and political strategies. There were many individual or collective acts of resistance, but these rarely find their way into the historical record. Some families in ER&S houses tampered with electricity meters.[43] Others refused to participate in the company's garden competition, used by ER&S to encourage workers to keep their houses in good repair, thus lowering maintenance costs and the cost of living.[44] Results for every year were published in the *Mercury* for all to see, another pressure to encourage tenants' participation.[45] Those who lived near the railway lines at the government subdivision risked trespassing fines to collect coal that slid off overfilled waggons. Free lectures and instructions did not easily convince the youth of Port Kembla of the merits of working-class respectability—New Year's Eve celebrations at Port Kembla often resulted in the destruction of property, and vegetable gardens were common targets for young thieves.

While class politics at Port Kembla originated in the industrial struggles of local industry, it soon moved into town-based organisations. In March 1913 the Port Kembla Political Labor League appeared on the political landscape. Table 5.1 reveals the importance of ER&S labourers and the intriguing inclusion of a storekeeper on the committee. The secretary of the EEA, Charles Clifford, was also secretary of the new league, and it proved immediately popular. The league had sixty names of interested people prior to the foundation meeting. In May 1913 it held a social dance at Simon's Hall, raising £20 in what was reportedly the highest attendance for such a function at Port Kembla.[46] With Clifford as secretary and at least four men from the EEA—including the president, E. Newtown—on the committee, the influence of the union was clear. The league also attracted local storekeepers, such as T. Wells and local barber W. P. Laughlin, as well as Alexander Pascoe, blacksmith at the Public Works quarry.

Table 5.1 Occupational backgrounds of the Port Kembla Political Labor League Executive and Committee, 1913

Position	Name	Occupation
President	Alexander Pascoe	Blacksmith
Vice-presidents	John Fitzpatrick	Labourer
	J. O'Malley	?
Committee	Frederick Forrester	Labourer, ER&S
	Raymond Chesher	Labourer, ER&S
	Thomas Jenks	Labourer
	T. Wells	Storekeeper
	E. Newtown	Labourer, ER&S, and President, EEA

Source: Illawarra Mercury, 28 March 1913.

ER&S workers, with the support of some local storekeepers, developed the Labor League into an influential local organisation. It represented an alternative forum to the Progress Association for residents to air their grievances. Indeed, the movement of class politics from the industrial workplace into town-based organisations coincided with a drop in popularity of the Progress Association in 1913. In June 1913, the same month that the Labor League held another successful social dance (a 'plain and fancy dress ball'[47]), the *Mercury* reported:

> Is it dead? Several prominent townsmen would like to know whether the
> Port Kembla Progress Association is dead or gone, as it is six months since a
> meeting was held. If the association has become deceased it is probable that an
> endeavour will be made to form a P & C [parents' and citizens'] association.[48]

An attempted reformation meeting in July 1913 resolved that, due to
the small attendance, membership fees should be reduced to one shilling
per year.[49]

From a position of increasing strength the working-class representatives
at Port Kembla moved class politics to the town centre and into the very
stronghold of localist politics, the Progress Association. There was some hint
of this change in 1912 when the EEA and the Progress Association held
joint meetings.[50] Word of the new strategy must have passed around for in
September 1913, 130 people turned up to the annual general meeting of
the Progress Association, as both sides marshalled their forces. A ballot was
held at the meeting and the results published in the local paper. The elections ended in a stalemate, with neither the labourers nor the staff from
ER&S gaining a clear ascendancy on the new executive.[51] The Progress
Association became a site for political conflict characteristic of class politics,
rather than the negotiation and truce of localist politics. This was ultimately
detrimental to the association and it faded from the political scene, replaced
by the active and healthy Labor League.[52]

The increasing strength and broad front of class politics at Port Kembla
culminated in the industrial conflicts of the late 1910s and 1920. In September 1917 the AWU (which had taken over from the EEA in 1916),
stopped work in sympathy with the railway and waterfront workers during
the General Strike. The new award that resolved the strike in December
1917 was accepted by the AWU, although it was 'the opinion of the members . . . that the award was in no way commensurate with the cost of living
at Port Kembla'.[53] The end of the war raised expectations that pre-war wage
levels would be restored, and dissatisfaction simmered as the branch tried
unsuccessfully to have the award wage altered in the face of post-war
inflation.[54]

Discontent was exacerbated by industrial downturn at Port Kembla.
At ER&S the blast furnace closed down in late December 1918 and one
hundred men were put off for a month.[55] In March the next year another
hundred men were laid off, and finally in June, a shipping strike and a
depressed market for copper led to the closure of all ER&S furnaces. The
company had been unable to sell any copper since October 1918, and it was
trying to finance its continued operations with the sale of gold. Workforce
numbers fell from a peak of 600 in 1918 to 400 in 1920.[56]

Construction work began at MM in early 1918, and these workers provided an injection of numbers to the AWU at Port Kembla. Many of these new workers at MM also appeared to be more militant than ER&S workers, and they led the early moves towards industrial action. In April 1919 workers at MM met to discuss a new award handed down by the state Arbitration Court. The men claimed the minimum rate of ten shillings a day did not take into account the rising cost of living. By the end of the year joint meetings of AWU members at ER&S and MM were claiming a basic wage of thirteen shillings a day. In December ER&S management abruptly pulled out of negotiations and the workers at MM were further inflamed when MM management claimed that the Board of Trade case due for the next year would not apply to them. The local branch was becoming increasingly interested in strike action, and the state secretary of the AWU had to remind branch members that they were not allowed to strike without central executive permission.[57]

Just before Christmas 1919, 500 workers from ER&S and MM (close to the total combined workforce at that time) went on strike. Members from the AWU and FEDFA were involved, and the company agreed to submit the dispute to the Wages Board in mid-February—the strike having lasted almost two months. Both unions managed to achieve a virtual 100 per cent compliance in the order to strike, demonstrating the strength of the unions and working-class solidarity. The AWU generally shunned strike action and preferred arbitration; however, the Port Kembla branch led the way this time and all state branches went on strike a few months later over the 44-hour week.[58]

The uneasy relations between management and workers at ER&S and MM had broken out into more sustained class conflict. The industrial conflict at Port Kembla mirrored nation-wide developments. Historians Connell and Irving have noted the increasing working-class militancy from 1910 to 1920, while Turner argued that the period from 1919 to 1920 'exploded in the most costly series of strikes Australia had yet known'.[59] It was not just a case of management versus workers, however, as the local petit-bourgeoisie played a decisive role in the strike of 1920, the origins of which can be seen in the growth of commercial Port Kembla in the 1910s.

In 1911 the local petit-bourgeoisie formed the Storekeepers' Association, indicating a degree of independence and a willingness to pursue their own interests.[60] As the petit-bourgeoisie became an established part of local life in the 1910s, their everyday interactions in the main street drew some closer to their predominantly working-class customers. This was reflected politically in the involvement of prominent storekeepers in the Political Labor League. Well-known storekeepers like T. Wells, W. P. Laughlin and

Robert Shipp (for a time) were active in the league from the late 1910s. Laughlin, the town's barber, was its president in 1914, 1915 and 1917, while Shipp was a successful Labor League candidate in the local government elections of 1920.[61]

Such links were not unusual in the Labor Party of the early twentieth century. In Sydney from the 1880s storekeepers and workers commonly formed municipal alliances. Labor ideology was broad enough to include small storekeepers and local businessmen. Even in its more radical moments, Labor's critique of capitalism rarely extended beyond large monopolies, banks and 'parasitical' middlemen who made up the 'money power'.[62] The development of such links between the petit-bourgeoisie and the working class at Port Kembla gave class politics a firmer grounding within the town. While the primary site for class conflict and class politics was the industrial workplaces of Port Kembla, the increasing strength of working-class politics in the 1910s extended its influence beyond the workplace to the town centre. By forging links with the working class, the petit-bourgeoisie was crucial to this development.

By 1920 the local petit-bourgeoisie were economically reliant on their working-class customers, politically linked to the working class through the Labor League, and socially close through the daily round of shopping and socialising that occurred in the main street. This was an important context for their role in the strike of early 1920. To survive months without wages the strikers at ER&S and MM formed a Distress Relief Committee 'to organise fund raisers and receive donations'. Local fishermen contributed cartloads of fish, and quarry workers passed the hat around at a special meeting.[63] The working class was willing to aid their striking comrades, but so too were local storekeepers. There were 'periodic collections among tradespeople', and donations were also forthcoming from 'leading professional and commercial men'.[64] The *Illawarra Mercury* said of the owner of Fairley's general store that 'Mr Fairley's kind treatment of the men during the crisis has been commented on'.[65] In early February, Shipp organised a benefit at his theatre that raised £40 for the strikers. When the strike settled, a meeting of the workers officially thanked him. Three years later, the AWU offered Shipp membership of the union, but union officials informed the branch that he was ineligible.[66]

Storekeepers often supported striking workers in industrial disputes throughout Australia. In such cases local business people were supporting the social fabric of the town, as much as unions themselves.[67] There was also a degree of self-interest involved, for many storekeepers relied on a 'good name' with their mainly working-class customers, which could be threatened if support was not forthcoming. However, there is no evidence of storekeepers being pressured to provide strikers with credit or donations at Port Kembla, and on the whole, their support appears to have been freely and generously given. Whatever their motives, the intervention of the store-keepers in the strike of 1920 showed the strength of this third political force and brought class politics into the town centre.

Re-establishing 'Order' in the 1920s

Following this peak of industrial unrest and class conflict in 1920, class politics at Port Kembla ebbed in the 1920s. An important context for this decline was the severity of the post-war recession; unemployment and underemployment, together with the rising cost of living, were not con-ducive to radical industrial action. By the end of 1921 the Mount Lyell Coke-works and the Public Works Department quarry were temporarily closed, and ER&S had worked only intermittently during the year because of the drop in world copper prices.[68] In 1921 the Wollongong Benevolent Society had 230 requests for assistance as compared to 170 for 1920, reflecting the worsening regional situation.[69]

While there were economic reasons for the decline in working-class militancy, the fate of the One Big Union (OBU) at Port Kembla demon-strates the particular local conditions which undermined the class politics that had culminated in the strike of 1920. Some historians have seen the eventual failure of the OBU as a victory for labourism, but from this per-spective it was the ideology of localism as much as labourism that finally brought about its failure.[70]

The OBU was a syndicalist revolutionary strategy initially inspired by the Industrial Workers of the World, although a more moderate version gained the increasing support of the working class at Port Kembla from 1917. The strategy envisaged an industrial takeover of the major parts of the capitalist economy by a united working class. As part of a strategy to create that unity, the New South Wales Trades and Labour Congress estab-lished the Workers Industrial Union of Australia to secure 'the abolition of capitalist class ownership of the means of production—whether privately or through the state—and the establishment in its place of social ownership by the whole community'.[71]

The AWU at Port Kembla were keen supporters of the OBU.[72] The idea was strong among Illawarra workers because of the influence of the Miners' Federation.[73] In October 1918 the AWU Port Kembla branch moved that the AWU constitution be changed, 'thus establishing democratic adminis-tration and cementing the One Great Union principle'.[74] The moderate AWU executive, however, was not so enthusiastic, and relations between the union and the Workers Industrial Union deteriorated. In July 1919 the

AWU's newspaper, the *Worker*, complained of the 'blowfly, maggot creating, white-ant tactics of the W.I.U. of A'.[75]

Branch members at Port Kembla became increasingly frustrated with their executive over the delays to the OBU strategy. In November 1922 the branch resolved that membership tickets from workers whose union had signed the Workers Industrial Union preamble should be interchangeable with AWU tickets.[76] In January 1923 the branch moved that 'the consumation [sic] of the O.B.U. should not be further delayed'.[77] By this time the AWU executive had changed its approach to the OBU. As the *Worker* noted, if the OBU stood for 'political action and arbitration' and not 'madness, direct action, sabotage, dissension and destruction of the union movement' as embodied by the Industrial Workers of the World, then the AWU would support it.[78] The OBU offered the AWU executive a chance to become the centre of a new organisation with considerable industrial and political muscle, and this non-revolutionary interpretation of the OBU became dominant. In 1924 the OBU was dealt a final blow by the failure of a provisional council, representing the unions interested in the OBU, to achieve registration in the Commonwealth Arbitration Court.[79]

The conservative executives that dominated unions such as the AWU, along with the state-organised arbitration system, hampered the radical OBU strategy, but local conditions at Port Kembla also highlighted the difficulties of building links with other unions. The AWU's award at MM and ER&S gave preference to members of the AWU, so the resolution offering membership to kindred OBU organisations could not be legally honoured. Moreover, there was a faction within the local branch who were more concerned about protecting local members' jobs than creating large cross-union industrial organisations. This was apparent in January 1922, when a motion was passed 'that holders of AWU tickets be given preference above all others when putting men on'.[80] For these men the threat of competing with other workers for jobs activated their local loyalties and overrode their class affiliations.

The radical edge to the OBU was lost and working-class radicalism was contained by forces that were both local and national, but developments within the labour movement were only one factor in the growing conservatism at Port Kembla in the 1920s. The involvement of the petit-bourgeoisie in the strike of 1920 benefited striking workers and brought class politics to the town centre, but apart from these specific moments of class tension, the commercial centre was a powerful unifying symbol of the locality, and by developing economic, social and political links with the working class, the long-term impact of the petit-bourgeoisie throughout the 1920s was to reinforce localism. The apparent classlessness of the main street, and its role as a forum for cross-class interaction, reinforced a growing political consensus that placed town interests above all others.

There were other forces promoting town interests too. Throughout the 1920s ER&S, and to a lesser extent Australian Fertilizers and MM, continued their paternalistic industrial strategies. This activity increased cross-class interaction and worked to smooth over industrial conflict. In March 1925 at the combined picnic day for employees of ER&S, MM and Australian Fertilizers, the *Mercury* correspondent observed: 'There was much comment in connection with the harmonious nature in which the administrative staff mingled with the employees, being for all the once on an equal basis'.[81]

The focus of middle-class political activity widened beyond industry in the 1920s. There is no direct evidence, but this change in strategy may have originated in the apparent failure of paternalism to quell the rise of the class loyalties at Port Kembla. Certainly ER&S was looking for new solutions—a system of bonus payments, associated with the new scientific management strategies, was instituted in 1919—but the overwhelming response was a new style of paternalism or welfarism which extended to the organisations of town society. Beginning in the early 1920s, the local middle class began participating in and dominating a range of influential local organisations. Moreover, new industries had joined ER&S at Port Kembla, and a company-based paternalism would no longer reach the majority of local workers. The Port Kembla middle class had to branch out into other areas of local society to encounter workers.

The Port Kembla Returned Sailors' and Soldiers' Imperial League sub-branch, for example, was formed in 1920.[82] The league had a cross-class membership with middle-class men such as E. A. White (ER&S), Thomas Downie (shipping agent, retired wharfinger, and past president of the Progress Association), H. P. Greenwood (manager at MM) and Dr Noel Kirkwood filling most of the leadership positions. The petit-bourgeoisie were active, with members such as H. F. Banfield and C. F. T. Jackson, and there were working-class members too, like Jack Warrington, Ted Livermore and Patrick Meurant, labourers from ER&S and MM.[83] In March 1921 about sixty members attended a Returned Soldiers' meeting, which gives some indication of their local support.[84]

Such organisations were important forums for cross-class interaction and the demonstration of middle-class political leadership. Friendly societies performed a similar role, and were increasingly popular at Port Kembla in the 1920s. In 1923 friendly societies directly or indirectly affected around 860 people at Port Kembla, or 41 per cent of the local population. Athough this was slightly less than the state average for 1930 of 47 per cent, it was nevertheless a significant proportion.[85]

The cross-class nature of friendly societies is highlighted by their membership lists. In 1928 the Independent Order of Oddfellows opened a branch at Port Kembla.[86] By 1932 there were thirty-four members consisting of seventeen labourers, nine skilled workers, one storekeeper (the local newsagent T. J. McCann), and three middle-class members.[87] This mixed membership ensured that social interaction was not class-specific, not only in the fortnightly transaction of lodge business at meetings, but in the round of social engagements that were a vital part of friendly society activities.[88] Middle-class and skilled working-class men dominated friendly societies' executives, although labourers formed the numerical majority in most lodges. With the middle class providing the leadership of these organisations, which stressed class co-operation and brotherly respect, friendly societies were institutions that worked against class conflict.

Those prominent in friendly societies often had a strong sense of civic responsibility and were busy participants in local society. The list of the financial members of the Independent Order of Rechabites, formed in January 1927, contained the names of George Simon, Thomas McCann and George Humble, all members of the Port Kembla Progress Association.[89] The cross-over in membership suggests that friendly societies and the Progress Association sprang from like-minded individuals who were energetic local citizens, and strong supporters of the ideology of localism.

After a number of years of inactivity, the Progress Association re-formed in February 1922, signalling its return as an important forum for local politics in the 1920s.[90] The immediate reason for its re-emergence is not clear from the available records, but an important context were two pressing local issues that required attention. Firstly, the Central Illawarra Council and the Public Works Department had been involved in a long-running dispute over the maintenance of a bridge on the Wollongong–Port Kembla Road. The bridge had fallen into disrepair and was particularly dangerous, and one of the first actions of the new association was to forward a petition from Port Kembla residents to the Minister for Public Works. Secondly, as noted previously, competition with Wollongong was often behind the political mobilisation of Port Kembla residents, and this may have been the case with the revival of the Progress Association, as Wollongong Council had lobbied the Minister for Local Government, George Cann, to absorb a section of the Central Illawarra Municipality (properties on the southern side of Mount Keira Road), and had further designs on capturing Port Kembla as well.[91]

More generally, the Progress Association arose out of the social and cultural context in the 1920s which was so locally centred. A meeting in November 1924 demonstrated the extent and the character of town-based political unity. The association convened a meeting regarding the inadequate water supplies experienced by residents. A resolution was passed calling on the state Member for Wollondilly, William Davies, to approach the Minister for Public Works, R. T. Ball.[92] The representatives of Port Kembla's middle class, working class and storekeepers were working together, even voting together for the good of the town, and those who voted for the resolution included the ubiquitous H. R. Lee; James Perry, secretary of the local branch of the AWU; and Robert Shipp.[93] Common issues could unite members of the Progress Association—the state of the local environment and the provision of services. On certain issues, locality could transcend class.

While local loyalties were strengthened in the 1920s, other allegiances did not simply disappear. They remained present ready to be reactivated in the right conditions. Industrial conflict, for example, could break through the apparent unity of localism and reveal the competing class allegiances of locals. In March 1923 there was a brief strike at MM over pay rates involving 200 men. One man who decided to work during the strike was asked by a deputation of workers to leave: 'He was escorted to the gates by some hundreds of men and given a "send-off" amidst hoots and cheers'.[94] This event demonstrated the solidarity of the workers and their ability to enforce class allegiances against the occasional transgressor. Another strike at MM in February 1924 exposed the competing loyalties of class and locality, when poor attendance at the fortnightly Progress Association meeting was reportedly due to 'some members being on business in connection with the strike at the MM Works'.[95]

Strikes most clearly revealed class loyalties, but local unions were themselves influenced by localism in the 1920s, their politics moderated by the ties of kinship and the cross-class links that characterised the town. Some unions like the AWU were drawn into the town-based alliance. Prominent members of the AWU such as Jack Mathews, Fred Finch and E. Scott were active in the Progress Association. The policies of the local branch of the Waterside Workers' Federation (WWF) were moderated by the kinship links that transcended divisions between employees and employers on the waterfront. George Sloan, secretary of the WWF from 1928 to 1936, was the brother of Ben Sloan, one of the four stevedores working at Port Kembla. Richard Dodd, branch auditor was the brother of Robert Dodd, another Port Kembla stevedore.[96] William Bailey, a waterside worker in the late 1920s and 1930s, and an opponent of the dominant moderate faction, recalled: 'There was such a lot of relations in the union at that time . . . The stevedores would pick their relatives . . . and some other men would borrow money off the stevedores so they would give them a job.'[97] The moderate faction within the branch ensured its survival (until 1936 at least) because those proposed for branch membership were usually friends or relatives of members.[98] These local kinship and social networks had undermined union militancy and compromised the effectiveness of the branch.

Sectarianism was another potentially divisive issue, but local efforts minimised the political impact of any religious conflict at Port Kembla. The conscription referendums of 1916 and 1917 had stirred sectarian conflict throughout Australia, and in the early 1920s the issue became prominent in the Illawarra. At Wollongong the Union Jack was burnt in the May Day March of 1921 and the New South Wales Protestant Federation passed a resolution condemning the action.[99] The Protestant Federation was active on the south coast and was accused of trying 'to stir up sectarian strife among the workers' during the 1922 state elections.[1] Catholics and Pro-testants traded letters and articles in the local press accusing each other of dividing society and threatening the moral order.[2]

At Port Kembla though, there was a conscious and public effort to avert religious conflict. In March 1922 the three managers of the local in-dustries, E. A. White (ER&S), H. P. Greenwood (MM) and R. J. Craig (Aus-tralian Fertilizers), all prominent Anglicans, officiated at the St Patrick's Day celebrations at Port Kembla. A few months later, after the annual Roman Catholic Bazaar, a 'prominent worker in connection with the bazaar' was quoted by the *Illawarra Mercury*: 'So far as Port Kembla is concerned the sectarian question is dead—we received support from all denominations. It was one of the pleasing features of the bazaar.'[3]

Throughout the 1920s localist politics effectively managed to gloss over or divert local political tensions, although industrial conflicts revealed the continuing presence of class politics at Port Kembla. The influence of cross-class organisations and the rhetoric of town unity drew the political loyalties of locals away from class and union. It was not a matter of one type of politics replacing another, but rather the coexistence of different loyalties and identities that were brought to different situations. Class politics re-mained strong in the industrial workplace while localist politics dominated the town centre, and appeared to speak for the majority of local inhabitants in political dealings with the Council, Wollongong-based interests, the state government and other relevant parties. From the late 1920s, however, localist politics confronted more serious threats—increasing working-class activism and a deteriorating economy.

The Breakdown of Town Alliances

From 1926 there was renewed activity from the unions at Port Kembla that went beyond occasional industrial action. In May 1926 the FEDFA went on strike at the Public Works quarry demanding a 44-hour week.[4] The next month there were moves by the Wollongong branch of the Labor Party and unions such as the WWF, the Carpenters and Joiners, the AWU and the Meatworkers, to re-form the Illawarra Trades and Labour Council, which had been dormant since 1917.[5]

Industrial conflict in the late 1920s, like previous incidents that decade, revealed hidden political divisions, but it also widened those divisions in a more comprehensive attack on the image of town unity. The timber-workers' strike, which began at Port Kembla in March 1929, precipitated a public disagreement about the merits of the strike. Two members of the local middle class, S. C. Jones, engineer from Australian Iron and Steel Ltd (AI&S), and F. H. Rickleman, a metallurgist at ER&S and later works super-intendent, wrote to the *Illawarra Mercury*: 'At the present time in this district a comparatively small number of men have been compelled to strike against the Industrial Arbitration Award, whose rulings they cheerfully accepted for many years because conditions have been favourable to them'.[6] This overview of the strike presented the strikers as a minority in the district (thereby implicitly evoking the localist rhetoric of unity), driven to in-dustrial action by opportunism and compulsion. The correspondents were especially riled by a demonstration one week earlier outside the timber yard at Port Kembla, near the train station at the northern end of the main street. During a picket of the yard, one man who chose to work was verbally harassed and 'escorted' home by members of the picket, much like the incident at MM six years earlier, and he didn't return to work the next day. Jones and Rickleman's letter continued: 'The demonstration which took place outside the South Coast Timber Co.'s mill last week is one which the majority of unionists will deplore. If the aim of the organisers is to further depress local industry and so aggravate prevailing unemployment and distress, it will be conceded that they may be quite successful'.[7]

The striking workers were presented as acting against the interests of the district. The demonstration was targeted particularly because unionists had publicly expressed their anger and exposed the absence of unity at the very heart of the symbol of cross-class unity and harmony—the main street. The unionists had defiled the symbolic unity of local society.[8]

These emerging divisions were reinforced the following week when a letter in reply signed by 'Timber Worker' from Port Kembla appeared in the *Illawarra Mercury*:

> [Jones and Rickleman's letter] showed that men who drew big salaries are out of touch with modern thought ... If Messrs Jones and Rickleman followed their argument through to its logical conclusion, it would be better for this country if the workers were reduced to the same standard of living as Chinese coolies ... It is very nice for men like Messrs Jones and Rickleman to preach contentment, their bank balances will not be reduced, except perhaps they may be shareholders in the timber company.[9]

'Timber Worker' emphasised the different class positions of Jones and Rickleman—their higher wages, their bank balances and the possibility they might be shareholders—all characteristics that the striking timber-workers undoubtedly did not share. This focus on difference further undermined the image of unity and common interest which localism had presented throughout the 1920s.

The paternalism of ER&S, an important force behind localism, also waned with the economic decline of the company in the late 1920s. The company backed away from many of its activities in local society. The Port Kembla Industries Co-operative Store, jointly run by ER&S and Australian Fertilizers, had failed to achieve the loyalty and support of sufficient numbers of customers at Port Kembla. It was sold to Frost Brothers in March 1928.[10] The political focus on the town and town-based unity encouraged by the paternalism of ER&S dissipated, as operations at the copper smelter were reduced to a bare minimum by 1929.

Unemployment and the influx of itinerant workers in the late 1920s initially led to a resurgence of localism around the issue of providing jobs for local men before 'outsiders'. In 1926 municipal representatives from Port Kembla used the Council to appeal for state government projects to ease local unemployment, and in 1928 the Progress Association wrote to the major companies at Port Kembla asking them to employ local men before others.[11]

But the depth of the crisis overturned many of the conditions that supported localist politics. Although the political rhetoric of 'jobs for locals' continued, by 1930 the barometer of the local political alliance, the Progress Association, was having trouble attracting members and interest was falling away.[12] Discussions were held about how to get people interested in the Association. During a Progress Association meeting in January 1930, 'a lengthy discussion eventuated regarding the matter of getting people to attend to the meetings of the association . . . However the discussion eventually lapsed without any decision being arrived at for improvement.'[13] The decline in popularity of the association demonstrated the breakdown of the uneasy political truce that it represented. By 1930 localist politics was a waning political force.

Politics at Port Kembla was characterised by the shifting relationship between localist and class politics. Localist politics, as embodied by the Progress Association and other town-based political alliances, gained strength from the material conditions of local society—a town-centred labour market, intermittent work patterns, paternalistic companies, and the cross-class interactions of everyday life and local organisations. These diverse forces came together in the 1920s, reinforced by an ideology of localism that pitted 'locals' against 'outsiders'. However, class politics was ever-present, centring on conflict between ER&S management and its workforce, and culminating in the strike of 1920 at ER&S and MM. In the late

1920s class allegiances again emerged from beneath the layer of town loyalty through industrial conflict and economic downturn.

The relationship between the two types of politics, then, was an uneasy coexistence of separate loyalties. As both types of politics waxed and waned it was not a matter of the replacement of one type of politics by another, for both had their origins in Port Kembla's economic and social structure, and both had their strong areas—in the industrial workplaces for class politics, and in the town centre for localist politics. It was when one type of politics entered the domain of the other—for example, when the working class tried to take over the Progress Association in 1913, or when unions in the 1920s were infused by localist sentiment—that it can be most clearly stated that one particular way of organising politics was dominant. From 1900 to 1930 it was localist politics that appeared to represent Port Kembla's legitimate political voice, and crossed over to influence unions, the industrial workplace and the working class generally. The Great Depression signalled new challenges to town-centred politics, reactivating class allegiances and ushering in a new competing force—the Illawarra region. Before looking at these challenges, however, it is necessary to outline the very different experiences of one particular group.

6

Kooris and Port Kembla, to the 1970s

WHILE TOWN DEVELOPMENT and growing attachments to locality were important components of the formative period of industrial society, not all locals shared equally in this vigorous local social and political milieu. Local Kooris were largely spectators of industrial growth and its attendant social relations. The emerging industrial society of Port Kembla resembled that of country towns throughout New South Wales, where there were clear divides between non-Aboriginal and Aboriginal society.[1] Industrialising Port Kembla, however, had a particular impact on Koori lives, affecting their access to natural resources, occupation of different campsites, and position in the labour market. By the beginning of the post-war boom in the late 1940s the essential features of the relationship between the town and the Aboriginal community were in place. The community was located both socially and spatially on the fringe of the town's society, and its inhabitants occupied marginal positions in the labour market. Koori residents were subject to a more regulated and interventionist legislative regime than white residents, represented most clearly by the New South Wales Protection Acts. Despite these hurdles, Kooris were not hapless victims of industrial growth, and maintained tangible relationships to place. In fact, evidence of Koori-led political campaigns for security and certainty in land tenure dates from as early as the 1920s.

The following chapter addresses the silences that surround local Koori history. In the public space of the town, and in the popular memory of many white residents, the events described below are not well known, and the places are rarely acknowledged to have significance for Kooris. To understand the relationship between Koori society and the town of Port Kembla during the industrial age, it is important to place the analysis within a broader context. A discussion of the relevant features of traditional society, the impact of European invasion of the Illawarra region, and estimates of the Koori population are necessary. After a hiatus in the late nineteenth century, industrial development at Port Kembla initiated a renewed process of dispossession and dislocation that culminated in 1942 with the removal of Kooris from Hill 60, a site of considerable economic and spiritual significance. This powerful historical legacy is one that still shapes Koori lives today.

Traditional Society

Archaeological evidence from the south coast of New South Wales suggests that Kooris occupied the area at least 25 000 years ago.[2] Following climatic changes, the coastal population increased markedly 5000 years ago, as the stabilisation of sea levels led to the creation of food-rich lagoon areas on the coast.[3] The overwhelming impression of early European accounts was of a well-populated area. There were sightings of numerous people and scattered fires by James Cook and Joseph Banks in 1770, and the explorers Bass and Flinders encountered significant numbers of Kooris at Lake Illawarra and Illowra (Red Point) in 1796. A large number of family groups and clans lived near the fertile areas of Nitoka (Port Kembla), Tuckulung (Tom Thumb's Lagoon) and Coomaditchie Lagoon.[4]

Kooris of the Illawarra were part of the Wadi Wadi people, and they shared a common language, Tharawal, with Kooris north to Botany Bay, south to Jervis Bay and west to Campbelltown and Camden.[5] They lived in bands of between twenty and fifty; men primarily fished and hunted, while women fished, gathered food, cared for children and introduced them to the land. Movement between these bands and other cultural groups for ceremonial or marriage reasons was common. In 1796 Bass and Flinders encountered Kooris near Nitoka who were from the Eora people of Port Jackson. In 1816 two Kooris, Bundle of the Wadi Wadi and Broughton from the Dharuk people (who lived to the north and west of Sydney), guided settler Charles Throsby on an overland route from Liverpool to the Five Islands District and on to Jervis Bay.[6]

Movement of bands or family groups was constant, although coastal groups were more sedentary than people living beyond the Illawarra escarpment because the supply of food from the coastal environment (fish, waterfowl and other wildlife) was less seasonal than inland environments.[7] Illowra (Red Point) was an ideal spot from which to base an economy on seafood. A good vantagepoint surrounded by water on three sides, Illowra had easy access to four beaches, two lagoons and one large lake.[8] Three nearby off-shore islands (subsequently named Big Island, Martin's Island and Rocky

Island by settlers; their Koori names are not recorded) were also important parts of the local economy.[9] The coastal people fished using bone hooks, spears, nets and carrels made of tea-tree bush and specially dug channels.

The relationship to the land was complex and multi-faceted, and has received considerable attention from anthropologists and historians.[10] The fragmentary evidence that survives from the Illawarra suggests that family groups had links with particular areas through traditional lands and sacred sites. The Timbery family lived around Tom Thumb's Lagoon and Berkeley, the Hooka family lived near Dapto, and the Bundle family around Wollongong, for example.[11] They moved over other areas, however, in a complicated mix of land-owning and land-using groups. A band could move into the territory of its neighbours if permission was granted and correct procedures were followed. Exogamous marriage and travel for ceremonial or trading purposes also encouraged movement between different groups. Illowra (and many other sacred sites) had strong emotional and spiritual meanings, as places to bury the dead and a sacred place where people originated in the Dreaming—a rich cosmology that embodied relationships between the spirit world and everyday life, between people, land, animals and plants.[12]

The Arrival of Europeans

The European invasion of the Illawarra, which gained momentum in the 1810s with the influx of cedar cutters and the declaration of the first land grants in the area, overturned many of these relationships. This was a common experience in many regions throughout the growing colony of New South Wales, but there were some local differences. In the Illawarra there was no period of warfare between the colonial government and Kooris, like that which occurred in the Campbelltown and Hawkesbury areas.[13] In 1816 the *Sydney Gazette* reported that the 'natives' in the Five Islands District were 'very amicably disposed towards us' and noted their 'general mildness of manners'.[14] Nevertheless, authorities could not always control the actions of settlers and escaped convicts, and frontier violence of a less organised, but no less brutal, kind occurred. In 1818 two local settlers, Cornelius O'Brien from Yallah and Lieutenant Weston from Dapto, were investigated by a Sydney magistrate, D'Arcy Wentworth, following a letter from Charles Throsby alleging unauthorised punitive expeditions against Kooris in the area. Wentworth concluded that O'Brien and Weston had acted with 'great indiscretion' but refused to consider charges of murder. Governor Macquarie reacted angrily, writing to Wentworth complaining that he was 'treating this wanton attack on the Natives with so much levity and indifference'.[15]

This photograph of a section of the new AI&S hot strip mill from a 1955 company publication illustrates the celebration of new industrial technology characteristic of an age where industrial society reigned supreme. The workers in the photo are tellingly unnamed and dwarfed by the machinery.

This aerial photograph from 1955 shows the location of the new AI&S hot strip mill. The image of the new industrial buildings shows clear evidence of airbrushing, typical of promotional photos of this era and type.

Concreting Wentworth Street in 1937. Some residential premises are still visible in the foreground, while most of the commercial premises were located in the middle and north-western sections of the street.

Wentworth Street looking north-west in 1991 and showing the intersection with Fitzwilliam Street. From the mid-1990s sex workers standing on this corner became a common sight. The kerbside trees represent Council attempts to beautify the declining commercial centre.

Men at work on the foundations of the AI&S blast furnace. Mud and pools of water reveal the effects of recent heavy rain. A farmhouse can be seen in the distance.

This set a theme for race relations in the region. Violence on the part of the non-Aboriginal inhabitants was tolerated or not reported, and efforts by colonial administrations to protect the 'natives' were generally ill-fated. As early as the 1830s European occupation represented a significant threat to Koori life and culture. By the end of the nineteenth century traditional patterns of land use were in complete disarray. Some Kooris maintained economic relationships with the newcomers (albeit unequal ones) as domestic servants, rural labourers or fishers, but generally they avoided white contact and tried to carry on their lives in the face of an increasingly interventionist state and a growing European population.

Dispossessed of their land, Kooris had moved to four main areas along the south coast by 1900. There was a large community at Nowra and nearby Wreck Bay, a La Perouse settlement (established in 1878), and two smaller communities at Port Kembla and Minnamurra. The regional focus of white influence in the nineteenth century sharpened into a more specific control over land and land use for Kooris in the twentieth century. This was indicative of state- and nation-wide trends as government policy became more interventionist from the beginning of the twentieth century, with increasing attempts to control the location and everyday running of indigenous settlements.[16] By the 1940s, these developments crystallised into a policy later known as 'assimilation', a concerted, often forcible, attempt to 'absorb' the Aboriginal community 'into the general life of white civilization'.[17]

Port Kembla and Berrwarra Point

Despite the development of more interventionist government policy, small areas of vacant land in the Illawarra provided some respite from government control and white contact. In the late nineteenth century Port Kembla was one such area, close to Wollongong but not intensively populated or farmed, with large areas of vacant crown land. In fact, it was the Koori rejection of the government reserve at Berrwarra Point, 6 kilometres south of Port Kembla on Lake Illawarra, which led to the increasing importance of Port Kembla for Kooris in the twentieth century.

In 1894 the New South Wales government body, the Aborigines' Protection Board (APB), established the Berrwarra Point reserve at the mouth of Lake Illawarra. The APB provided huts, a fishing boat, tackle and a boat shed, hoping that local Kooris would move to the reserve and become self-supporting.[18] In 1899 a missionary from the Australian Aborigines' Mission (AAM), John Vidler, took control of the reserve. AAM was a non-denominational society that grew out of informal contact with the La Perouse Koori community.[19] Vidler had some success, and benefited from the support of the well-known 'King' of the 'Illawarra tribe', Mickey Johnson, who had made a public conversion to Christianity in 1898. Johnson accompanied Vidler on his trips around the Illawarra, undertaken to raise money for a church at Berrwarra Point, which was built in late 1899.[20] However, Berrwarra Point was not popular, and the number of Kooris on the reserve never exceeded twenty, mostly Johnson and his family. Vidler suggested to the APB that the reserve should be moved to Port Kembla, arguing that it would be more successful there. The APB disagreed, claiming that fish and fowl were plentiful at Berrwarra Point and that it was not desirable for Kooris to live near Port Kembla because the APB believed it was likely to become a large population centre. Subsequent events proved Vidler's appeal for a transfer to Port Kembla was well founded. AAM's missionary work was more successful at Port Kembla because local Kooris preferred the town to the Lake Illawarra reserve. Despite police visits to Koori camps at Port Kembla and Bombo (just north of Kiama), Kooris could not be persuaded to go to the reserve.[21]

Ill-health forced Vidler to retire in 1900, and AAM concentrated its efforts on Port Kembla. The move to Port Kembla, however, did not suit all sections of local Koori society. Mickey Johnson and his family remained camped at Lake Illawarra. At a meeting held at Port Kembla in July 1900, Johnson complained that his people had to walk all the way from Lake Illawarra to Port Kembla and the mission had provided no refreshments. Johnson himself had invested a lot of energy in helping raise funds to build a church at Lake Illawarra, and the unpopular reserve may have reflected badly on his reputation as a regional Koori leader.[22]

Nevertheless, many other Kooris preferred Port Kembla. In 1903 the AAM's journal, the *Aborigines' Advocate*, reported that no work had been done at Lake Illawarra since 1899. In 1904 the APB visited Lake Illawarra and found it deserted—even Johnson and some of his family had moved to Minnamurra:

> A number of the houses constructed of galvanised iron were found to be unoccupied and as the aborigines cannot be induced to reside on this reserve, it was decided to make use of this iron (which was in excellent condition) at the Roseberry Park and Wallaga Lake Settlements.[23]

The APB put a brave face on the failure of the Lake Illawarra reserve by referring to the successful retrieval of scrap, but the true significance of the reserve's failure was that it highlighted the Koori preference for Port Kembla.

Whether Kooris living at Port Kembla maintained traditional associations with the land in this locality is impossible to say with any certainty. Koori people throughout the state had shown a strong ability to adapt and survive, and traditional relationships to the land were still relevant in places.

In addition, while upheaval and displacement may have severed many of the original Koori links to the area, new connections may have grown in their place. As Peter Read found of the Wiradjuri people: 'These days the towns as much as the creeks and hills focus Wiradjuri identification, but it is the same country, and the family alignments, bound by kin and marriage ties, form the core of local identity'.[24] Furthermore, Aboriginal culture could be as dynamic and adaptable as other any other culture, and there is no reason to assume that associations formed in the late nineteenth and early twentieth century were inauthentic or less culturally meaningful. Critics of native title claims often argue that claimants were not the traditional owners, while in the same breath arguing that non-Aboriginal people can develop deep connections with the land.

As well as these cultural meanings, Port Kembla had political and economic meanings for Kooris. They rejected Berrwarra Point and the APB's control; Port Kembla represented an area some distance from government reserves with opportunities for economic self-sufficiency. The beaches and lagoons surrounding Port Kembla offered considerable possibilities for survival based on fishing, as they had done traditionally; possibilities the growing European population was also discovering. From at least the 1870s the Saddler and Timbery families lived near Tom Thumb's Lagoon, fishing for a living.[25] Wonwongorong (a hill on Red Point renamed Hill 60 after World War I) also provided a retreat from white influence and control. Non-Aboriginal professional fishers, such as the Masseys at Berkeley (then appropriately called Fishtown) and the Burnses at Lake Illawarra, had cornered the trade on the lake, but white competition at Port Kembla consisted of small operators only, many of whom also worked at the local industries. Fishing represented a means of survival that merged traditional knowledge and skills with the demands of a growing non-Aboriginal population. By the 1920s Kooris were netting fish on Fisherman's Beach which were sold directly to local non-Aboriginal residents, or the catch was packed in crates and transported to Wollongong by my great-grandfather, William Bright.[26]

Fishing could not provide the sole basis of a viable local economy because of seasonal variations. Consequently, the numbers of Kooris at Port Kembla fluctuated, many travelling to the south coast to work in the market gardens of the area. The high season for agricultural work was January to April. Joan Wakeman, who lived at the Koori settlement on Hill 60 as a child, remembers travelling to the south coast: 'I used to go down and do seasonal work every now and then to earn a few bob'.[27] In 1954 anthropologist James Bell found that during the year most adult male Kooris at Port Kembla had been 'either on farms on the south coast or in industrial occupations in Port Kembla, Wollongong or Sydney'.[28]

Close links with Kooris at Nowra, Wreck Bay, La Perouse, and the north coast of New South Wales also promoted movement up and down the coast.[29] When Nelly Timbery drowned in Salty Creek in 1901, her mother was reported to be 'on a visit to the Richmond River'.[30] Danny Bell, who spent some time on Hill 60 fishing during the 1920s and 1930s, often moved between there and La Perouse.[31] In fact, a small settlement established at La Perouse during the Great Depression was named 'Hill 60', probably by people such as Bell who moved between the two areas.[32]

Given these conditions, finding an accurate estimate of the Koori population at Port Kembla is difficult, especially since the government authorities that collected such records were unaware of the extent of population movement and the reasons for it. These factors commonly led to underestimations of the local Koori population. The 1901 Census, for example, estimated thirty-nine 'Aboriginals' in the entire municipality of Central Illawarra. The APB and AAM had more regular direct contact with Kooris. The APB estimated seventy-one 'Aboriginals' in the 'Wollongong' area while AAM found seventy-six 'Aboriginals' at Port Kembla in 1901.[33]

There is also oral history evidence concerning the numbers of Kooris at Port Kembla. Joan Wakeman recalled that: 'Port Kembla was one of the main areas the Aboriginals lived, although they used to go up and down the coast'.[34] Dick Henry, whose mother lived at Hill 60 in the 1920s and 1930s, said of Port Kembla: 'Yes well it was more of a central place—people would pass through Port Kembla rather than go through the bush. Along the beaches was the easiest way to travel in them days'.[35] Joe Hill, a non-Aboriginal fisher who lived on Hill 60 from about 1913 until the depression, suggested a population of 'a couple of hundred, but it's hard to estimate because they were scattered around, a few in the scrub, one man here, a family here'.[36] The overwhelming weight of these recollections suggests a significant population of Kooris at Port Kembla. Given the variable nature of the population, the dubious status of some of the official figures and the strength of oral evidence, a reasonable estimate of the Koori population at Port Kembla in 1900 is eighty. Residence at Port Kembla, however, may have been punctuated by periods away for economic, social or cultural reasons, or forcibly broken by government transfers to reserves or institutions.

Industrial Growth and Koori Lives

In 1900 local Kooris had the option of living at Coomaditchie Lagoon, Hill 60, Salty Creek or Tom Thumb's Lagoon. Their occupation of these areas around Port Kembla, however, never gained legitimacy in the eyes of the government authorities that, according to white law, owned and controlled the land. In the early part of the twentieth century the process of industrialisation and town growth brought about what historian Heather Goodall called 'a new dispossession'.³⁷ These local factors were played out in the context of a state-wide policy regime of assimilation, which represented a more aggressive attempt to merge and absorb Aborigines into the white community. Aborigines at Port Kembla were vulnerable to this policy but also insulated from its full effects. Port Kembla Kooris were vulnerable because they represented a segment of the indigenous population who was seen to be especially troublesome. The 1939 annual report of the Aborigines' Welfare Board, a successor to the APB, noted that 'uncontrolled Aboriginal camps' on the fringes of white townships were proving difficult to manage since 'the Aborigines, in most instances, steadfastly refuse to remove [to reserves or stations], preferring to remain where they are handy to the town for employment, and where they can participate in the amenities of town life'.³⁸ Similar comments on the difficulties that the board and its successors faced with Aborigines outside formally controlled areas surface throughout the 1940s and 1950s.³⁹ While being defined as a 'problem' group, being outside Welfare Board control did offer some benefits, chief of which was greater personal and family freedom. After World War II especially, the assimilationist legislative and administrative regime was far more effective on tightly controlled reserves and, to a lesser extent, stations. This regime was less able to control totally the lives of Port Kembla Aborigines.

Freedom from government control, however, also entailed a complete lack of security of tenure, and the demands of a growing industrial town soon affected local Kooris. The first dislocation occurred in 1904. The Public Works Department complained to the APB about a number of Kooris living on land resumed for the harbour works near Tom Thumb's Lagoon. The APB investigated and asked the Kooris to relocate to one of the APB's reserves. One family went to Roseberry Park on the far south coast, but the rest refused to leave. Throughout the state, Kooris went to great lengths to avoid missions if possible, and those at Port Kembla were no exception. The APB asked Public Works to reconsider the eviction, but the department insisted on removal, as the APB reported: 'The police were asked to see that as little hardship as possible was allowed to arise through the compulsory removal of these people from their camping place'.⁴⁰ The removal of Kooris from Public Works land at Tom Thumb's Lagoon is reflected in the official Aboriginal population figures for Port Kembla, which drop from seventy-one in 1901 to thirty-three by 1905.⁴¹ AAM, which had maintained contact with Kooris in the area following Vidler's retirement, found only a few families remaining at the port.⁴²

It is unclear where these people went—probably to the south coast or La Perouse—but many eventually returned, so that by 1914 there was another large camp of Kooris on crown land at Salty Creek, not far from

Tom Thumb's Lagoon. However, Public Works had resumed land in this area earlier in the year, and again decided to have the camp removed, destroying or relocating the homes. Some Kooris moved to Perkin's Beach, while others headed south to Nowra or north to La Perouse.[43] From a reported sixty-seven in 1914 the population dropped again to thirty-nine by 1919.[44]

Besides land resumption caused by Port Kembla's industrialisation, the power of the state government, through its local representative the police, to remove individual Kooris from the area was another factor that severed links to the locality. In 1912 Annie S. (described as an 'Aboriginal') was charged with 'having no visible means of support'. According to the police she 'was living at Port Kembla and leading a [*sic*] immoral life'. Sergeant Noble stated before the court: 'I think it would be a charity to herself if she was sent to Long Bay'. The court agreed. She was sentenced to three months' gaol.[45]

In the 1900s and 1910s the state government reinforced its control over Koori lives, and refined the legislative apparatus for regulating where Kooris lived. The *Aborigines' Protection Act* of 1909 gave the APB power to remove Koori children over fourteen years old living on reserves from the care of their parents. Amendments to the Act in 1915 enabled the APB to take all Koori children from their families on reserves, and further changes in 1918 extended these powers to Kooris not living on reserves, like those at Port Kembla.[46] Little written evidence of the operation of the Act at Port Kembla has survived except this newspaper report from 1918:

> Last week two black girls had been taken in charge by the police for the purpose of sending them to a home in Cootamundra. They were placed in the yard at the police station awaiting a conveyance to take them to Wollongong. Whilst the back of the police officer was turned they scaled the fence and made off in the direction of the cokeworks. The police gave chase, and after a run of over a mile, the two girls were re-captured and subsequently forwarded to the home.[47]

From the 1920s urban expansion towards Hill 60 put more pressure on Koori living places, and Kooris were under constant threat of eviction. The Port Kembla Golf Club built a nine-hole course on the lower reaches on Hill 60 in 1923. Local non-Aboriginal resident Jean Payne remembers: 'There were [Koori] camps right at the bottom [of Hill 60] of course, but when the golf course was [built] there they went higher up didn't they, on the hill'.[48] The club considered expanding to eighteen holes in 1929. Elements within the Council wanted to evict Kooris from Hill 60 and declare it a public park.[49] The issue came to the attention of the Association for the

Protection of Native Races, a group of city-based white liberal philan-thropists, intellectuals and religious leaders who were concerned about the living conditions of Aborigines.[50] Some of their members visited Hill 60 in late 1929:

> Mr Cooper, Mr Sullivan and Mr Morley, paid a surprise visit and inspected the homes which they found to be cleanly, and quite suitable to the needs of the people concerned, they were certainly unsightly, were built of galvanised iron, kerosene tins, very cleverly put together, with sometimes an extension of canvas. They were almost entirely hidden by Ti Tree, and the only ground of objection appeared to be their nearness to the Golf Links.[51]

Alderman Mathews, former president of the local branch of the AWU and the Political Labor League, was asked by the Council to investigate. He reported: 'No one has complained of them and no one asked for their removal. They earn a decent living fishing.'[52] The APB also investigated and found twenty-five Kooris living there, none of whom were dependent on the board's rations.[53] The APB too believed that the Council was motivated by concern for the adjoining golf course. Plans for an extension to the golf course were shelved and eventually the club moved to Windang. The Council also dropped the idea of a public park on Hill 60. In this case the Koori occupation of Hill 60 was protected with the help of white pressure groups and sympathetic white aldermen.

Kooris were not completely isolated from the non-Aboriginal society and economy, and the growing town offered some benefits. In 1904 the APB reported that many of the Kooris at Port Kembla 'were in constant employment in the locality', either as fishers or coal trimmers at the harbour.[54] After the arrival of the railway line in 1916, some of the fish caught in the waters off Port Kembla ended up in Wollongong markets. Approximately a dozen Koori men (Roy Burns, Jackie Andersen and Stan Speechley among them) worked on the waterfront during the 1920s and 1930s, and some Koori women worked for white women in the town as domestic servants. Rose Johnson, widow of the late Mickey Johnson, divided her time between Minnamurra and Port Kembla in the 1920s. While at Port Kembla she often worked as a domestic for local white families.[55] Sarah Drury recalled that a Koori girl worked as a domestic in her grandmother's boarding house in the mid-1920s. She also remembered Kooris bringing around large vats of prawns caught from Lake Illawarra to sell in the town. Kooris did find employment at Port Kembla, but were clearly on the fringes of the labour market.

It was fishing that enabled Kooris to establish a settlement on Hill 60 not completely dependent on their marginal position in the township's labour market. Fishing provided a source of food and income, and merged traditional knowledge with the realities of survival in the twentieth century. Hill 60 gave an excellent panoramic view of surrounding waters and when a school of fish was spotted people would launch boats from Fisherman's or Perkin's Beach.[56] Beryl Beller, later a resident of La Perouse, recalls her days on Hill 60 in the 1930s:

> I remember when I was small, going down to the beach and helping my dad and grandfather haul for fish. We would sit on the sandhill which was called the lookout, and watch for fish to swim past, then run down and push the boats into the water. When the nets were back on the beach we would put the fish into wooden boxes. The men then took them and they were sold.[57]

The Koori experience of Port Kembla, then, was characterised by a number of dispossessions and dislocations from camps at the edges of the town. This process was initially propelled by government plans for the Port Kembla harbour, and further hardship was caused by the growth of residential and urban facilities for the white township in the 1920s. But it is also apparent that distance from white influence was something actively sought by Kooris, and despite the dispossessions, camp sites around Port Kembla, especially Hill 60, became important areas for local people. As Joan Wakeman stated: 'Hill 60 was more like Aboriginals wanted to live in those days. Just shacks and freedom and happiness, it was really beautiful'.[58] Many non-Aboriginal residents understood the area as 'off limits'.[59] White children would only tentatively venture onto Hill 60, frightened by prevailing racist ideology, or simply by an intuitive understanding that this was Koori space. The appreciation of Hill 60 had resonance with traditional links to the land, and was also modified by the political meaning of the hill as a place of their own, away from white contact, and its economic meaning as a base for a lifestyle centred on fishing. Hill 60 became a locality in itself, separate from though linked to non-Aboriginal society at Port Kembla.

In the 1920s Kooris took steps to secure their occupation of Hill 60. Evidence of this campaign to achieve security over land is mediated through non-Aboriginal sources, but it is clear that Port Kembla Kooris made representations through the state Fisheries Department to the local Council asking for just under one hectare of land on Hill 60. Council debated the issue in 1927: 'It is understood that they [local Kooris] are perturbed at the apparent insecurity of their present quarters and desire provision to be made for the permanency of the fishing station'. Alderman Lee was reported as saying that 'there was no objection to the places, as long as proper provision is made in regard to sanitary conveniences'. Further evidence of Koori concern over their uncertain tenure came in the same year. Joseph

Timbery, an Aboriginal fisherman residing at Hill 60, wrote to the Council concerned that the behaviour of other residents would threaten his tenure. The Council replied that his lease was not under threat. There was no official recognition, however, of the legal status of the Koori occupation of Hill 60.[60]

The case came to the attention of the APB in 1929, the board seeking to support Aboriginal claims for some security of title. A letter from the APB to the Department of Defence makes it clear that local Kooris had sought assistance from the department as the owner of significant portions of the area. The secretary wrote:

> I beg to advise that a number of Aborigines who have, for many years past, been living near the town of Port Kembla, on a site known as Ti Tea Hill [Hill 60] have been served with a closing order by the local Shire Council. My Board is prepared to help these people provided they have some sort of title to the land on which they reside ... It is understood that a number of them have lodged application with your Department with a view to securing some such title, and I now beg to ask that their application be, if possible, favourably considered.[61]

The surviving Department of Defence records do not include any details of the department's response; however, these records and other secondhand references indicate that local Kooris were conducting a campaign to secure title to part of the area. This amounts to evidence of one of the first land rights campaigns conducted in the Illawarra region. Kooris sought out relevant local, state and federal authorities and wrote letters detailing their position and requesting assistance. Again, however, the Koori claims were not acted upon and there was no recognition of their occupation of Hill 60.

This lack of recognition made the Koori possession of Hill 60 vulnerable to further incursion, and in the late 1930s the Department of Defence decided to fortify the hill, and the area surrounding the eastern breakwater. This latter location on the Military Reserve near the breakwater was another favourite camping area. The military's plans for Port Kembla developed as the world situation worsened. After some discussion the Department of Defence decided in August 1938 to construct a battery observation post on Hill 60 but leave the provision of fittings and equipment until wartime. Likewise, gun emplacements near the eastern breakwater were to be temporary only, and the guns transferred in case of war.[62] The plans expanded to include a command post, an operational battery observation post and two permanent 6-inch gun emplacements with guns *in situ*, together with accommodation and amenities for the 13th battalion. The work had begun with day labour in July 1939, offering some work for local men, including my grandfather, Hugh Halcrow, a former farrier and ER&S employee. By February 1940 the emplacements and associated buildings near the break-water were virtually complete, while the foundations for the Hill 60 battery observation post had been laid.[63]

There was no public record of the removal of Kooris from Hill 60, since war-time censorship precluded any public announcements of defence preparations. Department of Defence records, as one would expect, maintain a rigid focus on the plans and progress of construction. One source, a memoir written by a former army officer who served at Port Kembla, indicates that the removal occurred in September 1942.[64] The removal is also present in the collective memories of Koori and non-Aboriginal people in the area, as Kooris were moved down the south coast or to Cooma-ditchie, the last remaining Aboriginal camp at Port Kembla.[65] Coomaditchie was a traditional camp site beside a freshwater lagoon, a short walk from Perkin's Beach, but in other ways less suitable than Hill 60. The area was gazetted a 'reserve' in February 1929. It offered no views of the surrounding ocean, and during the depression the Council established a large camp for the unemployed adjacent to the Koori camp, making conditions there overcrowded and placing further strain on the natural resources that Kooris were so dependent on.

The loss of Hill 60, coming on top of the other dispossessions in the preceding forty years, was a major setback for Kooris. By the mid-1940s Coomaditchie Lagoon was the only local area where Kooris lived. Land at Port Kembla had come under increasing control and scrutiny, especially through government land resumptions, while population growth, environmental destruction and land clearance destroyed natural resources. These changes meant that by the 1940s Kooris, like the local white working class, were dependent on the limited opportunities for wage labour. Fishing continued, but after 1945 other casual work—waterfront labour, day work on the Council sanitary carts, or seasonal labour in the market gardens of the south coast—became more common Koori male occupations.

Links between Kooris and non-Aboriginal society at Port Kembla were tenuous and distant. Some characteristics of town life were amenable to Kooris. The Whiteway Theatre was not racially segregated, and the Council was more sympathetic than its counterparts in Dubbo, Brewarrina, Yass and Condobolin, although this sympathy rarely extended to direct support. Yet white society was largely unconcerned about the plight of Kooris. The most telling demonstration of this was that threats to Koori living places were never seen by local whites to be threats to the locality itself. White oral history also voices this division, revealed in the language of 'us' and 'them'. One respondent recalled of the local Kooris, 'there were a few up on Hill 60. We didn't have any contact with them and mostly they stayed up there.

You'd see a couple of them around the street at times'.[66] This was a common characteristic of these oral narratives. Much like white itinerant labourers, Kooris were seen as transients or visitors to the town centre and were never afforded membership of 'local' society.

Post-war Experiences

After 1945 the Koori community at Port Kembla continued to assert their rights and seek certainty in the face of unclear tenancy. A shortage of housing and poor living conditions remained important problems. One 1961 study initiated by Monash University found that poor conditions related to Aborigines being 'an always available source of cheap labour for the seasonal agricultural requirements of our south coast's economy. There can be no other reason'.[67] Employment or family ties attracted Aborigines to the area, yet overcrowding and Housing Commission rules against multiple occupancy required many to rely on the overstretched and expensive private rental market.

In the early 1960s there was a public controversy over the state of the Official Camp at Port Kembla, including the living conditions of thirteen Aboriginal families resident in the camp. The camp, 'humpies and tin sheds under the eternal threat of eviction', had no sewerage, reliable water supply or electricity. The campaign to improve conditions for Aborigines involved the South Coast Trades and Labour Council, various local clergy, and the Aboriginal Advancement League.[68] The Aborigines' Welfare Board had approved only six homes and was keen to evict other occupants because they were 'too light-skinned'.[69] Since the early 1900s some Aboriginal men had worked on the Port Kembla waterfront as coal trimmers and waterside workers. In 1961 the Port Kembla branch of the WWF, through some of its Aboriginal and progressive non-Aboriginal members, alerted the South Coast Trades and Labour Council to the plight of Aboriginal families at Coomaditchie. These links between a well-established local union and local Aborigines were a significant exception to the local division between Aboriginal and non-Aboriginal society.

In the 1960s the policy of assimilation was modified, and eventually abandoned, in New South Wales at least, in 1969. The Aborigines Welfare Board was abolished and the existing legislation, notably the Protection Acts, were repealed. Control of Aboriginal Affairs was vested in the Minister for Social Welfare working through the Directorate of Aboriginal Welfare. The policy emphasis was on greater consultation and self-determination, exemplified by the newly created Aborigines Advisory Council. In 1970 the directorate reported that 'there is no implicit desire to demand the subjugation of Aboriginal identity'.[70] Half a century of formalised assimilation policy had failed to absorb the Aborigines into white society. Pockets of indigenous resistance had remained strong against this policy imperative. Yet the policy had also failed to deliver adequate living conditions for most Aborigines in the state, something it had specifically aimed to do in order to 'uplift' Aborigines to 'white standards'. The legacy included settlements like Coomaditchie that had inadequate housing, ill-suited to family and cultural needs, but also included a generation of Aborigines who had survived against the odds and maintained their cultural, family and personal identity as indigenous people. These survivors in particular would lead the next stage in the struggle from the 1970s for land, compensation and social justice.

By the mid-1960s Coomaditchie was a ramshackle collection of a dozen weatherboard houses, home to sixty-nine people.[71] Its location in Korrungulla Crescent away from the main road to Warrawong was a blessing as far as white residents were concerned. The view in parts of non-Aboriginal Port Kembla was that white generosity had been abused. Houses had been destroyed, and burnt for firewood, so it was said. This story was told and retold. One non-Aboriginal respondent, whose house in Cowper Street overlooked the Coomaditchie housing area, recalled:

> See the first lot that they built those houses down there, they ended up there was only two left. They ended up pulling them down and using them for firewood, but now they've built some nice ones. You can see them straight across there. See that red roofed one [points out the window] that's a two-storey one and they're quite nice homes they've built for them now.[72]

At Port Kembla, and throughout New South Wales, the idea of Aboriginal residents burning the wood from government homes was one that white residents found particularly irksome. Given the history of Aboriginal contact with white administration and authority, disdain for its philanthropy was well-founded. Aborigines knew that the rhetoric of uplift and welfare was not matched by real improvements in living conditions and racial equality. Burning homes for firewood was a response to poverty and lack of resources, as well as an effective way to thumb their noses at a haughty and hypocritical white society that promised equality and delivered racism.

Housing conditions remained a key issue in the 1970s. In 1976 one student from the University of Wollongong found seven Aboriginal households in the Kemblawarra area, with other clusters of Aboriginal households in the nearby suburbs of Warilla, Barrack Heights, Koonawarra and Berkeley.[73] Over the period 1900 to 1970 Port Kembla's suburban development effectively shifted Aboriginal groups out of the town to its margins or to satellite suburbs. Movement to Port Kembla continued for employment or family reasons, but housing shortages and a lack of culturally appropriate accommodation remained unsolved problems. A report by the Reverend Terry Fox in 1974, a Catholic priest from Fairy Meadow just north of Wollongong, found a three-year delay for Housing Commission homes, and a twelve-month wait for House For Aborigines homes. Fox was especially critical of Housing Commission officers in enforcing the maximum occupancy rules, and commented that 'Several incidents in the last few days would indicate that the Commission officers lack the sensitivity and understanding in *serving* (?) the needs of the Aboriginal community'.[74]

From the mid-1970s land rights legislation, initially in the Northern Territory and then slowly extending to other jurisdictions, has seemingly offered a chance for indigenous groups to secure the certainty that they have searched for since white occupation. In isolated areas of the continent parcels of crown land have been returned to indigenous ownership. In the more densely settled parts of south-eastern Australia, like the Illawarra, these opportunities are highly circumscribed. In 1995 a native title claim on Coomaditchie Lagoon under the federal government's *Native Title Act* of 1993 was rejected by the Native Title Tribunal on the basis that the lagoon was the subject of David Allan's original land grant in 1817. The land in question passed through various owners until 1939, when it was resumed by the state government and the local Council for recreation and future road and subdivision planning. Justice French found that Allan's original grant 'extinguished any subsisting native title on that land'. The claimants had argued, among other things, that the conditions of the original grant were not adhered to, and that local Kooris were not given notice or required to leave the area. On these two issues Justice French found that 'there is no evidence that the condition was breached', and that the crown was under no requirement 'to give notice to such persons as may have been traditional owners of the land'.[75]

A wave of publicity surrounded this case, focusing on whether the claimants were the true descendants of local indigenous groups. Such criticisms, largely irrelevant since the case was unsuccessful, fail to understand that dispossession, dislocation and removal were not options for Kooris but policy goals of successive white administrations and forcibly secured by white authorities. The few indigenous people who can trace direct links to specific country are fortunate accidents in a process of colonisation that destroyed such links and broke up clan groupings.

This chapter covers a period that has significant implications for indigenous and non-indigenous relationships of the present day. Patterns of urban and social marginalisation accelerated with the onset of industrial society. Nonetheless, a concerted political struggle for access to land emerged as early as the 1920s. The latter period awaits an indigenous writer armed with the imprimatur of the Koori community to take the Koori stories of Port Kembla into the public sphere. Such knowledge resides within specific family groups in the Illawarra and has filtered into the university environment through the Aboriginal Education Centre at the University of Wollongong. In these forums, history means something quite different to the Western concept of an open discourse freely available to all for posterity or for academic analysis and debate. History there is the intensely personal stories of family and kin, oppression and struggle. It remains to be seen whether the local indigenous community wants such stories to have a wider currency.

For the non-Aboriginal community, knowledge of local Aboriginal history remains limited to a few dedicated specialists. A recent Council-sponsored heritage survey of Hill 60, drawing extensively on my own research, represents the first major public acknowledgement of the importance of the area to local Kooris. There remains no public recognition, however, of the Koori habitation of Port Kembla and surrounding areas. Early camping grounds at Tom Thumb's Lagoon and Salty or Allan's Creek are altered beyond recognition, buried under tonnes of rubble, artificial waterways and industrial development. Hill 60 still affords a remarkable view of the coast, but tourists and locals alike are encouraged to consider the military history of the area and enjoy the view. As they look out upon the beautiful coastline, few realise they are standing on Aboriginal ground.

7

The Challenges to Locality, 1890 to 1947

A<small>FTER</small> 1945 P<small>ORT</small> K<small>EMBLA'S</small> political and social life was exposed to powerful outside influences. These challenges to locality were as diverse as changing transport options, large-scale industrial growth, the influence of the Wollongong political elite, and political regionalisation. They had their origins in the late nineteenth century, were reinforced in the following decades, and became ascendant in the period after World War II. This chapter charts the rise of a contending series of developments that challenged the long-term viability and integrity of a self-sufficient and inward-looking locality. These changes provide a crucial context for understanding post-war Port Kembla.

This chapter firstly details the long-term challenges to the Port Kembla locality, including changes in transport services, spatial developments at the edges of the town, and the reorganisation of state administrative boundaries. Then it turns to factors that specifically aided the regionalisation of the Illawarra, such as the tradition of regionally organised politics in the Illawarra and the changing management strategies of Port Kembla companies. Finally, the effects of the Great Depression and the changing political and social landscape of the 1930s and 1940s are discussed.

Long-term Challenges to the Locality

New transport options, dating from the late 1910s, began to undermine the locally based nature of Port Kembla society. Delays in the establishment of effective and affordable transport to and from Port Kembla provided an opportunity for the development of local shops and services in the town. However, by 1920 new railway and transport services were beginning to strengthen links between regional towns, facilitating the regionalisation of the Illawarra.[1]

One of the most important of these developments was the inauguration of the first rail service to Port Kembla in January 1920. This train service allowed male working-class commuters working at Port Kembla, and living elsewhere, mainly in Wollongong, easier access to Port Kembla, providing they could afford the weekly fare of 2s 2d.[2] In 1920 approximately 300 men from the combined workforce at Electrolytic Refining and Smelting Company of Australia Ltd (ER&S) and Metal Manufactures Ltd (MM) of 800 lived in Wollongong, with a smaller number from Dapto, Unanderra, Fairy Meadow and Corrimal.[3] Passenger trains to Port Kembla consolidated the earlier introduction of workers' trains from Stanwell Park (on the coast 27 kilometres north of Port Kembla) to Wollongong in 1908.[4]

The rail service also provided easier access to Wollongong for Port Kembla residents, modifying the close relationship between the dependence on local services and the development of local identity outlined in Chapter 4. Until 1961 Port Kembla lacked a secondary school; because of the train service to Wollongong, Port Kembla children attended schools there—Wollongong High, St Mary's Catholic Girls School or the Christian Brothers' Catholic Boys School. Edith Neaves attended St Mary's from 1924 to 1925, travelling by train every day from Port Kembla with 'half a dozen' other girls. Colin Warrington also commuted by train to Christian Brothers.[5] Morgan Simon attended Wollongong Technical College in 1932 to complete his intermediate certificate. In March 1924 over 13 000 tickets were issued at Port Kembla station, indicating the extensive number of locals who travelled away from their locality by train.[6] The experience of secondary education in Wollongong had a significant impact on Port Kembla children, for it exposed them to people and places beyond their town, and memories of travelling to Wollongong have an important presence in the oral narratives of the generation who grew up in Port Kembla in the 1920s and 1930s.

In the 1930s the motor car and omnibus further increased mobility. In the preceding decade Council debates regarding speed limits and road maintenance indicated the growing presence of motor transport.[7] Although car ownership at Port Kembla was initially restricted to the staff from the local industries and local doctors during the 1920s, by the 1930s some petit-bourgeois and working-class families had access to cars as well. During the depression local baker Bob Rees travelled to Wollongong by car to collect money from the Department of Labour and Industry for the food relief tickets presented at his family's store. A few working-class households could borrow trucks or delivery vehicles for a short period. By 1939 one in four Australian families had access to a car.[8]

In a growing regionalisation of consumption and leisure, trips to Wollongong by car or bus were common by the late 1930s. Sarah Drury and her husband often spent Friday night in Wollongong shopping or eating takeaway fish and chips in their Dodge utility, 'watch[ing] the people walk up and down Crown Street'. Late-night shopping on Fridays was popular, and many young women and men would go on from the stores to dances at the Wollongong Surf Club or the Returned Servicemen's Club.

Better transport threatened certain interest groups within Port Kembla, notably the petit-bourgeoisie who relied on local customers, but such developments did offer tangible benefits to locals. There was opposition from some at Port Kembla to the train service to Wollongong.[9] For example, in April 1918 the Progress Association decided that the rail service was not a priority and did not appoint delegates to a conference on the issue scheduled for the next month. The president of the Wollongong and District Citizens' Association, M. J. Wilson, complained that 'opposition arose from the Port Kembla end; it was that end which was blocking the whole business'. However, highlighting the complexity of local reactions to transport improvements, others at Port Kembla supported the introduction of passenger trains. Ted Livermore, a local resident representing the Port Kembla branch of the AWU, reportedly told a public meeting at Wollongong:

> if the passenger service was established to Port Kembla it would be the making of the town, and would not be detrimental to its progress, as some people seem to think. He was sure that it would be the means of a number of people settling in Port Kembla and would also induce people to build.[10]

In other cases local groups, such as the storekeepers, had conflicting interests in improved transport. The storekeepers feared that their customers would travel to other towns to shop, but they also desired better delivery services for their own goods. At a public meeting in support of the train service, J. G. Fairley, owner of the largest Port Kembla store, protested that 'he experienced difficulty in getting his goods conveyed to his Port Kembla branch'. Robert Shipp complained to the Parliamentary Standing Committee on Public Works in 1923 of the inadequate transport facilities, which prevented him from securing fresh chaff for his Port Kembla store.[11] Access to the 'outside world' was not always an imposition by regional or Wollongong-based interests, for some locals actively sought the benefits of improved transport too.

Other long-term developments exposed the locality to outside influence. Industrial and suburban development beginning in the late 1920s compromised the previously distinctive spatial boundaries of the town, formerly an important context for the growth of local identity. The most significant alteration to the town's distinctive boundaries came in 1927, when the Hoskins steel works was established on a site north of Port Kembla on the road to Wollongong. While Australian Iron and Steel Ltd (as the company became in 1928) was officially called 'AI&S, Port Kembla', the blast furnace and the surrounding mills and foundries were closer to Cringila and Warrawong. Previous industrial development had been located close to the town centre, but as AI&S grew it bridged the gap between Port Kembla and Wollongong, symbolic of the increasing integration of Illawarra towns.

In the 1930s the growth of new suburbs around Port Kembla also blurred the spatial boundaries of the town. Cringila, 3 kilometres north-west of Port Kembla, was an amalgam of two housing estates, Steeltown housing estate which opened in the late 1920s, and Belvedere estate which opened in the mid-1930s. In 1934 Charles Hippisley opened a mixed business and unofficial post office in Newcastle Street, Cringila. In 1935 a primary school for 70 to 80 pupils was built, and by the early 1940s the population had grown to 665. By 1947 the population was 773 living in 194 dwellings.[12]

Warrawong, only 2 kilometres south-west of Port Kembla, also grew at a fast pace from the mid-1930s. The *BHP Review* commented in 1936: 'Warrawong over a period of two years has emerged from its natural bush state to a township of 500 people with a post office and a modern shopping area'.[13] By 1947 Warrawong's population increased to 1566. Windang, primarily a tourist and fishing town 6 kilometres south of Port Kembla, also grew in the late 1930s, the population reaching 153 by 1937 and 661 by 1947.[14] These new industrial suburbs became the focus of population growth, and the centre of new migrant communities, in the post-war era.

These developments complicated political and social boundaries on the margins of Port Kembla. In the mid-1930s Cringila was understood by some to be a 'suburb' of Port Kembla and in that sense dependent on its larger neighbour, but some residents in these new suburbs were finding their own voices and breaking away from Port Kembla's political representation.[15] In 1934 some Cringila residents found it 'discourteous and extraordinary' that the Port Kembla Ratepayers' Association believed it was entitled to speak for Cringila on the location of their new school.[16] From the mid-1930s these nearby towns attracted shops and services, and formed their own Progress Associations. These competing localisms ultimately blurred the boundaries of the Port Kembla locality, and undermined the apparent unity and legitimacy of Port Kembla's political voice.

From the mid-1930s the state government facilitated further challenges to the locality of Port Kembla through a series of planning and administrative reforms. These reforms distanced political and administrative power from the locality, and reinforced the moves to regionalisation. In previous decades localism at Port Kembla benefited from outside political domina-

tion by the farmer-dominated Council, but in this case the array of government committees were more formidable opponents, often beyond the direct
influence of locals. Furthermore, Port Kembla-based representatives who
were once vigorous supporters of localist causes were co-opted onto many
of these organisations.

In 1936 the Port Kembla and Environs Planning and Advisory Committee was given the task of balancing industrial and residential development in the Port Kembla area.[17] The members of this 'committee of experts'
(as the Minister for Works and Local Government, E. S. Spooner, called
them) included a lecturer in town planning from the University of Sydney,
officials from such government departments as Public Works and the Valuer-
General, as well as the engineer of the Central Illawarra Shire.[18] The committee began drawing up plans for the construction of roads, the allocation
of areas for industrial, residential and recreational use, and the provision of
new water, sewerage and electricity infrastructure. The results of its work
included the construction of the Port Kembla Olympic Swimming Pool in
1937, and the bridge at Lake Illawarra in 1938. In 1938 the committee's
name was changed to the Illawarra Regional Planning Advisory Committee
and its scope extended to include the area from Stanwell Park to Shellharbour. In 1936 another committee, the Port Kembla Housing Committee,
investigated the housing shortage at Port Kembla. They, along with Spooner,
planned the construction of a 'Temporary Settlement' in Wattle Street,
Warrawong, which was completed in 1938.[19]

In 1941 the state government divided New South Wales into seventeen
administrative units, known as 'regions'. In the 'Illawarra' region, the
Illawarra Regional Development Committee assumed responsibility for
planning, and took on a major role after 1945.[20] The committee consisted
of representatives from each of the Illawarra Councils (Robert Shipp from
Central Illawarra), and officials from the Public Works and Lands Departments. In 1952 the committee was joined by another regional planning
body, the Illawarra Regional Planning Authority.

The work of the Illawarra Regional Development Committee culminated in the single most important municipal reform in the Illawarra in the
twentieth century. In September 1947 the Central Illawarra Council amalgamated with the local Councils of Bulli, Northern Illawarra and Wollongong, to form the Greater City of Wollongong. Often presented as a great
step forward for the region, the move had less positive implications for Port
Kembla. Opportunities for the local articulation of political issues and
democratic participation were restricted. Political interests at Port Kembla
had campaigned for municipal autonomy from the early 1920s. Municipal
reform did not come about until September 1934 when the Central Illawarra
Municipality was proclaimed a shire with three ridings. This change failed

to please Port Kembla-based aldermen (who all voted against it) and can be generally seen as a victory for the rural representatives on the Council. Riding A, which included Port Kembla and nearby towns such as Windang, Berkeley and Warrawong, had four councillors and a population of 7760, while Riding B, which included Mount Kembla, Unanderra and Figtree, had the same number of councillors with a population of only 2500.[21]

The issue of local government boundaries came up again in 1946, when a state government inquiry into the Council boundaries of the region was announced. Port Kembla representatives formed the Campaign for Port Kembla Municipality and gathered a petition with over 830 signatories. The movement secured the support of nearby localist groups such as the Kemblawarra, Primbee and Mount Kembla Progress Associations.[22] Localist politics at Port Kembla was at its most influential, as Port Kembla itself appeared to be rivalling Wollongong as a natural hub of municipal administration. The mayor of Central Illawarra even argued that any newly amalgamated Council should be called the 'Greater Kembla'.[23] However, at the point of its greatest power, perhaps because the threats were so ominous, localist politics was nearing its demise. With the authority of these new planning bodies, and the force of the state Labor government and Wollongong-based interests behind it, the amalgamation option with Wollongong as the administrative centre became the preferred model. The bitter politics of the amalgamation would plague the new Greater City of Wollongong Council for at least a decade.[24]

These local government and planning reforms amounted to a regionalisation of the political and economic boundaries used for administration and control. State government committees, 'experts' and now a regionally based Council gained control over some major aspects of life at Port Kembla— the management of industrial development, the provision of local services and housing.[25] The ability of residents to exert influence over their local environment declined as opportunities for local political participation were restricted or were incorporated into political forums with a broader regional focus. This situation was not substantially altered until the early 1990s when more progressive Councils opened up local government through mechanisms such as the Neighbourhood Committees, which functioned as the latter-day heirs of the Progress Associations.

The Challenge of Region

Like the influence of the state government's planning reforms, many of the forces that undermined locality promoted region as its replacement. Regionalisation had its origins in the growing regional basis of the labour market in the Illawarra, but its strength was also built on a tradition of regional political involvement in Port Kembla that dated back to the campaign to secure a safe harbour for the Illawarra in the 1890s. The South Coast Harbour League, a coalition of Illawarra-based mining and shipping interests and state and municipal representatives, led this campaign. Organised by W. H. Rees, an auctioneer and real estate agent from Wollongong, representatives from the contending Illawarra sites for the harbour (Bellambi, Wollongong and Port Kembla), agreed to abide by the government's decision on the best site. This gave the Harbour League credibility with the state government, and once the Parliamentary Standing Committee on Public Works concluded that Port Kembla was by far the most desirable location for a deep-water harbour, the league focused on lobbying for Port Kembla in the late 1890s.

The Wollongong political elite were influential, but regionally based groups like the Harbour League gained credibility and ultimately greater strength because of their district-wide membership. The league successfully presented its vision for a harbour at Port Kembla in terms of a broad regional interest, and opponents were derided as 'sectional' or 'parochial'. Of the Newcastle-based opposition in the New South Wales parliament, for example, Premier G. H. Reid said that he had 'never seen in the House a greater glare of local self interest voting against a public work'.[26]

The *Illawarra Mercury* was also influential in focusing regional attention on Port Kembla. The paper's editor in the 1890s and 1900s was Archibald Campbell, a free trade liberal and state member for the electorate of Illawarra from 1891 to 1903. As a representative of the electorate, he took a regional rather than town-based approach. He was heavily involved in regional politics and regional organisations like the South Coast Tourist Union and the Illawarra Mutual Building Society.[27] Between 1896 and December 1898 the *Mercury* gave considerable coverage to the struggle to have the Port Kembla Harbour Bill passed, and Campbell harshly criticised the bill's opponents. In one editorial he described the Newcastle-based Labor members who opposed the bill as 'mere provincialists of a very mediocre type' whose 'absence from parliament would be a distinct gain to Labor'.[28]

Once the *Port Kembla Harbour Act* passed, Campbell's editorials continued to suggest that the construction of the harbour at Port Kembla was vitally important for the whole Illawarra. In 1900, for example, the paper editorialised that the success of the district was dependent on the construction of the harbour.[29] Port Kembla, according to the interpretation circulated by the *Illawarra Mercury* and organisations like the South Coast Harbour League, was a place of great consequence for the entire region.

In 1910 S. R. Musgrave succeeded Campbell as editor and followed the tradition established by Campbell in backing regional interests. Musgrave was involved in regional pressure groups such as the Wollongong and District Citizens' Association, a Wollongong-based organisation with a strong regional focus formed in 1913. An editorial in 1917 revealed his regional attitudes. That year Charles Hoskins publicly announced his intention to build a steel works at Port Kembla if the state government would construct a railway line from Moss Vale to Port Kembla. Musgrave was excited at this prospect, but sounded a note of warning: 'To help forward this progress the residents will have to be roused to a spirit of community life which is at present lacking. Progress will not be achieved by shirking the duties of citizenship as so many of our residents do at present.'[30]

This 'community life' was not based on any one town, but on the Illawarra district. Indeed, Musgrave understood localism to be an impediment to 'progress'. The editorial continued, 'And when it comes to select a route for that railway petty parochial ideas will have to be abandoned in the interests of the whole community'.[31]

The *Illawarra Mercury*, under Musgrave, was an ideologically diverse paper, promoting regionalism at the same time as providing space for the celebration of localism. Correspondents from most of the major towns wrote regular reports under the headings of 'Port Kembla', 'Dapto', 'Corrimal' and others. This fostered interest in local affairs and created images of self-sufficient town-based societies. However, the more powerful message, contained in editorials and campaigns for regional development, was the privileging of regionalism over localism. Before Port Kembla-based political groups had been able to articulate concerns specific to Port Kembla in the late 1900s, broader regional interest groups defined the economic and political meanings of the town. These Illawarra-wide understandings of the town were persistent challenges to the boundaries of an autonomous locality.

The *Illawarra Mercury*'s regional preference continued after World War II. It is perhaps no surprise that the *Mercury* was firmly behind the local government amalgamation of 1947, and in the 1950s the town-based reports disappear altogether as the paper actualised its regional bias in its own content. As a result, information on specific towns in the Illawarra is much harder to uncover for this period than for the period before 1950.

In the continuous lobbying between the regions of New South Wales and the state government, the towns and political organisations of the Illawarra were to some extent united by a principal rival—the Newcastle region. As a region similar to the Illawarra (through the importance of coalmining, and later the steel and metal industries), competition with Newcastle for public investment heightened regional feelings in the Illawarra. When the Parliamentary Standing Committee on Public Works reported in favour of the Port Kembla proposal in 1897, opposition from Newcastle, expressed through Newcastle-based members of parliament, became more heated and engaged in what the *Sydney Morning Herald* called 'stone-walling tactics'.[32] In 1898 Alfred Edden, Member for Kahibah, spoke against the Port Kembla Harbour Bill in the parliament. Comparisons between Port Kembla and Newcastle were, Edden argued, unwarranted:

> It is of no use to institute a comparison between Newcastle and the twopenny-halfpenny place such as that where it is proposed to construct this work. What is the use of comparing Port Kembla with a harbour where you may see up to two hundred vessels lying?[33]

Newcastle was a generally reliable port for the northern coalfields, whereas the southern coal trade was hampered by the lack of a reliable, all-weather harbour, so the possibility of a deep-water harbour at Port Kembla threatened Newcastle's comparative advantage, a fact not lost on Newcastle political interests.[34] The *Newcastle Morning Herald* published editorials identifying the Illawarra, and Port Kembla specifically, as 'rivals' of Newcastle.[35]

Opposition from Newcastle resulted in considerable anti-Newcastle feeling in the Illawarra. Even after passage of the *Port Kembla Harbour Act*, the resources given to Newcastle were constantly compared to the situation in the Illawarra. A public meeting at Wollongong in March 1902 passed a resolution urging the government 'to provide more improved wharves and loading appliances to expedite shipping' at Port Kembla. One speaker claimed that 'at Newcastle it was a case of asking and receiving'.[36] In 1903, after years of drought, economic downturn and public spending cutbacks, lobbying for the rapid completion of Port Kembla harbour became explicitly linked to the future of the whole Illawarra, and opposition from Newcastle appeared to be a direct threat to the viability of the region. In 1904 the editor of the *Mercury* wrote: 'The district without a harbour is like a bird without its wings ... Illawarra is entitled to first recognition from the treasury of NSW; and if Newcastle is to come in, then treat them both on terms of equality!'[37]

From the 1920s regional political organisations gained an even higher profile in the Illawarra. A signal of the growing concern for regional political co-ordination came in 1920 when a meeting of aldermen and the usually parochial Progress Associations of the south coast called for greater co-operation between all towns. At the meeting Alderman N. S. Smith of Wollongong Council recognised the political value of regional co-operation: 'Different Governments would pay more attention to the needs of the Coast if a cohesion of all governing bodies took the place of the present system of making important wants known by disconnected and single advocacy'.[38] Such regional co-operation became common in the 1920s as regionally based groups—the Cross Country Railway League, the South Coast Tourist Union, the Illawarra Chamber of Commerce and the Wollongong and

District Citizens' Association among others—began to dominate development politics in the Illawarra. The Illawarra Chamber of Commerce, for example, was formed in 1920 with E. A. White from ER&S filling the president's chair. Made up of Port Kembla industrialists and professional and commercial men from Wollongong, it lobbied for transport and communications improvements in the Illawarra, including the upgrading of Port Kembla harbour and the construction of a railway line from Moss Vale to Port Kembla.[39] Another group, the Wollongong and District Citizens' Association, was formed and led by a self-consciously regional leader, J. F. Beatson, an alderman on Wollongong Council and mayor on numerous occasions from the 1890s to the 1920s.[40] In 1920 Beatson claimed that the association represented not only Wollongong, but the 'district generally' and predicted that 'Illawarra was bound to progress if civic pride was kept alive as the district had all the essentials necessary for greatness'.[41] After his death in 1927, Musgrave wrote in Beatson's obituary that 'His desire always was to work for the advancement of the Illawarra district, rather than his native Wollongong'.[42]

These lobby groups increased regional political co-ordination but they also drew former Port Kembla-based political leaders into regional politics.[43] The secretary of the Water Supply League from the early 1920s was H. R. Lee from ER&S. Lee, who had formerly been so active in local society, moved into many of these regional organisations in the 1920s, including the Water Supply League and the Cross Country Railway League.[44] By 1931, two years before his death, Lee was secretary of the Australian Mines and Metals Association and advising industrial officer to the New South Wales Chamber of Manufactures.[45] Robert Shipp, one of Port Kembla's most successful localist politicians, moved from municipal representation in the early 1920s to serve on state government planning committees in the 1930s. Eventually he was elected alderman to the new Greater City of Wollongong Council in 1947 in a Council structure that he had initially opposed. Shipp's career alone says much about the changing spatial organisation of municipal politics. Prominent managers at Port Kembla also became more involved in regional politics. J. P. Caddy, W. E. Jones (MM), R. J. Craig (Australian Fertilizers) and Cecil Hoskins (AI&S) were active in the Illawarra Chamber of Commerce from 1930.[46] These moves were indicative of the widening political boundaries of the region's well-off petit-bourgeoisie and middle class.

Working-class men also became more regionally organised. In June 1926 the Trades and Labour Council in the Illawarra region, dormant since the 1917 General Strike, was resurrected.[47] With the onset of the Great Depression, however, the Labour Council lost its impetus. The number of unemployed and non-unionised workers who had came into the area overwhelmed it. Richardson, in his history of the Illawarra labour movement during the depression, notes the Labour Council began to 'function merely as a sounding board for workers discontent'.[48] Despite the collapse of the Labour Council, the depression represented only a temporary setback to the regionalisation of the labour movement. Most unionists were convinced that further regional organisation was necessary for the effective representation of Illawarra workers, and building links between the coalminers and the unions covering the growing steel works became vitally important in re-establishing a healthy labour movement.

Another force for regionalisation in the Illawarra in the 1930s was the new management strategies pursued by Port Kembla's major industries, which severed the close links between industry and locality. The older approach, as exemplified by ER&S's attempts to create a company town, became less influential. The largest industry in the 1930s, AI&S, did not show any great interest in the town itself, being more concerned with strategies for controlling and managing its workforce. Its arena for political action, especially after the BHP takeover in 1935, was state and federal politics rather than local.[49]

By the late 1930s MM had developed a management style that combined welfarism with a strong concern for efficiency and order. A company history written in 1939 noted: 'A prominent feature throughout the Works is Cleanliness and Tidiness, the value of which in efficiency, as well as from a psychological point of view, is fully realised by the management and employees alike'.[50] Representations of the works from company's publications give an indication of MM's self-image. One picture from the 1939 publication shows a clear graphic of the works, superimposed on a photograph of the town. MM stands out as an efficient, clean and ordered area, while the rest of Port Kembla appears cluttered, untidy and dirty. Likewise, AI&S airbrushed photographs of industrial buildings as represented by the image of the hot strip mill reproduced in the illustration following page 116. At the centre of the AI&S and MM approach from the 1930s was the control and arrangement of the workplace; the town of Port Kembla was peripheral to such strategies.

The Great Depression

By 1930 these forces for regionalisation, and the regionalising labour market outlined in Chapter 2, had such an influence on Port Kembla society and politics, that regional factors, along with class and locality, must be introduced into the analysis. The conjunction of regionalism, localism and the depression experience at Port Kembla produced contradictory outcomes that require careful analysis. The onset of the depression initially halted the growing influence of region as some locals attempted to re-assert the boundaries of the locality against 'outsiders'. In other ways, however, the depression hastened the decay of the locality's boundaries, and ultimately the long-term trend towards regionalisation continued largely unhindered.

One reaction to the depression, common in many towns throughout Australia, attempted to isolate the labour market from the full effects of nation-wide unemployment. In 1932 the Port Kembla Relief Committee, which included prominent labour identities like Alderman Jack Mathews, E. Scott and Fred Finch, resolved that 'Port Kembla was loaded with more than their fair share of unemployed from other parts'.[51] Alderman Mathews was a vigorous supporter of Port Kembla workers and demanded that they be given preference in municipal works. In 1933 the Council's Health Committee recommended that no residents from 'other municipalities' be allowed to erect camps in the Central Illawarra. While it was impossible to seal off the locality from the depression, such responses demonstrated the continued presence of localism and the way local allegiances were reactivated by an economic crisis.

Not only labour leaders, but some local workers too focused on 'outsiders' who were taking local men's jobs. There was an adverse reaction to Lithgow workers, many of whom had followed Hoskins Iron and Steel Ltd to Port Kembla, because they were seen to be taking the jobs of locals. A BHP publication relates the story of J. Mathews, who transferred from Lithgow to Port Kembla in 1928: 'local people had not exactly welcomed the newcomers from Lithgow, in some cases openly resenting the fact that they were taking jobs which might have been filled by local men'.[52] The precise impact of Lithgow workers on the Port Kembla labour market is difficult to ascertain, although many did have previous experience in steelworking and, therefore, somewhat better chances of securing work. The presence of such stories in the oral and written evidence reveals the conflict that occurred at the social boundaries of the locality.

Paradoxically, attempts to isolate local workers from the effects of the depression, far from bringing Port Kembla together, actually revealed the limitations of the localist rhetoric. Attempts to exclude non-ratepaying citizens from being considered 'locals' demonstrated that the principal electorate of localism was a select group of male ratepayers. This can be seen in the renaming of the Progress Association as the Port Kembla Ratepayers' Association in 1932, and in moves by the Ratepayers' Association in 1933 to encourage the Council to 'take action with a view to restricting or stopping the number of unemployed from other municipalities building humpies etc in this district'.[53] The Ratepayers' Association represented a smaller constituency at Port Kembla, for many living in unemployed camps, boarding houses or overcrowded rental accommodation did not pay rates, and others left destitute by the depression could not afford to pay.[54]

Similar moves, which highlighted the growing division between local political organisations and the unemployed, came from within Council itself. In 1933 Alderman Shipp moved that Council give preference to 'unemployed ratepayers' for relief work on Five Islands Road near Port Kembla.[55] For its part the broader interests of Council were in protecting its own revenue base of ratepayers. Itinerant labourers always had a tenuous relationship with local society, but during the depression the Ratepayers' Association, Port Kembla aldermen and other local bodies such as the Relief Committee sharpened these divisions, attempting to impose an increasingly exclusive definition of who was a 'local'.

The depression didn't only affect itinerant workers. Few sections of local society were left untouched. The broad impact was to divide Port Kembla, discrediting appeals for local unity, and clearing the way for increasingly powerful regional interests. Morgan Simon recalled that 'there was no or very little class distinction in those days [before the depression], but you did get a bit more of it in later years'. Simon believed that in the 1930s some 'people [at Port Kembla] had more money than others [at Port Kembla] and they built beautiful homes'. Simon's views, influenced by the experience of living within sight of the unemployed camp at Coomaditchie, were different to many respondents who claimed that the depression united Port Kembla. Ces Catterel, a boy of twelve in 1930 whose father worked for the Public Works Department, recalled: 'It brought them together, as I say. People could help each other if somebody had vegetables, perhaps a lemon or something—you wouldn't go and buy any, you'd give them out to your neighbours. So it helped that way.'

This apparently contradicts the argument that town unity was undermined by the depression; however, such memories call upon a specific understanding of what constituted Port Kembla. In Catterel's case, his memory of unifying effects is bounded by an understanding of Port Kembla as constituted by the group of families, like his own, who lived near the Port Kembla Power House and worked for the Public Works Department. These workers had a tradition of mutual aid and reciprocity. In late 1929 they all decided to work half-time and spent off weeks fishing and gardening, rather than lose half their workforce.[56] Co-operation and mutual support were limited to these family, neighbourhood or workforce groups, but these memories are presented in terms of the whole town helping. Colin Warrington specifically recalls that 'if anyone was in trouble, in close proximity to the street where he lived, well, these people—neighbours, friends and family—would help'.[57] Respondents often projected memories formed in the consensus of the 1920s onto the Port Kembla of the depression. The broad alliances of the 1920s, however, were shattered through the conflict and division of the depression, and the scope of the bonds of reciprocity and mutualism substantially curtailed.

Spatially too, the depression foregrounded divisions in the town's social geography. It became less tenable to understand Port Kembla as a united town when there were such identifiable areas of misery and deprivation alongside wealth and affluence. In the 1930s new expensive areas of Port Kembla were developed which had a disproportionate number of middle-class residents. In Robertson Street 57 per cent of those in the paid workforce were from middle-class occupations—foremen, doctors, accountants and clerks, to name the most common. In Bland and Donaldson Streets, 25 per cent of residents were in middle-class occupations, and this was twice the average for the whole of Port Kembla.[58] At the same time, three camps for the unemployed sprang up on the margins of the town, remaining throughout the 1930s. In 1932 there were over 1000 people living in humpies, shacks and tents made with material scavenged from industrial sites, ex-army tents and recycled kerosene tins. Even within the town itself Military Road and Darcy Road took on a dowdy appearance, and in the newer subdivisions jerry-built homes or tents pitched on blocks of land were reminders of the crisis.[59]

The depression also undermined the role of Wentworth Street as a symbol of local unity. Echoing the industrial conflicts played out in the main street in 1929, the town centre became the focus for clashes between the police and unemployed men in the early 1930s. On 12 May 1931 unemployed workers at Bulli, Wollongong and Port Kembla demonstrated against the presence of police at the food relief depots. At Port Kembla an unidentified man addressed a crowd at the corner of Allan and Wentworth Streets, only to be arrested by a squad of police from Wollongong. The police charged the crowd and Alexander Slade, an unemployed man camped at Port Kembla, was knocked unconscious by a constable (after an Inspector Gibson had hit him across the face with a whip) and arrested for indecent language. Later, at Slade's trial, two members of the Relief Committee, Alderman Jack Mathews and Fred Finch, gave evidence that the police had charged without provocation, and the constable had hit Slade without reason. The charges against the unemployed man were dismissed. This event caused considerable bitterness in Port Kembla. Alderman Mathews noted in court that when he remonstrated with Inspector Gibson on the day the inspector had replied, 'We have to keep law and order Mr Mathews', to which Mathews had responded, 'It is the most cowardly thing I ever saw. You will hear more of this.'[60]

Following the violence, the relief depot became a potential flashpoint as unemployed men assembled every week to collect their relief dockets under the watchful gaze of police. On 17 May further scuffles broke out as police refused to allow members of the local Relief Committee to issue food relief dockets. That afternoon, a protest meeting attended by 200 people condemned the police baton charge of the previous week and their inter-ference in the provision of food relief.[61] The mood in the town centre was nervous. The Traders' Association, fearing further outbreaks of violence, and perhaps rioting and looting, requested that Council keep the street lights on all night.[62] The town centre's role as a unifying symbol was tainted by political dissent and heavy-handed police intervention that occurred there during the depression.

As the local social geography and symbols of local unity fractured, so too did town-based political alliances. The depression drove economic and political wedges between former partners in the local alliance. The petit-bourgeoisie, who had enjoyed good relations with working-class customers, reined in the provision of credit and became less forgiving to debtors. From 1920 to 1926 there was very little legal action by storekeepers at Port Kembla in the Wollongong District Court; however, from 1926 to 1931 some local stores were suing not only suppliers but also customers to recover money owed.[63]

This distancing of the working class from the storekeepers was often emotionally difficult for storekeepers. John Philpot, who started work in his father's general store, Philpot's, in 1927, remembers the financial dif-ficulties that food relief brought—'My worst recollection was of getting the money from the government'—but he also recalls that dealing with the unemployed 'was a constant strain'. Storekeepers were interacting less with women customers with money, and more often with dispirited unemployed men offering food coupons: 'People would come to us and say they had work but nothing to eat or to dress themselves with and I was only a boy and my father was the softest touch and he'd give them boots and clothes and that would be the end of it'.[64] The change in the gender of customers was crucial in bringing the petit-bourgeoisie closer to the alienation and anger of unemployed men, and distancing working-class women from their formerly close contact with the town's storekeepers.

The change in relations between the working class and the storekeepers has entered the oral record of the working class in the form of an ambi-valence about the petit-bourgeoisie during the depression. Edith Neaves remembered sociable contact with storekeepers, but also recalled that Phil-pot's used the depression to sell old stock—in fact, the same stock that John Philpot remembers his father giving away:

I remember I went up to Philpot's and he got an old pair of shoes out of the box that had been there since the shop opened I think—pointy toes and laced fronts—they were the funniest shoes I ever put on. I didn't ever wear them. I would rather go bare footed. He got rid of a lot of his old stock that way, old Philpot . . . it wasn't really right but he did it and I think a lot of that went on.

The local middle class also sought to distance themselves from the consensus of the 1920s, and the depression galvanised them into new forms of separate political action. Some turned to the paramilitary organisation of the New Guard; J. P. Caddy, MM's general manager, was allegedly a prominent member, while others in senior management at MM and AI&S were also suspected of involvement. A focus on whether particular individuals were involved in the New Guard—despite the absence of clear evidence—has obscured other more important conservative responses to the depression.[65] Caddy also helped establish a united conservative response to organised labour through the organisation of the United Australia Party. For this he used the resources available to him through his industrial contacts. In November 1932 he wrote to Sir Colin Fraser, company director and leading figure in the Collins House Group, asking for a £50 donation to the newly formed branch of the party at Port Kembla. 'With the help of the companies' wrote Caddy, 'we are endeavouring to stir up the people in our electorate to a sense of their responsibilities'.[66] Another manager, Cecil Hoskins of AI&S, was active in the All For Australia League, an organisation of Sydney-based businessmen which acted as a respectable front for recruitment to the Old Guard. Like Caddy, Hoskins used the resources of his company to help finance operations.[67]

Working-class Mobilisation

After the worst of the depression, the space left by the discrediting of localism was filled by working-class mobilisation. Unions had struggled through the depression, but improved economic conditions from 1934 slowly helped turn around union membership and influence.[68] Strike funds were replenished as workers achieved some permanency, and the numbers of unemployed men camped around the town, who had represented such a threat to unionism, slowly decreased.

It was not just economic recovery that led to working-class mobilisation. The years of consensus politics in the 1920s had left a conservative mark on local workers that was not easily removed. In 1933, the general superintendent at ER&S, F. H. Rickleman, commented that 'the daily paid employees are on the whole an excellent lot of men'. However, he identified a possible threat from 'outside intervention from both sides'.[69] Indeed, many of the new union leaders of the mid-1930s were from outside Port Kembla, and had arrived during the depression.[70] Shunned by established local labour and civic leaders at Port Kembla, it was these men who turned local workers, embittered by their depression experiences, towards industrial action and growing militancy.

This mobilisation was primarily expressed through union organisation and industrial conflict. The first tentative sign of a new working-class activism came in July 1934 with the bricklayers' strike at AI&S, outlined in Chapter 2. Communist activists at AI&S took heart from the strike and urged workers to 'get into your unions, follow the lead of the miners, oust reactionary leaders and put militant leaders in office, who can and will give a correct lead in the struggles that take place'.[71] The industrial conflicts of 1936 demonstrate that local unions were becoming progressively more confident. That year the Federated Ironworkers' Association (FIA) and the Moulders' Union demanded a 40-hour week and a 3d per hour increase at AI&S. As the Industrial Department at AI&S noted, the FIA 'gave notice to the company that it intends upon starting a policy of direct action'.[72] The FIA and the WWF also engaged in a ten-week stoppage over the dismissal of a union delegate, Norman Annabel, and consequently the FIA was deregistered by the Commonwealth Industrial Commission.[73]

In 1937 the old kinship networks that had compromised the WWF's effectiveness were swept away by new radical leaders, who were successful at branch elections. The new secretary, Ted Roach, was a former Unemployed Workers' Movement activist, member of the Communist Party, and, importantly, a newcomer to the area. He, along with other 'militant transferees', as one historian of the WWF describes them, joined the branch in 1936.[74] Reflecting the broad front of working-class mobilisation, the FIA also gained a new militant leadership under Pat McHenry in 1937.[75] AI&S's Industrial Department reported in May 1938 that McHenry had 'immediately entered upon an active campaign of union organisation throughout the metal trades and metal refining industries in this district'.[76] By 1940 union mobilisation was extensive. The Industrial Department reported that the unions were 'taking full advantage of the present abnormal circumstances [war-time] to launch an offensive to achieve maximum gains'.[77]

The *Dalfram* dispute of late 1938 and early 1939, well-covered by labour historians, shows the extensive nature of working-class mobilisation in the Illawarra.[78] The *Dalfram* berthed in Port Kembla in mid-November 1938 to load pig iron for the Japanese port of Kobe. On 18 November the WWF refused to load the ship, arguing that the pig iron was being used by the Japanese military against China and that it might eventually be used against Australia. The waterside workers, and other working-class organisations at Port Kembla, had shown an increasing interest in militarism throughout the 1930s, and in the fate of the Chinese people during the Japanese invasion.[79] The dispute was the culmination of a decade of growing political activism by waterside workers both at Port Kembla and in other ports throughout Australia.

The conservative federal government, under Prime Minister J. A. Lyons, responded to the WWF boycott by arguing that foreign policy was not the concern of unions, but of a democratically elected government. When an end to the dispute was not forthcoming, on 6 December Attorney-General Robert Menzies applied the *Transport Workers Act*. This legislation, dating from 1929, required workers to obtain a licence to work on the waterfront. No workers registered, evidence of the extensive solidarity that had developed in the region's working class, but a more serious threat to the continuation of the dispute came a few days later when AI&S closed down, arguing that it could no longer continue operations. This lockout engendered considerable bitterness towards AI&S, left 4000 workers unemployed for the Christmas holidays, and effectively cut off much of the local financial support from unionists. On 21 January 1939 the WWF agreed to load the *Dalfram* under protest, and the government promised a review of the policy of trading with 'aggressor nations'.[80]

The *Dalfram* dispute facilitated new unity in the Illawarra labour movement, which had previously been divided between supporters and opponents of the controversial former Labor premier J. T. Lang.[81] When the waterside workers first announced their refusal to load the ship, for example, the Illawarra Trades and Labor Council immediately declared its unanimous support and established a committee of nine members to organise support for the local branch of the WWF.[82] As the dispute progressed, it began to have implications beyond the labour movement. The strikers received wide-ranging support from storekeepers, church leaders, the New South Wales Trades and Labour Council, some left-wing Labor politicians and intellectuals. Thus a broad coalition of groups within the Illawarra and elsewhere united against Attorney-General Menzies and the imposition of the *Transport Workers Act*.[83]

The regional mobilisation of the working class in the Illawarra replaced localist politics as the focus of Port Kembla politics. Within unions and the Labour Council, the working class developed their own separate area of class politics away from localist politics. In conditions where local workers saw their interests as best served by their union and their main antagonists as 'the company' or the federal government, a political alliance based on locality was no longer tenable. Though they never completely dominated the labour movement in the Illawarra, communist influence in the Miners' Federation, the WWF and the FIA was considerable and their ideas presented people with new ways of analysing local politics and society. The

A postcard dated 1916–18 with notations added at the time indicating different areas of Port Kembla such as the 'Aboriginal camp' on Hill 60 and Percy Laughlin's 'Barber Shop'. The notation 'This hotel has no license' dates the handwritten additions to between 1915 when the hotel was complete and 1917 when it received its first liquor licence.

An aerial view of Port Kembla in 1930. In the left foreground men can be seen alighting from the early-morning train from Wollongong and the northern suburbs such as Thirroul, Bulli, and Fairy Meadow. The commuters, mostly employed by the new steel works, symbolised the increasing regionalisation of the labour market in the 1930s. Beyond the station and the Ulladulla Brickworks site are the ER&S company houses in Darcy Road with the nearby sports ground.

The government quarry at Port Kembla, showing four large steam-powered cranes and loaded trucks waiting to be taken to the new breakwater construction site, c. 1900–10.

The Empire Hall was the first theatre in Port Kembla, built in 1915 by a company that included senior staff from ER&S and local businessmen.

The area that was once Tom Thumb's Lagoon and nearby wetlands, at centre, became the Port Kembla inner harbour. This 1962 aerial view shows the Port Kembla–Wollongong Road bridge, now demolished.

communists argued that improvements in the standard of living could not be achieved through local organisations lobbying government, but through the revolutionary overthrow of the capitalist system. Local companies were part of the problem, rather than allies, and the industrial workplace, rather than the town, became the focus of political activity.

Working-class mobilisation also aided the progress of regionalism as a replacement for localism. Despite town-based appeals for job protection, regional organisations such as the Labour Council and Labor politicians, such as state Member for Illawarra William Davies, highlighted the plight of unemployed men throughout the Illawarra. Some unions at Port Kembla such as the FIA had significant links with Lithgow men (their secretary, J. Ward, and many of their active members were from Lithgow) and this moderated their position on local preference. As the labour market became more regionalised in the 1930s, calls for job protection more often assumed an Illawarra-wide focus, not only from unions, but also from the state government. In 1936 the Minister for Labour and Industry, J. M. Dunningham, met with officials from AI&S to discuss the possibility of employing more 'south coast men'.[84]

At Port Kembla the principal organisations promoting localist politics struggled in these conditions. This was partly because class politics and industrial conflict now dominated the political scene, but also because the broad move to regionalism had undermined the political value of localism. At a meeting called to discuss the need for an ambulance at Port Kembla in March 1936, the aptly named J. Humble claimed that Port Kembla did not need its own ambulance: 'if Port Kembla's request had been successful then Corrimal, Dapto and other places would want one. It was obvious the services would overlap.'[85] This concern for regional efficiency was a new feature of these usually parochial associations. There is a striking contrast between the demands for local services expressed by these organisations in the 1920s and their new modest tone. By the 1930s the political and structural move to region had infiltrated the very organisations at Port Kembla that had typically fought against regional involvement.

Yet in the 1930s there was only a tentative cultural change that mirrored this broad shift to region. Localism had suffered a severe setback during the depression, as a town-based identity was discredited and some locals retreated to smaller social units such as the family, kin and workmates. However, following the confluence and strengthening of the challenges to locality, and its gradual replacement by region in the 1930s, there was no immediate growth in regional loyalty. Despite some signs of new expectations on political leaders—in August 1940 a correspondent named 'Silent Worker' complained about the Central Illawarra Council in the *Illawarra Mercury*: 'To get men to act in a district rather than town sense seems utterly impossible'—there is little evidence of increasing regional loyalty, particularly in the oral record.[86]

Local identity persisted partly because it was organisations dominated by men and a male labour market that regionalised. Women were affected by these changes, but even in the late 1930s and 1940s women were still active in a very localised informal economy. It was primarily men who travelled on trains and drove cars and trucks in and out of Port Kembla. If regionalisation had differential effects on women and men, it also did not completely overturn many of the characteristics of 1920s Port Kembla society. Daily interactions in the main street continued and links with neighbours as well as kin remained town-centred, despite the challenges to the integrity of local society.

However, given the extent of the attacks on locality and the comprehensive moves to region, a more important explanation hinges on the durability of the culture of localism. Loyalties that developed during the heyday of localism were strongly held by the generation that grew up with Port Kembla. This was the generation who came to Port Kembla as children in the late 1900s and 1910s, like Edith Neaves, Morgan Simon and Ursula Lindsay, and, despite living through a period of tremendous historical change, they held onto their notions of identity and belonging forged in the 1910s and 1920s. This also accounts for the transference of memories of a united town in the 1920s onto an obviously divided town during the depression. The culture of localism, in fact, did not have a simple deterministic relationship to the changing material conditions of local society. As Morgan Simon recalled, the growth of the nearby suburb of Warrawong from the mid-1930s 'took a lot of people out of Port Kembla but it still was good old Port. Everyone seemed to know that they were part of Port Kembla even though you do your shopping over at Warrawong.'[87]

While some challenges to locality diffused or undermined the boundaries of the Port Kembla locality, others encouraged new spatial boundaries based on the Illawarra region. Regionalisation was fostered by the growth of a regional labour market, regional political organisations, and improvements in transport. The structures and social relations of Port Kembla became porous and diffused, slowly merging with regional structures. The cultural effects of these changes were more ambivalent. A self-sufficient locality had been challenged at many levels—economic, political and social —but for many Port Kembla still retained its symbolic and cultural importance. After 1947 a curious paradox predominated: continuing expressions of local attachment existing within an economic and regional context inimical to such views.

8

Industrial Society Supreme, 1945 to 1970

AFTER 1945 INDUSTRIAL, economic and administrative changes under-mined the locality of Port Kembla even while localist sentiments remained culturally important. Industrial development and high levels of migration, together with continuing and intensifying regional influences on the structures of locality, represent major components of the post-war Port Kembla experience. Industrial society was elevated to new levels of dominance, and the post-war rhetoric of industry, science and progress submerged locality into region, or denied reference to place at all. Connections to distant localities multiplied as European migration, BHP reliance on US technology and a diversifying export trade diluted the Anglo-Imperial dominance of the formative period. While the formative period saw a profound elaboration of locality and town-based society and politics, the supreme period glossed over the spatial context, further dividing industry and locality.

Central to this division was a fundamental reorganisation of the structures of locality by the scale of industrial development and regionalisation. Immigrant workers and their families from Southern and Central Europe altered the social structure and the nature of the labour market, and re-vitalised the informal economy.

Post-war Regional Context

Having survived the crises of depression and war, the Illawarra boomed. The region became the fastest growing in Australia, barring Canberra where population growth was stimulated by public spending and the growth of the federal government. The population of 'Greater Wollongong', which included the northern suburbs to Helensburgh and the southern suburbs around Lake Illawarra to the boundary with the Shellharbour municipality, increased from 62 960 in 1947 to 149 496 in 1966. The population in the area of Port Kembla, Cringila and Lake Heights increased nearly three times over the same period, from 8271 to 23 089. Other nearby industrial suburbs experienced growth that was even more spectacular. The Housing Commission suburb of Berkeley had a mere 103 residents in 1953, mostly fishers and their families living by the lake. By 1966 this was a major suburban centre with a population of 9170. The population of the older rural town of Dapto also increased to around 9207 from a higher base of 1603. Nearby Primbee and Windang also grew; this was more a matter of consolidation than rapid growth, with the combined population of these contiguous suburbs rising from 1152 in 1947 to 3761 in 1966.[1]

The lack of available land and the proximity of industry limited residential growth at Port Kembla. As Table 8.1 shows, Port Kembla's population increased by less than 3000 from 1947 to 1961.

Table 8.1 Population and housing at Port Kembla, 1947–61

	1947	*1954*	*1961*
Population	4 960	6 570	7 830
Males	2 730	3 558	4 495
Females	2 230	3 012	3 335
Occupied dwellings	1 159	1 665	1 862

Source: Commonwealth Census, 1947, 1954, 1961.

Unlike the period before 1945, housing stock kept pace with increasing population. A major state housing construction programme accompanied significant industrial expansion, and this accounted for the difference between the pre- and post-war experiences. The huts, tents and kerosene-tin shacks were no longer a major feature of industrial growth. Average occupancy levels remained at around 4.2 people per occupied dwelling, though higher rates characterised areas of migrant location such as Cringila. Table 8.1 also shows the 1947 gender balance at Port Kembla was approximately 55 per cent male to 45 per cent female. This was a significant move towards parity as the industrial community became more established and working-class families more settled. In the next twenty years, mostly through continued male-dominated migration to the steel works, the gender balance remained at this level, with similar ratios in 1954 and 1961.

The increase in labour demand at the steel works, and the high turnover levels for labour did not overwhelm the regional housing market for two major reasons. Firstly, workers and their families could move into the newer industrial suburbs around Port Kembla. Secondly, with the increasing availability of the motor car, and continued reliance on rail and bus networks, workers could live outside Port Kembla and commute to work. The local labour market of the 1920s and 1930s was regionalised. The growth that flowed from the expansion of the heavy industries at Port Kembla spilled out to other nearby areas, and throughout the region.

The Formal Economy

Industrial growth in steel making and its related industries underpinned population expansion, and continuing demand for migrant labour in particular. Post-war expansion centred on Port Kembla's largest industry, AI&S. The expansion on AI&S land, located well away from the town's centre, continued rapidly in the post-war period. Such industrial expansion reinforced the already growing division between town and industry and eventually allowed industrialisation to be captured and named by a regional, or Wollongong identity. Where AI&S had employed one in seven of the region's male labour force, by 1961 it employed approximately one in every four. The dominance of AI&S in the regional economy was complete. Such were the dimensions of these changes that by the 1960s the 'steel town' of Port Kembla had given way to the 'steel city' of Wollongong.

International connections in the post-war era continued the trend established in the formative period as the United States replaced Britain in technological and financial affairs. As US involvement in the Australian economy became more pronounced, so did its role as a supplier of technology and training for AI&S. By 1965 Australia was United States' fifth largest target for overseas investment, and more than one-quarter of the manufacturing industry was in American ownership.[2] Ties to Britain nonetheless remained strong. AI&S continued sending staff to Britain, and an agreement was signed with the British Iron and Steel Foundation in 1949 to exchange personnel for experience and training.[3] Links with the United States, however, expanded rapidly. In 1948 AI&S secured designs and specialist advice for the planned new Number 3 blast furnace from A. G. McKees of Cleveland, Ohio. In 1953 BHP managing director, Norman Jones, travelled to the United States and Canada for discussions with steel industry leaders, making arrangements for Australian personnel to gain experience in US hot strip mills, as a prelude to the introduction of this technology in Australia.[4]

The first of the major post-war developments at AI&S—a new merchant bar, rod and strip mill—was completed in 1949, costing £2 million. A flat products division was established at Port Kembla, in anticipation of a post-war demand for consumer goods such as cars, refrigerators and washing machines that required flat thin steel. Eventually, iron and steel capacity geared up to feed the new mills through the construction of a second integrated steel works, known as the Number 2 steel works, west of the original works and closer to Wollongong and adjacent to the future site of the Port Kembla inner harbour.[5]

By 1953 Port Kembla's Number 3 blast furnace was the largest blast furnace in the country, surpassing BHP Newcastle's Number 3 furnace with a daily output capacity of 2450 tonnes. AI&S also produced more steel than Newcastle. In 1954 Port Kembla produced 944 980 tonnes of ingot steel while Newcastle produced 926 497 tonnes. This development received constant comment in the regional media, and from state members of parliament from the region looking to justify increased government expenditure. As the Member for South Coast, Jack Beale, noted in 1955: 'Greater Wollongong is a key city, and since 1953 it has become the greatest steel centre in the southern hemisphere'.[6] Beale's comments also highlight the inexorable shift to new spatial scales as 'Greater Wollongong' became linked to steel industry development. Throughout the 1950s, steel production, coke-making and power plants were upgraded, a new sinter plant was completed in 1957, and a fourth blast furnace in 1959. The construction of Number 4 blast furnace only confirmed this regional boosterism, for the new furnace marginally exceeded the daily tonnage capacity of the Number 3 furnace. By the end of the 1950s the older Number 1 steel works, together with the new Number 2 works across Five Islands Road, employed 22 884.[7]

While the focus was on AI&S, other firms, commonly with a BHP link through share ownership and interlocking boards, were also expanding. John Lysaght invested £9 million in the new cold reduction reversing mill at Port Kembla in the mid-1950s. BHP acquired a majority shareholding in Lysaght in 1970, and the company was eventually bought out by BHP in 1979. ER&S, the oldest and most traditional of Port Kembla industries, also invested more than £3 million in new furnaces, processing and plant control technology from 1958 to 1963. One of the few outside the ambit of BHP, ER&S was owned by Broken Hill South and North Broken Hill Pty Ltd from 1948 to 1980. Even by 1972, however, the plant employed only 675, a figure that highlights BHP's dominance of the regional economy.[8]

The completion of the new government-built inner harbour in 1960 underlined the state government's commitment to make Port Kembla a major industrial and shipping centre. The ambitious inner harbour scheme involved the dredging, and infilling, of Tom Thumb's Lagoon, and the construction of a new and expanded port facility. This project had been anticipated by the *Australian Iron & Steel Limited Agreement Ratification Act* of 1936 by which a large area of public land was sold to AI&S, including the lagoon itself. Later, post-war reconstruction plans put forward by regional planning authorities and local members of parliament argued that limited capacity in the harbour would hinder Port Kembla's industrial development. The state government passed the *Port Kembla Inner Harbour Construction and Agreement Ratification Act* in 1955, authorising the construction of an inner harbour, at an estimated cost of £5.25 million, exclusive of land resumptions. The Act proposed the construction of an artificial harbour of approximately 40 hectares to a depth of approximately 9.75 metres in an area occupied by Tom Thumb's Lagoon, the natural tidal lagoon and wetland area. A 140-metre channel would join the outer and inner harbour, and new roads, wharf accommodation and a railway marshalling yard were to be built.[9]

The construction of the inner harbour had far-reaching, and largely unanticipated, consequences. The scale of industrial growth not only overwhelmed the locality and blurred its formerly distinct boundaries. Projects such as the new inner harbour involved the physical destruction of places that were local landmarks and fondly remembered sites of childhood play and informal economy activities. Port Kembla's inner harbour development resembled the reclamation and expansion of Port Waratah at Newcastle under the 1953 *Newcastle Harbour Improvement Act* which also involved the 'reclamation' of wetlands. Such major public works projects were typical of the 1950s, and underline the dominance of industrial society. Other projects of this ilk at Port Kembla included the construction of the Number 6 jetty which was approved in 1953 at a cost of £725 000, and extension of the inner harbour loading and transport facilities approved in 1961, costing a further £2.5 million.[10] The power of industrial society was such that plans for the reclamation of the beach area near MM were seriously contemplated in the 1960s. The Illawarra Regional Development Committee formulated the plan in order to create additional industrial land. It would have involved dumping millions of tonnes of rubble and slag on the shallow sea floor between the outer harbour and Big Island off Hill 60, thus destroying the marine habitat and creating a new coastline.[11]

The new inner harbour also changed the way Port Kembla connected with nearby towns. The 1955 Act required the closure of the bridge over the Wollongong–Port Kembla road. The bridge and the lagoon had represented an important physical and psychological boundary between Wollongong and Port Kembla since the 1890s when Wollongong coal trimmers traversed the rough footbridge over the lagoon to work at Port Kembla. During the debates over Council amalgamation in 1946 Central Illawarra Council clerk and local Labor Party identity Fred Finch, in arguing for a Port Kembla-based municipality, remarked that 'there was a natural boundary between Port Kembla and Wollongong—Tom Thumb's Lagoon'.[12] To make way for the new harbour, however, the bridge and the lagoon were destroyed, and the road effectively closed to through traffic in 1960. Separate plans were made for road access via Springhill to Warrawong and Port

Kembla.[13] In October 1961 state member for Wollongong–Kembla, R. F. X. Connor, noted that the closure of the Wollongong–Port Kembla Road led to a 'complete revolution in the travelling habits of my constituents in particular and constituents in adjoining electorates'. Connor spoke of 25 000 people who had 'to acquire new travelling habits and . . . seek new routes by which to travel to and from work'.[14] The closure of the direct route to Wollongong and the eventual construction of an alternate route made Port Kembla a detour off the main road south. This had major implications for the existing commercial infrastructure in Wentworth Street. Like country towns bypassed by new highways, Port Kembla lost its through traffic. The modest local population growth detailed above was not enough to ensure the long-term viability of the existing commercial premises. Springhill Road, from Wollongong to Warrawong via Lysaght's Spring Hill works, cut through a hillock west of Port Kembla. The road cutting was like a scar in Port Kembla's commercial heart, bleeding customers from Wentworth Street either to Wollongong or to the new retail growth area of Warrawong.

The local labour market was comprehensively absorbed by a regional labour market. Electoral roll surveys based on a Port Kembla labour market are no longer appropriate for the post-war period. Census figures, although not comparable to the electoral roll figures provided for the earlier period, can still provide basic information on the regional labour market, of which Port Kembla was a significant part. In general, the contours of the post-war class structure that included a working class, a middle class and a petit-bourgeoisie continued from the formative period. The regionalisation of the labour market, however, make it less meaningful to refer to a 'local class structure', especially as the middle class and some petit-bourgeoisie increasingly moved from Port Kembla to the more salubrious suburbs of Wollongong, such as North Wollongong, Mangerton, and Figtree.

By 1961 Greater Wollongong (that is, the post-1947 Council boundaries) had a male workforce of 43 861. There were 21 965 in the manufacturing sector, 4916 in building construction, 3870 in mining, and 2989 in transport and storage. These were predominantly waged employees, with the vast majority employed at AI&S or its subsidiaries. In commerce 3942 men were employed, in finance and property 593, and 1094 in hotels and amusements. This was a remarkably narrow formal economy, thus leading to a situation where the fortunes of AI&S decided the fate of the region. AI&S dominance also affected the female labour market. There were few employment opportunities for women in a formal economy dominated by heavy industry. There were 2687 females employed in commerce, 1938 females in the community, professional or business sector, 1214 in clothing and knitted trades, 372 in finance and property, just to name the most numerous areas.[15]

It is not possible to cover all of the diverse paid working experiences in this economy. The steel works alone employed 25 000 workers by 1960. Quite apart from specific effects on the labour market, industrial society pervaded all aspects of regional life. Its effects were felt in households where male breadwinners worked shift work, and through less direct influences such as the powerful industrial logic applied to areas of life beyond work.

The wages of workers at ER&S, outlined in Chapter 2, can be followed into the post-war period. At ER&S waged employees secured a major new award in October 1951 which ushered in the 44-hour week and access to sick leave, among other new conditions. More industrially powerful steel unions had recently won many of these conditions. The basic male wage at ER&S was set at £8 13s per week. Ladlers and furnacemen were still the highest-paid waged employees. They earned the basic wage plus 47 and 54 shillings respectively. Cleaners and sweepers earned 18 shillings above the basic wage. Some workers who handled noxious material or strong acids were given a shilling per week bonus 'to compensate for damage to clothing'.[16] By the time the ER&S award of 1959 came into force, new types of benefits were available, including long-service leave and the supply of free gloves. The male basic wage was set at £13 14s per week, with furnacemen and ladlers still topping the pay rates at plus 70 and 55 shillings respectively.

With sections of the white-collar workforce becoming unionised, the Federated Clerks' Union made some inroads at ER&S. A new award covering clerks came into force in July 1946, giving them a 44-hour week, with 30-minute lunch breaks and a war loading backdated to June 1945. Male clerks over 24 years of age earned a minimum of £6 0s 6d per week. Female clerks over 23 earned £3 10s 3d per week. It would be another twenty-five years before equal pay for women and men doing equal work became a legal reality. Most of the award entitlements won in this period for clerical and waged employees alike were negotiated by a workplace conciliation committee, which consisted of representatives of management and the relevant unions. Disputes rarely resulted in industrial action.

The new migrant workers also alleviated labour shortages, although firms such as ER&S employed proportionately fewer migrants than AI&S as they did not experience the high labour turnover of the steel works. Initially migrant workers at ER&S were 'displaced persons' from Eastern and Central Europe. There were 52 'displaced persons' employed at ER&S by June 1950, out of a total workforce of 527. By the mid-1960s the ethnic composition of the ER&S workforce had diversified to the extent expected of a workplace with limited labour turnover. While 305 or 63.4 per cent of the waged employees were Australian-born, there were 47 born in the British Isles, 30 from Italy, 27 from Yugoslavia, 15 from both Poland and Germany, and smaller numbers from other European countries.[17]

But AI&S was undoubtedly the most significant influence on the regional economy in the post-war period. In November 1949 the basic wage at both the Port Kembla and Newcastle steel works was £6 10s to £6 12s. By 1967 workers with a trade, such as a boilermaker's fitter, were earning $111.90 plus approximately $12 in bonuses at AI&S.[18]

The diversity of work experiences at AI&S in the post-war period defies simple description. The works was expanding rapidly, especially once the Number 2 steel works came on line, and construction or modification of plant was almost a constant process. High labour turnover and an increasingly larger workforce created a depersonalised workplace with constant change, a heavily managerial emphasis and few personal relationships between foremen and workers to modify this predominant managerialism. The older ER&S returned to welfarist or paternalist management strategies, suitable for its stable and relatively small workforce. By contrast, AI&S developed a complex administrative structure to manage workforce issues but committed relatively fewer resources to retaining workers or encouraging company loyalty. Immigration programs were a vital part of the AI&S labour process. Only minimal effort was needed to attract and keep workers since AI&S had a reliable supply of contracted workers through its special immigration programmes. By 1952 approximately 20 per cent of BHP's Port Kembla and Newcastle workforce were 'displaced persons', usually tied to the company by two-year indentures.[19]

Migration

Migration was the major component of post-war population growth, and was central to the continuing industrialisation of the region. In the Illawarra from 1947 to 1966 the rate of population growth from natural increase was 12.27 per cent per five years, while the rate from net migration was 23.22 per cent.[20] Port Kembla's social structure, labour market and satellite industrial suburbs changed irrevocably. The Port Kembla remembered by Anglo-Australian residents who had grown up in the period from the 1910s to the 1940s was radically altered. In a decisive change to the pre-war structures of locality, the new migrant Port Kembla was like a separate locality, operating through separate family, kin and institutional networks. While sharing the same local space and infrastructure, the new migrant Port Kembla was a locality within a locality. To this day, migrant Port Kembla created after 1947 maintains an uneasy relationship to the older Anglo-Australian Port Kembla forged in the formative period.

By 1961, after almost two decades of industrial expansion and immigration, the Port Kembla industrial complex was surrounded by increasingly diverse communities of post-war migrants. Migrants from Britain and Ireland, Italy, Greece, Germany, and other continental European countries overwhelmingly dominated employment in the labour-intensive unskilled areas of the steel works, and in some other high-turnover manufacturing industries. The labour demand for such work, and the inequities operating in the labour market, shaped the ethnic mix at Port Kembla and its nearby suburbs. Locality-specific figures are not available, but local economist John Steinke compiled a list of the birthplaces of all residents living within five minutes' drive of the Port Kembla shopping centre for the years 1961 and 1966, shown in Tables 8.2 and 8.3.

Table 8.2 Birthplace of residents living within five minutes' drive of Port Kembla shopping centre, 1961 (national groups under 25 excluded)

Place of birth	Males	Females	Total	% of population
Australia	2 354	2 262	4 616	62.8
United Kingdom & Ireland	278	196	474	6.5
Greece	135	77	212	2.9
Germany	131	96	227	3.1
Italy	690	268	958	13.0
Malta	37	20	57	0.8
Netherlands	13	12	25	0.3
Poland	44	20	64	0.9
Other European	476	159	635	8.6
Other	33	22	55	1.1
Totals	4 206	3 140	7 346	100

Source: J. C. Steinke, *Future Prospects of Port Kembla Shopping Centre*, Wollongong University College, [1969?].

Table 8.3 Birthplace of residents living within five minutes' drive of Port Kembla shopping centre, 1966 (national groups under 25 excluded)

Place of birth	Males	Females	Total	% of population
Australia	2 255	2 237	4 492	56.3
United Kingdom & Ireland	317	244	561	7.0
Greece	176	133	309	3.9
Germany	72	53	125	1.6
Italy	497	308	805	10.1
Malta	31	25	56	0.7
Netherlands	14	16	30	0.4
Poland	41	26	67	0.8
Yugoslavia	835	171	1 006	12.6
Other	50	32	451	5.6
Totals	4 564	3 420	7 984	100

Source: J. C. Steinke, *Future Prospects of Port Kembla Shopping Centre*, Wollongong University College, [1969?].

In 1961 the dominant ethnic group at Port Kembla was the Australian-born from Anglo-Celtic backgrounds. The religious differences among this group continued to be important in the post-war period. As Chapter 4 noted, such religious differences, particularly between those of Catholic and Church of England denominations, constituted an 'ethnic' difference of sorts, though it reflected class difference as well. Table 8.2 shows that the sex ratio among this Anglo-Australian group was close to parity. This reflects the more established nature of this community and the decline in single men or married men whose families lived elsewhere. Among the recent migrants such as the Italians or the Poles, the ratio of males to females was much higher, reflecting the early stages of male-dominated worker migration. Spouses and siblings (if any) joined married men after a settling-in period, while single men either returned to their place of origin to find a bride or married in the local ethnic community. These patterns of migration were similar to those experienced by Anglo-Australian families in the formative period. Although place of birth is by no means an assured indicator of ethnicity, these figures do communicate the cultural origins of a large number of the overseas-born.

By 1961 Port Kembla's ethnic mix included large numbers of Italians, Germans, Poles, Ukrainians, Lithuanians, and Greeks. In the next five years however, significant changes to that mix occurred. The most dramatic was the increase in the number of 'Yugoslav' migrants, overwhelmingly Macedonian in origin. Their prior presence at Port Kembla is somewhat obscured by Table 8.2 since they were included in the 'Other European' category. The first half of the 1960s, however, saw increasing numbers of Macedonians coming to Port Kembla and nearby industrial suburbs. The majority arrived in the late 1960s and early 1970s. The relative numbers of Anglo-Australian residents continued to decline, and some migrant groups such as the Italians and the Germans were clearly moving on from Port Kembla, establishing homes in other places throughout the Illawarra. The polyglot mix of 'Other European' expanded rapidly, reflecting the continued demand for labour at AI&S. The majority of these new arrivals were men, more than likely single or travelling without their families, bound for work at AI&S.

The Macedonian story highlights general features of the Illawarra migrant experience with some distinctive features as well. Early pioneer Macedonian migrants in the Illawarra in the 1920s and 1930s were the first links in a chain migration from specific parts of rural Macedonia. This area was undergoing rapid economic change, particularly with the reconstruction of agriculture, and industrial jobs in the north of the then Yugoslavia were not generally available to Macedonian migrants.[21] Consequently, Macedonians looked further afield.

One pioneer Macedonian migrant was Angele Brglevski from the village of Velusina, near Bitola. He arrived in Australia in 1936. After undertaking rural work in Victoria in the 1930s he moved to Port Kembla in 1941 and found employment at AI&S. Overall, there were just over one hundred Macedonians in the area in the 1940s, mostly men working at AI&S. Some like Brglevski arrived via rural work, while others had transferred from Lithgow with the Hoskins steel works. As Brglevski recalls, 'These 120 or so people helped bring hundreds of people from their villages to Australia'.[22] As a result of the financial and social support of these early pioneers and subsequent waves of Macedonian migrants, the overwhelming numbers of Macedonians at Port Kembla came from the Bitola region, Macedonia's second city near the border with Greece, or Ohrid, also in southern Macedonia.

Like many European migrants, Brglevski aspired to move beyond wage labour. He purchased a shop in 1949, and sponsored his wife to migrate in 1952, his father in 1954, and other family and friends in the 1950s and 1960s. His experience was typical. Male migrants arrived in the Illawarra alone, worked to establish their financial security and then sponsored wives or relatives to Australia. Tome Kokalevski came to Port Kembla in 1959 from the southern Macedonian village of Gorno Srpci. His uncle, who then lived in Newcastle, sponsored him. A married man with one child, his first task as he saw it was to work to buy a house and bring his wife and child to Australia. Once he had established some financial security, he sponsored his wife in 1961 and later other family members to migrate.[23]

The pre-war structures of locality centred on the reliance on local institutions, shopping in Wentworth Street and the common cross-class experience of locality. By contrast, the constituent parts of the post-1947 migrant locality of Port Kembla were family and kin groups based on common ethnicity. Few established institutions, whether in Port Kembla or elsewhere, were responsive to migrant needs, so the developing community relied on its own resources in the areas of finance, religion and recreation. Banks and other financial institutions refused loans to recent migrants. As the Immigration Advisory Council found in 1973, refusals were often on the basis that new arrivals could not 'provide a sound credit history'.[24] Government schemes for helping home owners were also based on holding money in approved accounts for at least three years, and so disadvantaged the recently arrived. Since relatives and friends in Australia sponsored the majority of migrants, they were ineligible for housing in Commonwealth hostels. Other government programmes offered accommodation to skilled migrants, but many Macedonian migrants were unskilled or were unable to have their qualifications recognised. Because of these factors, and other forms of subtle discrimination, disproportionately fewer migrants from Macedonia or from other Southern European countries enjoyed the benefits of Commonwealth assistance compared to British and Western European migrants.[25]

Such institutional shortcomings were addressed by an informal and widespread system of familial and ethnic group support. Established migrants sponsored their relatives and friends by providing money, offering assistance and support on arrival, and usually housing new migrants in the short to medium term. Neda Kotsofski, who arrived in 1957, sponsored migrants to Port Kembla: 'We would bring them here, feed them, find a room, find everything, then find a job, take [them] to the steel works, and then alright'. Mendo Trajcevski recalls that his father, who arrived in 1959, 'must have brought about twenty-five to thirty people. It was a snowball effect. Entire villages were reduced from 200 houses down to twenty houses.'[26] Such activity reached its peak in the period 1966 to 1975. Of the 601 clients of the Port Kembla-based Macedonian Welfare Association, 326 or 56 per cent arrived during this period.[27]

In the absence of assistance from financial institutions, private loans sealed by handshake alone were commonplace. The figures for average occupancy rates per dwelling increased decisively, especially in suburbs like Cringila where households catered for two or more migrant families. The close proximity of the migrant community in and around Port Kembla lent further significance to the network of social support among Macedonians. Ironically, these ethnic-based self-help networks, which grew in the face of an indifferent or hostile institutional environment, caused some resentment among Anglo-Australian residents who saw them as overly exclusive.

Macedonian migrants found some spiritual common ground in the Methodist Church in Wollongong, and later the Greek Orthodox Church in Wollongong. Levels of community organisation grew from the 1960s. One spur to organisational growth was the Skopje earthquake of 1963, which brought Macedonian migrants together to form an organisation to raise money for earthquake relief. Out of the relief effort came plans to build a Macedonian church in Wollongong, St Dimitrijac, which eventually opened in 1972. Sporting teams like Primbee United and Cringila United received migrant support from the Port Kembla and Cringila communities from the 1970s. Established organisations in Port Kembla, such as the Rugby League, Cricket, Bowling and Golf Clubs, remained remarkably isolated from such demographic changes. By the 1970s, though some had changed more than others, these institutions were like small enclaves representative of an older Anglo-Australian Port Kembla.

These self-reliant social networks and emerging migrant organisations had few points of contact with Anglo-Australian Port Kembla. Shopping was probably the most common form of activity that enabled contact between newer migrants and established commercial interests in Anglo Port Kembla. As one Macedonian woman recalled, neither she nor any of her friends were shortchanged by an Anglo-Australian storekeeper during that vulnerable period immediately after their arrival. On the contrary, most businesses in Wentworth Street welcomed the new customers, and some responded to requests for 'special' foods such as chillies, continental sausages, olives and European cheeses.[28]

By the 1960s new migrants were also becoming a part of commercial Port Kembla. Due to the intransigence of banks, migrant businesses were confined to those with cheap start-up costs. The areas that Greeks and Macedonians dominated were cafés, milk bars, and fish and chip shops. Businesses such as hotels involved the purchase of expensive liquor licences, and many other larger businesses required a significant amount of start-up capital. In the 1960s the Passadis family ran the fish and chip shop adjacent to the Commercial Hotel, which attracted considerable lunchtime trade from the nearby industries of ER&S and MM. Some Italian families, meanwhile, moved into fresh fruit and vegetables and, using the slightly larger resources of a more established ethnic community, the building industry and smallgoods. A German restaurant called the Nirvana was operating by the early 1960s in Wentworth Street. The Capri, an almost legendary Port Kembla Italian restaurant and nightclub that still survives in one form or another, was situated across the road.

The effect on the Anglo Port Kembla palate was modest but memorable. Mainstream restaurants such as the Open Hearth Hotel at Warrawong typically served a choice of fish or steak in the 1950s and 1960s. The Nirvana offered culinary experiences that few Anglo-Celtic residents had known, including veal schnitzel and sauerkraut. The Capri served pasta, seafood (beyond just fish), and wine with meals. As Paul Wand, who moved to Port Kembla in 1963 as a trainee metallurgist at ER&S, recalls, 'Port Kembla was to some extent on the cusp of the ethnic change in Wollongong'.[29] Port Kembla was the first and most common site of contact between Anglo residents and new migrant residents. In the less ethnically diverse suburbs of northern Illawarra, for example, European migrants were more of a rarity. This possibly explains the generally positive reception that migrants received in the town.

Migration also revived the ailing informal economy at Port Kembla. During the formative period industrialisation challenged wage labour alternatives, making the paid work of men more central to a family's survival and reducing the scope and importance of local links. Such trends continued after 1945, but migrants brought a new impetus to the informal economy. As the scope of the informal economy narrowed, its focus became Port Kembla's backyards and vegetable gardens. Migrants grew vegetables that were common to their diets. Macedonian Australians grew chillies, tomatoes and cucumbers, while Italian Australians grew tomatoes, zucchinis, and grapes, and brewed home-made wine. Virtually all migrant households kept chickens, and the Macedonians were known for keeping pigs, which occasionally brought them into conflict with their non-Macedonian neighbours.

The informal economy complemented the male industrial labour market, supplementing its resources and offering some breathing space against moderately lengthy work disruptions. There was widespread acceptance, however, that a steady job in the local industries was the major path towards advancement. Migrant workers in particular believed that their employment in the coke ovens or the open-hearth furnaces was a way to secure a good financial future for their families and ensure that their children did not have to do the same kind of work. Shift work, the predominant arrangement for labourers and tradesmen at AI&S, placed huge strains on workers' personal and familial resources, but they accepted its difficulties and even welcomed it for the extra income that it offered.

The importance of employment in the formal economy was such that pollution from Port Kembla industries, bar a few exceptional incidents, was accepted as a normal part of life. Indeed, the plume of smoke rising from industrial chimneys was symbolic of the prospect of regular work and the flow of money into workers' pockets. As one resident recalled, 'When there was smoke coming out of that stack there was money going into people's pockets'.[30] More than that, the visible symbols of industrial society were also seen as aesthetically appealing, even when pollution was identified as an issue. Commenting on the new ER&S stack completed in 1965, Mrs Whiddett remarked: 'That's beautiful. You ought to have been here where the little one was here and we'd get all the smoke of it. This was the worst area in Port Kembla when the little stack was there. We used to get all this fumes and smoke.'[31] The rhythms of industrial society became central and often highly regarded features of working-class life for both Anglo and migrant Port Kembla. Resisted both industrially and culturally up to the 1930s, from the 1940s regular industrial time was so firmly equated with prosperity for many working-class people that company time was now a friend rather than a foe—company time kept food in the pantry and the rent men at bay.

As industry became part of local society, its rhythms and routines infused every household and every social and religious event. Company time structured local time. Throughout Port Kembla sirens, hooters and whistles announced the beginning and end of every shift. Religious and other community groups took care to plan their fundraisers for the day or weekend immediately after pay Thursday. Local retailers learnt to expect the fortnightly fluctuations in their business as customers came in after pay Thursday, and the week before payday was characterised by little trade.

Company routines were not always predictable, and industrial processes not always as amenable to human control as the rhetoric of industrial society suggested. Explosions of furnaces were, and still are, a regular part of nearby suburban existence. In one case, a series of explosions at the ER&S wire bar furnace in August 1957 halted production for almost six weeks. A 'breakaway' in the furnace led to almost 200 tonnes of molten copper pouring onto the furnace floor. The molten material contacted water and triggered a series of explosions. Luckily, men working at the furnace had sufficient warning, and raced to safety before the blast.

Such explosions were an obvious danger in the workplace but they also impacted on nearby suburbs. Port Kembla residents saw sheets of furnace roofing iron flung hundreds of feet into the air by the wire bar furnace explosion. One Warrawong resident (some 2 kilometres away) said that the blasts sounded like 'a series of detonators being exploded under my house. The windows and the house were badly shaken.'[32] The image is telling. The explosion felt as if came from under the very foundations of this man's home. Industrial society was the bedrock of the regional economy and provided many of the cultural and linguistic metaphors for local residents.

Politics

Between 1945 and 1970 a broad consensus emerged over the desirability and management of industrial growth. Management, unions and most local communities were incorporated into a consensus view that heavy industry provided jobs, stability, and valuable products for post-war Australia. While conflict occurred around the edges of this consensus, the broad parameters of industrial society were remarkably well accepted by nearly all relevant groups. The formal economy remained a flashpoint for class conflict. However, the consensus of industrial society was such that serious challenges to its fundamental tenets were rare. A strong institutional consensus developed between unions, government and business based on centralised arbitration, yet the pace of construction, working conditions, and the size of the workforce at AI&S Port Kembla produced volatile rank-and-file class politics. This class politics found expression through union organisation but also through wildcat strikes and rank-and-file militancy, especially where union executives were perceived to be too closely wedded to the industrial age consensus. The focus of class politics, apart from some lone union voices interested in social and human rights, was almost exclusively on the industrial workplace. Historians have considered the post-war industrial relations of Port Kembla and the Illawarra at some length.[33] Rather than repeat this material, I will consider issues that relate specifically to the themes pursued here. Such was the dominance of AI&S, and the industrial issues that it threw up, that localist politics was all but obliterated with the partial exception of the issue of pollution, which the next chapter covers.

Central to this consensus was the active role of the state and federal governments, principally in the areas of infrastructure development, housing and immigration. Private ownership of major industries remained largely unchallenged, apart from a few critics on the far left. Earlier debates in the labour movement around nationalisation and the so-called 'socialist objective' were left behind. While nationalisation of steel was a crucial issue in post-war Britain, it attracted little if any attention in Australia. In the post-war era, as this one example shows, Australia drew far more heavily on the US rather than the British experience.

Unions, government, and BHP (which was in full control of its subsidiary, AI&S) came to a basic understanding over the use of migrant labour in 1949. After expressing some initial misgivings, the executive of the FIA agreed to allow the large-scale use of migrant labour at the steel works under certain conditions. This was no easy task for the FIA because the use of displaced persons was anathema to the White Australia policy, an article of faith for many in the labour movement. Moreover, there was some concern that BHP, particularly after its major trial of strength with the FIA in the 1945 steel strike, might use migrant labour to undermine the union.[34] The Minister for Immigration, Arthur Calwell, secured an agreement from BHP not to employ migrant workers in staff positions, and to enrol them in the relevant union. Most importantly, BHP management agreed to place migrant workers in the least desirable jobs. This was the origin of a dual labour market that structured employment at AI&S according to ethnicity for at least thirty years. The agreement, put to branch meetings in the last half of 1949, secured majority but by no means unanimous support.[35]

One crucial way in which the industrial society consensus incorporated unions was through the movement of migrant labour into the least desirable jobs available at the steel works. These migrants, of course, played a key role for BHP in providing a large labour supply during a period of unprecedented construction work and increasing production. For unions such as the FIA, however, migrants effectively provided a labour force that was streamed into lower-paid unskilled jobs, jobs that Anglo-Australian union members found less palatable. For the FIA, migrant workers also offered guaranteed membership under an arrangement negotiated between the federal government, the FIA, and BHP. The consensus was further strengthened when a more moderate leadership gained control of the most important union in the Port Kembla industrial sector, the FIA. Prominent militant Bill Frame lost the secretary's position at branch elections in 1952.[36]

AI&S required large numbers of workers for its Port Kembla expansion programme, yet the plant had been plagued by high labour turnover, and had generally failed to secure an adequate share of the existing labour market. The fact that migrant workers were tied into two-year contracts with a specific employer was highly appealing to BHP, and helped address their labour turnover problem. The links between BHP and migration planning became more apparent after 1948, as migration moved away from the displaced persons programme to large-scale immigration of other European refugees and economic migrants. By 1952 one of the federal government's key advisory bodies, the Immigration Planning Council, included BHP executive Ian McClennan, along with ACTU president Albert Monk.[37] BHP relished its role as an entrepot employer since it guaranteed access to a large, expanding and tied labour force. Nevertheless, in forging this alliance with the federal government, BHP had to give certain concessions, not the least of which was the offer to guarantee union membership of migrant workers and stream them into positions where they posed little threat to Anglo-Australian workers. In securing access to this labour supply BHP gave away some management prerogatives to state and union. It was, however, a small price to pay, and such compromises were central to the industrial society consensus.

Industrial conflict that did occur over the period was largely confined to legalistic and administrative forums, where union representatives negotiated with company representatives. While there were important disputes throughout this period (well-covered by existing labour histories of the Illawarra), it was not unusual for the AI&S industrial office to note that the industrial position was 'quite satisfactory'.[38] Beneath this legalistic and ritualistic conflict between unions and management, however, were more subterranean tactics of job control and subtle resistance, where the key players were rank-and-file union members and plant foremen. At this level, the industrial society consensus was less well established. Small, often daily, battles for influence and control were played out in the workplace. In one case, a labourer was dismissed for threatening a foreman. The foreman's report is probably a sanitised version of events. Foremen generally reported their own actions as reasoned and polite, although there is evidence of mistreatment, favouritism, even verbal and physical abuse. But the report does highlight the issue of a worker struggling for greater control over his working conditions.

> M. Ipcus was instructed by me at approx 1 pm to clean the head of grinder no. 1. This man argued that this was not his job alone, that other shifts should clean the machine also. I told him that this was so but that at present he got paid for keeping the machine clean . . . The man still argued about having to clean the machine after which he was firmly instructed to commence the job. He then said 'If ever I get you out of here I will kill you'. He repeated the threat and then started the job he was instructed to do.[39]

Ipcus was dismissed by the section manager. AI&S records are overflowing with such incidents. At the workplace foremen and workers were struggling daily over the control and direction of the work effort. Ipcus's comment 'If I ever get you out of here' is a recognition that outside the works different rules apply; that beyond the factory gates the authority of foremen and section managers was not absolute.

Threats were not the most common form of individual resistance to workplace authority. At the flat products shop in AI&S there were sixteen dismissals in 1960. The most common infraction was 'absenteeism', which accounted for thirteen of the dismissals. One man was dismissed for 'refusal of duty', another for 'failure to carry out duties', and one was deemed 'unsuitable'.[40] Absenting yourself was a passive form of resistance that took a worker out of their relatively powerless situation, a 'flight' rather than 'fight' response.

Minor battles over time—clocking on and off, overtime, double-time, time and a half—occurred throughout this period. In 1945 the AI&S Industrial Department undertook a careful study of the clocking on and off records for one Saturday shift in May. Out of a total of 569 workers whose time cards were studied, only three had clocked on before their shift began, thirty had started on time, 100 at one minute past, 196 at two minutes past and 240 at three minutes past.[41] Throughout the works whenever workers perceived that their efforts were being monitored, timed, and studied, wild-cat strikes typically resulted. Any suggestion that 'time and motion' experts were on the job drew swift and angry rejections of their methods by unions, largely focusing on the issue of time and work effort.[42]

The conflicting notions of personal and company time, as well as differing views on management and union authority, are apparent in a case involving the actions of C. Stevens, a boilermaker and union delegate in the AI&S sinter plant in 1967. After Stevens allegedly suggested to an engineer welder that work he was doing might provoke a demarcation dispute, management sought an interview with him. When approached in the change rooms a few minutes before the end of shift, Stevens told a foreman that he 'had no chance' of getting him to report to the superintendent since he was 'on his own time'. When the worker was summoned the next day for a discussion—not during his usual shift—he refused to answer any questions until he was informed whether he was being paid for presenting himself at the works. Once this issue was settled in Stevens's favour, he refused to discuss the exchange between himself and the welder, saying, 'Any discussion between he and me was Union business and I am not going to discuss it. It is none of your concern. I won't discuss any Union business unless the Union secretary is present.' This case shows an individual worker with a highly developed sense of his own rights and obligations; these rights and obligations were based on his union membership rather than his employee status. Ultimately a compulsory conference failed to resolve the matter, and Stevens was suspended for two shifts. Such notions were held not only by individual workers but were the basis of sympathy strikes right across the works. In this case, the boilermakers in the sinter plant went on strike in support of Stevens.[43]

The Port Kembla steel works, particularly sections such as the open hearth, the coke ovens, and the jetty, developed a reputation for rank-and-file militancy. A sample of these small unofficial disputes indicates the extent to which workers on the job were acting without reference to their union officials. On 1 December 1953 boilermakers in the coke ovens department stopped work over the attitude of a foreman engineer. The company refused a conference with the workers, and from 4 December all boilermakers were absent from work until a resumption on 7 December.[44] Stopping work was just one form of protest. Bans on overtime or specific kinds of work were instituted by nearly all groups of workers and could be the result of a dispute over pay, allegedly dangerous working conditions, or demarcation. Most of the major differences ended up in the NSW Industrial Commission.[45] In this managerial environment there was little room for local negotiation and conciliation. AI&S was wedded to the centralised industrial relations system, and rarely stepped out of legalistic procedures. Consequently, groups of workers usually took industrial action as the first option: experience had shown that conciliation was rarely effective.

The institutional players had major points of disagreement, but both had clear interests in maintaining either management or union control over the actions of the workforce. In August 1957 a conference of AI&S and FIA officials discussed a recent walkout of blast furnace employees. W. K. Jones from AI&S opened the discussion, saying that the company 'was concerned at the practice which had developed in the Open Hearth Department of men going on strike when another man is stood down'. Jones reminded the FIA that the Court of Industrial Arbitration had determined that unions were responsible for the actions of individual members. Long-serving Port Kembla AI&S industrial officer, V. R. Petney, remarked that

> the Company and the men have certain rights—the Company has the right to stand men down for misdemeanours and the men have the right to test the Company's actions in a proper manner. However the men will not respect the Company's right and this is more pronounced at Port Kembla—at Newcastle men take more notice of the Union officials whereas at Port Kembla there are certain factions operating in the ranks of the union itself, and it comes back to the proposition that the Union must take steps to take control of its own affairs.

Petney accurately pointed to the existence of rank-and-file militancy at Port Kembla, where dissatisfaction with moderate FIA leadership was present from the late 1950s until a major change in leadership in 1970. The union officials present, including Port Kembla branch secretary Tom Malcolm and FIA state secretary H. Hurrell, did not differ in their assessment of the problem. Hurrell noted that 'the Union was doing its best to straighten out the matter'. For Hurrell the men involved in the blast furnace walkout had 'acted in a hot-headed manner'. It is striking the extent to which both the management and the moderate FIA leadership of the time identified rank-and-file militancy as a common problem. For these unlikely partners in the industrial society consensus, rank-and-file militancy was one force within the institutional industrial relations nexus that they could not control.[46]

Other challenges to the industrial society consensus related to the streaming of migrant workers into the most difficult, dirty and dangerous jobs. In the 1950s and 1960s complaints from migrant workers were not clearly articulated through union structures dominated by Anglo workers, but evidence of their concerns occasionally surfaced. In 1950 two Lithuanian workers in the merchant mills were suspended for a shift for refusing to work as directed. A foreman directed these men to assist in cleaning a certain area of the mill. When pressed by the foreman, one man replied that they were willing to work but not on that particular job: 'When there is hard work always New Australians have to do it'.[47] In 1954 four Greek workers visited the AI&S time office with a journalist from the Greek-language newspaper. The ensuing discussion was recorded by time office staff and reported to the general manager. The workers had seen the Greek ambassador 'because of the way they had been treated here'. The reporter noted that the workers 'had claimed, among other things, they are given the worst and the hardest work'.[48]

The lack of adequate union representation of migrant workers, coupled with the widespread belief that migrant workers received the worst jobs, was one force behind the rank-and-file movements across the Port Kembla steel works. Within the FIA various rank-and-file organisations emerged, particularly in the 1960s. One such organisation, the Ironworkers Rank and File Vigilance Committee, produced an occasional broadsheet critical of union officials, especially secretary Tom Malcolm for 'not pushing workers' concerns vigorously enough'. The AI&S Industrial Department assiduously collected such publications, and it is significant that they were issued in Greek and Italian as well as English from as early as 1960.[49] After 1970, major Port Kembla unions became far more open to migrant issues, especially with the election of new FIA secretary, Nando Lelli.

The movement of large numbers of migrant workers into AI&S eventually influenced traditional union organisations. Class politics at Port Kembla was shaped by this ethnically divided labour market, yet as crucial as AI&S industrial relations were to the human experience of industrialisation, these battles were played out in contexts that had little to do with the locality of Port Kembla. The regional labour council, state and nation-wide wide labour movements, as well as directors in distant boardrooms and Sydney- and Canberra-based politicians were the key players. Industrial battles at AI&S effectively demonstrate the movement of class politics out of its local context.

Perceptions

While the formative period was characterised by an uneasy oscillation between localist and class politics, by the post-war period the power of industrial society muffled local voices and overwhelmed pre-war localist politics and its characteristic forms. Locality all but disappeared from view. In public relations documents, company management strategies, government-sponsored literature on the steel industry, and in census information, little mention was made of Port Kembla. Place no longer mattered, in what amounted to a distinct division between industry and locality.

This was the golden era of industrial society, characterised by confident expressions of progress and assertions of the value of technology. Operations at Port Kembla were underpinned by the notion that steel and other metal products were central to modern society. The formative period of industrial society experienced growing pains as rural interests chafed against the rising tide of industrialisation, and trade union and working-class organisations struggled to find a legitimate space within the new order. By the post-war period a consensus transcending class differences and widely held by most social groups had developed, although it was strongly contested at the edges as we have seen. At Port Kembla and throughout the region, post-war prosperity and industry-led economic growth raised such sentiments to their peak in the 1950s and 1960s.

Encapsulating the sentiments of industrial society at its zenith was the souvenir booklet produced by BHP for the opening of extensions to AI&S in August 1955. One of the opening pages contains photographs of the BHP board of directors, while almost surreal, colourised and retouched photographs display views of the new machinery. The workers in these photos are unnamed and dwarfed by the giant machines that were the heroes of industrial society, as shown in a reproduction of one of the images following page 116. The usual information on local services and settlements that graced such company publications in the pre-war era was absent. Moreover, the use of colourised and retouched photos indicates that the excesses of the industrial age were actively censored. The realities were too harsh for simple photographic reproduction.

The 1955 commemorative booklet emphasises the capital expenditure, and construction of industry on the former tidal swamp with piles as long as 27 metres reaching into bedrock. These metaphors help link to the overall theme of progress with anchored stability. The buildings were, reassuringly, built on solid foundations, despite all appearances. Beneath an old reclaimed swamp were long and anchoring foundations that reached down to the very bedrock of industrial society. The themes of building solid industrial foundations out of the insubstantial and treacherous 'swampland' are common in both Port Kembla and Newcastle. Such was the power of industrial society that it was able to transform the very landscape on which industry was situated into something more useful, substantial and productive.[50] This was apparent in private industry and public works, as the destruction of Tom Thumb's Lagoon and the construction of the inner harbour demonstrates. The new mill was also a triumph of continuous production. The flow diagram contained in the 1955 booklet suggests the logical and almost effortless progress from steel slabs to value-added products such as coiled strip and tin plate. The simple application of technology had tamed the strength of steel and created a product vital to post-war industrial growth.[51]

The opening ceremony for the new mill, with the guest of honour Prime Minister Robert Menzies, showed the same concern for a veneer of modernity and aesthetic appeal. Some 22 750 square metres of silver foil and 1365 metres of blue satin decorated the mill. For this day at least the mill was transformed from a grimy, dusty, hot and noisy workplace to something that matched industrial society rhetoric. The prime minister, amplifying the optimistic, modernist mood, spoke of a company that was 'not some tired old organisation but an organisation that is full of lusty youth with a remarkable record of achievements'.[52]

The hallowed notions of progress, modernity and increased growth through industrial production were broadly held across the political spectrum. In 1953 state Labor Member for Wollongong–Kembla, R. F. X. Connor, summed up the ethos of industrial society accurately:

> We live in the age of steel. Each age has its identifying characteristics but historians will record this period as the steel era. Steel means power and strength, and the industrial potential and economic resources and defence possibilities of any country are reckoned in terms of steel.[53]

The powerful forces that regionalised Port Kembla's economy and society, or denied reference to place at all, received one final but significant boost that sealed the destruction of an autonomous locality based on Port Kembla. A major change in census categories occurred in 1966. Port Kembla statistically disappeared, replaced by the larger Wollongong Statistical District. It is far easier to find figures on Port Kembla's population and housing in the 1911 and 1921 Census than it is from the 1966 Census onwards. This move sealed the victory of Wollongong interests, who, from as early as 1898, had coveted Port Kembla's development, and had wished to capture and control that development for their own benefit. If 1947 marked the end of the political possibility of Port Kembla-based local government, this 1966 change marks the effective end of Port Kembla as a separate administrative and statistical entity for planning purposes. This statistical sleight of hand was the symbolic end of a century-long process that saw Port Kembla slowly enveloped by regional suburbanisation, and a centralising administrative power located in Wollongong. By 1966 Port Kembla was, at least according to the Commonwealth statistician, a suburb of Wollongong.

The construction and expansion programme at Port Kembla throughout the 1950s and 1960s appeared to justify the effusive expressions of the importance of iron and steel production that characterised the period. Even at the end of the financial year in 1970, BHP reported strong demand for steel products, a domestic economy growing at 8 per cent and the highest volume of orders received in the company's history in the second half of the period.[54] However, BHP dominance contained the seeds of later trouble. As the steel works towered over the regional economy it narrowed its economic base, making it the most industrially dependent region in Australia. In the 1970s and 1980s industrial society came under increasing pressure from a world in recession, and from local residents who increasingly questioned the privileging of production over their quality of life. The split between industry and locality led to a growing number of locals with no investment in the continued operations of local industries. These industries had created a massive yet narrowly focused regional labour market, simultaneously ignoring the social, political and environmental context of the immediate surroundings. BHP and its subsidiary partners, no less than the communities reliant on their ongoing operation, would reap this grim harvest in the next thirty years.

9

The Dissolution of Industrial Society? 1970 Onwards

FROM 1970 MANUFACTURING INDUSTRIES began a long period of decline at Port Kembla, as they did throughout all industrialised countries. The industrial economy remained important, but a series of setbacks—long-term, deeply rooted trends, as well as short-term crises—challenged the core tenets of industrial society. By the beginning of the twenty-first century, components of Port Kembla's once confident and growing industrial economy were part of a heritage trail, the Industry World Theme Park. Sites of industrial production became locations for tourist consumption—at least that was the hope of those who established Industry World. Increasing numbers of residents questioned the value and long-term status of Port Kembla's industrial economy. The post-war consensus, shaky over industrial relations, was now fracturing over more fundamental questions such as the desirability and place of heavy industry in the region.

After struggling with the scale and impact of industrial growth for almost seventy years, the region quickly became immersed in the effects of economic decline. Even as the worst of the retrenchments of the 1980s passed, persistent long-term forces undermined the dominance of industrial society, including commercial decline, 'law and order' problems in the main street, and protests over pollution. The locality of Port Kembla was largely forgotten in what was an overwhelmingly regional crisis with strong national and international dimensions. But the specific features of the downturn created distinctive impacts on Port Kembla.

Formal Economy

The opening sentence of the 1975 Jackson report, the product of a committee of industry leaders, trade unionists and academics appointed by the federal government, was to the point: 'Australian manufacturing industry is in crisis'. The committee recognised worldwide economic problems but also identified a 'a deep-seated and long standing malaise' in the Australian industry. Policies of import substitution, tariff protection, and prosperity through continued immigration and population growth had created a manufacturing industry that was oriented to the domestic market. This market was comparatively small, growth was slowing, and demand was fickle. Capital investment had failed to keep pace with overseas competitors, and equipment was 'old, inefficient and overdue for replacement'. The next twenty-five years would be tumultuous for local industries, their workers, and the nearby communities. At Port Kembla the problems of rapid growth were replaced by the problems of economic decline and large-scale retrenchment.[1]

In 1972 BHP reported a decline in profits at AI&S, increasing industrial disturbances, and generally a 'severe downturn in the domestic and international markets'. The new basic oxygen steel making facility, Number 5 blast furnace, was completed that year with a capacity of 4500 tonnes per day, or more than four times the capacity of the original Number 1 furnace built in 1928. But there were commissioning problems with the new furnace. By 1975 the managing director of the steel division, J. C. McNeil, reported that demand had contracted further due to inflationary pressures, and the plant was working below capacity. That year the steel division returned a net loss of over $39 million.[2]

At the beginning of 1982 over 200 jobs were lost in the regional coal industry and these presaged larger retrenchments throughout 1982 and 1983. By mid-1984 over 11 802 jobs had been lost from the Port Kembla steel works through a combination of voluntary and forced redundancies.[3] The precise cause of these retrenchments is still not accurately known. Most relevant sources are still subject to the thirty-year rule and the vast majority of available evidence reflects on the consequences of the crisis rather than the causes. BHP management pointed to the world-wide downturn, growing international competition and increasing labour costs. In contrast, a trade union organisation, the Wollongong Workers' Research Centre, questioned the authenticity of the steel 'crisis'. According to an analysis commissioned by the centre, the crisis was created in order for BHP to secure further tariff and tax concessions from the federal government. There was no major threat to BHP's domestic market for steel from cheap overseas imports, and BHP had failed to reinvest in new technology in the 1970s.[4]

Whatever the causes of the downturn, its political fallout was significant. The federal government had played a crucial role in the domestic manufacturing industry since the origins of tariff protection in the early 1920s, but the crisis brought new responsibilities for this level of government.

Labor Prime Minister R. J. Hawke announced the steel industry plan in August 1983. The plan ran for five years from January 1984 and included an advisory committee of industry, trade union and academic members. The 1984/85 budget allocated significant federal money for steel regions, including Newcastle, Wollongong, and Whyalla. Infrastructure projects to broaden the economic base of steel-dependent regions, as well as education and retraining projects, were funded, totalling $70 million over the period 1983 to 1988. The Port Kembla grain terminal, for example, secured $1.9 million in federal assistance. A total of $30 million annually was allocated to the payment of bounties on Australian-produced steel in 1983/84 and 1984/85.[5]

After the recession of the early 1980s, BHP's commitment to steelmaking was questioned. The steel division returned to profitability in 1985, yet unions and some political interests felt suspicious that the new corporate culture of the 1980s and 1990s would eventually led to a major withdrawal of BHP from steel making. These suspicions were borne out in the long term. The company conducted a review of its steel division in 1997 that led to the closure of steel making in Newcastle in September 1999, and the loss of 2500 jobs. Forward planning suggested that Port Kembla would take over capacity from significantly curtailed, or closed, BHP operations in New Zealand and Whyalla. In 2001 however, the newly merged BHP–Billiton announced that the BHP Steel division would be floated on the stock exchange in mid-2002, effectively cutting the ties between the steel division and the parent company.[6] Other Port Kembla industries also struggled in the 1980s and 1990s. Port Kembla's oldest industry, ER&S, was taken over from Conzinc Rio Tinto Australia (CRA) in 1980 and became Southern Copper in 1990. After struggling to make a costly upgrade profitable and in the midst of industrial and pollution problems, Southern Copper was shut down by CRA in 1995.[7] In the wake of all of these labour reductions and industry closures, the links between the locality of Port Kembla and its nearby industries become even more tenuous. By the 1990s Port Kembla was no longer an industrial town, but a suburban area that happened to reside close to industry.

Port Kembla, indeed all of the Illawarra statistical district, was heavily dependent on employment in the steel works, or related to it. The extent of the industrial downturn was such that population levels actually dropped at Port Kembla in the period 1976 to 1986, as Table 9.1 shows. The population decline at Port Kembla was common across other manufacturing-dependent suburbs such as Berkeley (11.1 per cent decline), South Wollongong (9.2 per cent) Warrawong–Kemblawarra (7.5 per cent), and Cringila (3.1 per cent).[8] In the entire region, which at an administrative and political level is defined as all the local government areas of Wollongong, Shellharbour, Shoalhaven and Wingecarribbee, employment in the manufacturing sector declined from 29.8 per cent of the labour force in 1981 to 17.9 per cent in 1991. By 1998 the level of manufacturing sector employment had dropped to 15.1 per cent. The major sectors that increased included wholesale and retail trade (14 to 17.3 per cent), finance and business administration (5.7 to 9 per cent) and community services (12.2 to 17.8 per cent).[9]

Table 9.1 Population and housing at Port Kembla (includes Kemblawarra), 1976–86

	1976	1981	1986
Population	7 138	6 762	5 309
Males	3 748	3 528	na
Females	3 390	3 234	na
Occupied dwellings	2 351	2 176	na

Source: Australian Bureau of Statistics, 1976 and 1981, *Population and Housing Collection District Summary Data (NSW)—Postcode 2505*; Commonwealth of Australia, *1986 Census*.

The decline of the manufacturing sector, coupled with the reduced labour demand for those manufacturing industries still operating, had significant impacts on areas heavily dependent on industrial production. In 1976 the locality of Port Kembla had a labour force of 2849. There were 1487 males and 173 females, or 58.3 per cent of the total labour force categorised as 'manufacturing', indicating that the male domination of heavy industry remained largely unchanged. The other relevant sectors included 10.7 per cent employed in retail, 5.7 per cent in transport, and 0.6 per cent in community service. In 1986 Port Kembla's paid workforce numbered 2329, the drop a result of population decline and industrial retrenchments. The workforce included 46.1 per cent involved in manufacturing, 14.9 per cent in retail, 9 per cent in community service, and 7.3 per cent in transport. Such changes were characteristic of the effects of deindustrialisation in labour markets across many localities and regions in the industrialised world, with a significant decline in manufacturing employment never fully counterbalanced by a growth in retail and community services employment.[10] Within a decade trends that had persisted for over fifty years were reversed. The certainty of industrial society progress and growth was over, perhaps most clearly demonstrated by the rise in Port Kembla's unemployed from 3 per cent of the labour force in 1976 to an extraordinary 17.6 per cent in 1986.[11]

Even after the precipitous drop in manufacturing employment as a proportion of the total labour force, this sector remained important. Port Kembla's 1986 figure for manufacturing employment was almost double the average for the whole Wollongong local government area, and only exceeded in Cringila (64.1 per cent), and Warrawong (54 per cent). These latter-day industrial suburbs were more comprehensively a product of industrial growth alone. They lacked a more differentiated labour market, such as Port Kembla's, to provide other kinds of job opportunities. The age profile of Port Kembla and the surrounding industrial suburbs also shows the changing demographic structure of the population as the generations who arrived at the height of the industrial economy aged. By 1986 Port Kembla had 33.1 per cent of the population aged 50 years and over, which was one of the highest figures for any locality in the Wollongong local government area.[12]

The geography of occupational and class hierarchy was firmly entrenched by the 1980s, a result of the historical forces that shaped Illawarra industry and the locational factors that encouraged the concentration of particular kinds of workers in particular places. In 1986 the Port Kembla occupational structure showed the expected dominance of labouring and machinery workers, at 30 per cent and 18.4 per cent of the workforce respectively. At the same time, Port Kembla's older labour market and somewhat more diverse employment base showed in higher numbers of 'managers', 'administrators' and 'professionals' than in the newer industrial suburbs. In 1986, 3.7 per cent of the Port Kembla workforce were 'managers and administrators' and 7.3 per cent were 'professionals'; the same figures for Warrawong were 2 and 3.8 per cent. Nevertheless, these differences should be placed in context of the figures for the Wollongong City Council area as a whole, and for more salubrious regions. In the local government area, 17.7 per cent of workers listed their occupations within the 'labouring' classification while 12 per cent were under 'plant machinery'. The average for professionals was 12.5 per cent, while more salubrious areas such as North Wollongong–Smiths Hill and Figtree had professional rates of 21.9 per cent and 21.8 per cent respectively. The highest figure for the local government area was Stanwell Park, where the growing attraction of this area to middle-class academics, business people and other professionals was clearly apparent. After 1970, heavy industry struggled in a difficult economic climate and the centrality of industrial production to the economic future of the region was questioned. The industrial society consensus started to come apart, especially as the dominance of heavy industry was identified not as a strength but as a fatal flaw in the region's economy.

Some, not associated with industrial employment, went further and identified the absence of production and paid work as a kind of liberation. When industrial society dominated, regular paid work was a metronome for prosperity and wealth. As perceptions of heavy industry and its pollutants changed, however, new understandings developed. After World War II concerns over pollution levels, and their impact on people and the environment, encouraged an environmental consciousness that was often harshly critical of industrial production. For local residents who eventually formed the Illawarra Residents Against Toxic Emissions (IRATE) in early 1997, the closure of Port Kembla's oldest industry, Southern Copper, in 1995 was a symbol of freedom from smoke, sulphur dioxide and lead emissions. After the closure many claimed improved health and the revival of local wildlife.[13] However, a Japanese-led consortium, Port Kembla Copper Limited (PKC), purchased the plant in 1996 and embarked on an ambitious upgrade and reopening programme. By the middle of 2000 the new company had delivered its first consignment of copper to nearby MM. The resumption, however, was plagued with problems, more pollution incidents and local protests.

For IRATE and other locals, the five years between the closure of Southern Copper in 1995 and the reopening of PKC in 2000 represented a respite from pollution. For such groups the comings and goings of industry, and the presence or absence of its byproducts, mark out distinct meanings. The presence of industrial byproducts represented not prosperity but a degradation of local quality of life, while closure represented not economic decline but freedom from pollution. Groups such as IRATE have widespread support, a testament to the fracturing of the consensus of industrial society, at least locally.

Ethnicity

By 1975 four out of every ten workers in the Australian manufacturing industry had been born overseas. These workers were overwhelmingly concentrated in low-paid, unskilled jobs.[14] These national figures were reflected in Port Kembla's heavy industries, and had a profound effect on nearby communities. The older ethnic make-up of Port Kembla, apparent in the 1947 Census, had been completely overturned in the space of forty years. By 1986, 41.4 per cent of the locality's population had been born overseas, as compared to just 10 per cent in 1947. This was one of the highest rates for any regional locality, exceeded only by Cringila (55.5 per cent), Lake Heights (43.8 per cent), and Warrawong (46.9 per cent).

Proximity to the steel works and its overwhelmingly dominant labour market shaped the development of nearby suburbs throughout the post-war era. After 1970, however, Port Kembla was no longer the major point of arrival for many migrants. In 1981 a number of other suburbs had far larger proportions of migrants who had arrived within the past five years. The Housing Commission suburb of Bellambi had 16.4 per cent of all overseas-born with less than five years' residence, while Fairy Meadow with its large Vietnamese-Australian population had 21.1 per cent, and South Wollongong 19.7 per cent. Port Kembla had 8 per cent of all foreign-born with less than five years' residence, which was less than the average for the local government area of 10.1 per cent and was indicative of the new destinations for migrants in the Illawarra.[15]

The statistics for Port Kembla in Table 9.2 show that 48.7 per cent of the overseas-born were from Yugoslavia, 15.5 per cent from Italy, 9 per cent from England and Scotland, and 5.1 per cent from Greece. For Yugoslav migrants, the figures do not provide any breakdown in terms of region or ethnicity. Almost all of the Yugoslav migrants to Port Kembla were Macedonian, with most arriving in Australia between 1966 and 1975. However, migrant arrivals continued in the 1980s and 1990s, especially after the worst of the industrial retrenchments were over. Of the 601 clients of the Port Kembla-based Macedonian Welfare Association, 154 or 25 per cent arrived between 1986 and 2000.[16] While the largest overseas-born population in Port Kembla were from Macedonia, other nearby suburbs had much lower concentrations of Yugoslavs, greater numbers of Italians, and a sprinkling of Germans.

Table 9.2 Origin of overseas-born residents of Port Kembla and selected suburbs, 1986

Overseas-born residents	Port Kembla	Cringila	Lake Heights	Warrawong	Berkeley	Thirroul
Number	2 192	2 037	2 817	2 121	1 673	738
% of population	41.4	55.5	43.8	46.9	29.9	14.2
% from Yugoslavia	48.7	56.6	26.0	23.9	9.6	2.7
% from Italy	15.5	6.6	16.9	19.8	6.0	2.3
% from Germany	1.4	1.2	3.7	1.7	6.5	5.6
% from England/ Scotland	9.0	3.5	11.4	11.7	33.0	52.7
% from Vietnam	0.7	3.0	3.9	0.5	1.5	0.5
% from Greece	5.1	2.9	1.3	2.6	0.4	1.4
% from Holland	0.4	0.1	0.9	0.5	3.0	6.5

Source: Illawarra Regional Information Service, *1986 Census of Population and Housing—Census Data: Small Area Comparison: Statistical Data Series No. 3*, Wollongong, NSW, 1989.

While there was no absolute distinction in terms of ethnicity between these industrial suburbs, a number of trends emerged. Macedonian migrants moved to Port Kembla and Cringila, though some spread to other nearby areas. English and Scottish migrants clearly preferred the Housing Commission suburb of Berkeley. Government policy may have encouraged this since up to 1961 migrants were unable to apply for Commission homes until they had been resident for twelve months, and Anglo-Celtic migrants were typically longer-term residents.[17] The Italians were well-represented in Port Kembla, Warrawong and Lake Heights, but were less inclined to settle in Cringila and Berkeley. The Greeks, Dutch and Germans preferred Primbee, and the Vietnamese, who began arriving in the late 1970s, Lake Heights. The northern suburb of Thirroul is included to highlight the different ethnic make-up of these old predominantly Anglo-Australian mining towns.

The ethnic make-up of these suburbs suggested clear preferences but no rigid separation into ethnic 'enclaves'. The southern portion of the Illawarra, south of Wollongong towards Lake Illawarra and Shellharbour, was an area of high European migrant concentration. In contrast, to the north of the Wollongong, following the coastal train line that passes through old mining communities, the number of English and Scottish migrants was significantly higher. In Thirroul, for example, although 14.2 per cent of the population had been born overseas, more than half of those were from England and Scotland.

Commercial Decline

Until the 1950s the structure of retail and consumption in the commercial sector encouraged local shopping. As Ces Catteral recalled, 'very rarely would they [his parents] go to Wollongong for shopping unless they couldn't get something at Port Kembla'. Regular delivery rounds from local tradespeople enabled custom to flow through to local storekeepers. The cost of a bus fare to Wollongong made shopping there somewhat more expensive, and few working-class people had access to cars before the early 1950s. These structural features were underpinned by a strong sense of local loyalty. Len Ewart, who grew up in Darcy Road and later worked at AI&S, recalled that he did all his shopping in Port Kembla: 'Port Kembla first, Port Kembla second, and if there was anything left it didn't matter'. This was typical of the depth of commitment not just to local stores, but also to the idea that Port Kembla could provide for all daily needs.

Industrial growth initially encouraged commercial expansion at Port Kembla. In 1949 for example there were twenty-seven commercial premises in Wentworth Street that sold foodstuffs (grocers, butchers, bakers), and by 1966 the number had increased to thirty-three. In 1949 there were sixteen 'commercial' premises (banks, offices), and this increased to thirty-four by 1966. Industrial premises had likewise increased from five to twelve during the same period. The only significant decline occurred in the clothing and drapery retail trade, where shop numbers had dropped from nineteen to twelve.[18] Residents recall up to a dozen buses lined up in Wentworth Street in the 1950s and 1960s as many workers, especially migrant workers, did not have vehicles.[19]

Despite commercial growth, there were ominous signs. There were twenty-six vacant shops in Wentworth Street by 1966, as compared to six in 1956 and only one in 1949.[20] Transport changes and major supermarket development from the early 1960s challenged the centrality of established main-street shopping. Big W opened at Warrawong in the early 1960s, Westfield Shopping Town opened at Figtree in the 1970s, and Shellharbour Square in 1984. By the 1980s Wentworth Street was but a small player in the region's commercial sector. Warrawong in particular had space for shopping centre development and for large car parks. W. C. Wentworth III had aggressively developed the site from the late 1930s. The bypassing of Port Kembla through the construction of the inner harbour in 1960 funnelled trade towards Warrawong just as it turned Port Kembla into a detour on any journey south or north.

From the late 1960s the commercial decline of Port Kembla attracted the attention of regional planning bodies and the Council. Residents were fully aware of the process and some of its causes. M. Finch noted in 1976, 'the town is comparatively dead to what it used to be—ever since Warrawong shopping centre was built. It saddens you to think what Port used to be. The shops used to be busy, but now they're deserted. That's progress.'[21] Suggestions for revival included zoning Wentworth Street an 'ethnic' restaurant and nightclub area, and the encouragement of entertainment venues.[22] Throughout the 1980s and 1990s various local groups co-ordinated festivals and parades to help revive the main street and re-create the lost sense of social interaction, while Wollongong Council attempted street beautification. However, the economic forces associated with changes in supermarket retailing were powerful ones. These forces, together with the legacy of urban planning decisions that approved new urban space without adequately considering the effects on established areas like Wentworth Street, were impossible to reverse at least in the short to medium term.

Paul Wand, who left ER&S employment in 1985, and returned as managing director of Southern Copper in 1993, found that the 'shopping strip had become semi-derelict'. In 1992 fire destroyed the Whiteway Theatre in Wentworth Street, once a centre of local social life but largely disused from the mid-1980s. By 1998 the Wollongong Council's cultural plan noted the significance of the loss of main-street life for Port Kembla, Cringila and Berkeley residents, all swamped by the Warrawong and Wollongong behemoth. Unplanned urban growth undermined existing commercial and social infrastructure in main streets like Wentworth Street. This was not unique to Port Kembla or the Illawarra region, but common throughout Australia, and a process that is still occurring in many older mining and industrial towns like Newcastle, Broken Hill, Port Pirie and Rockhampton. Ironically, W. C. Wentworth III's work in developing Warrawong from the 1930s ultimately destroyed the very main-street shopping area that bore his family name.

Social Problems of the 1990s and Beyond

In the 1990s a rise in drug-related problems and visible street prostitution accompanied commercial decline of the main street. While Port Kembla had illegal and illicit betting houses and brothels from at least the 1920s, the decrimininalisation of prostitution in 1995 bought sex workers onto Wentworth Street. Conflicts between the sex industry on the one hand, and main-street commercial interests together with residents on the other, have continued throughout this period. For older Anglo-Australian and migrant residents, the rise of visible prostitution in Wentworth Street is a powerful symbol of local decline, especially when contrasted to the memories of the 1960s and earlier. Wentworth Street had been a vital forum for local social life, a shared space that facilitated local attachment and after 1945 an aid to migrant negotiation of life in Australia. Those who have not lived through or learned about these earlier experiences find it difficult to appreciate the full impact of a main street that has derelict shops, visible sex workers and a major drug problem.

The regulation and control of the sex industry, along with pollution, were the most significant political and social issues of the area. One community leader involved in both issues indicated that 'cleaning up the main street' would 'get the town going again', and much effort has been directed towards achieving a compromise between these disparate interests. One response initiated by the local police command and supported by Wollongong City Council evoked powers under the *Local Government Act* of 1993 to deal with 'anti-social behaviour'. The 'no loitering' trial—which involved police dispersing even small groups of people in targeted areas—created some protest as youth groups, community workers and other activists suggested that such laws would have an adverse impact on young people, the poor and indigenous people. In one case that has entered local folklore, a young man was allegedly fined for eating a pie on a park bench in Wentworth Street! Demonstrators subsequently held a 'mass loiter' in Wentworth Street in May 1999.[23]

The Council's evaluation of the policy concluded that it would have little long-term positive effect on anti-social behaviour. The Council turned to a consultative process that involved meetings with residents, sex workers, local traders, and police. The Port Kembla Safety Program was developed in September 2000 in an effort to respond to local concerns over prostitution, drug use, and harassment of both sex workers and residents in Wentworth Street.[24]

Pollution and the Revival of Localist Politics

The most important area where the supremacy of industrial society has come under increasing criticism is pollution. The skills and traditions of localism were mobilised to mount a number of withering attacks on industrial production. The lineage of this growing disquiet at Port Kembla can be traced back to the late 1930s. This long history, together with the severity of the industrial pollution, explains the depth of this political reaction. Such criticisms reached a peak in the late 1950s when a major public health study surveyed the health effects of pollution at Port Kembla. Another wave of local criticism from the 1980s focused on lead exposure and later other toxins. The two main targets of criticism were ER&S/Southern Copper/PKC and AI&S/BHP.

In the late 1930s concern about pollution was led by pioneering but lone voices like the FIA and the Port Kembla Ratepayers' Association. By the late 1940s these voices were joined by the local branch of the Labor Party, and aldermen on the newly established Greater City of Wollongong Council.[25] As early as 1945 residents signalled their concerns over pollution: 'Fumes and dust from the E.R. and S. chimney stack at Port Kembla were the subject of a deputation of residents from the town to last Monday's meeting of the Central Illawarra Shire Council'.[26]

One common area of concern was the effect of pollution on gardens. As a means to supplement household economies the garden was an important place. In times of economic hardship home-grown produce could generate income as well as provide food, a role that gardens at Port Kembla and elsewhere had performed in the 1920s and the Great Depression. Given the growing ideology of suburban life, and the central place of the home within it, damage to vegetable gardens also represented a threat to the sanctuary of the home, and the ability of everyone to maintain and improve their own domestic space.

This is exemplified in the *Illawarra Mercury*'s front-page coverage on 11 February 1959. The article headed 'Port Kembla folk "have had it"' included comments from several local residents about the depressing effect of fumes on their gardens:

Mrs. Brunning told me she had taken great pride in her garden and won several prizes in flower shows. An elderly woman, Mrs Brunning is an energetic member of the Australian Red Cross. She had hoped to make flowers available to the branch this year, as she had always done. 'But I'm afraid I've nothing left to give them this year,' she said.

A large photo showed 'fume damage to rhubarb in Mrs Brunning's garden at Port Kembla'.[27] The Brunnings were long-time residents of Port Kembla, and such people, together with the established political voices like the local branch of the Labor Party and the waterside workers, led the campaigns against pollution.

This particular period of intense local action and media coverage of pollution culminated in a major study of the effects of exposure to pollutants on local residents. Dr Alan Bell, from the New South Wales Division of Occupational Health, directed a two-year survey starting in 1959 that examined 947 Port Kembla residents. Bell found an unusually high level of mild chronic bronchitis among the sample group of 471, compared to a control sample from Corrimal, north of Wollongong. He attributed this to the presence of sulphur dioxide gas at Port Kembla, particularly in the summer months when prevailing winds blew the smoke plume across south-western Port Kembla towards Warrawong. Beyond these documented health effects, it is also significant that many residents believed they were affected although they showed no symptoms according to medical tests available at the time. Many also noted that they changed their social arrangements because of the presence, or the possible arrival, of pollution. The study indicates that the pollution had a wide-ranging impact on the lives of residents in terms of health, perceptions of their health, and social activities.[28] In response to this study and the passage of the New South Wales *Clean Air Act* in 1961, ER&S completed a new 200-metre stack by 1965 in the belief that the action of winds would disperse the pollutants and provide relief for local residents.

The focus of Bell's study was ER&S; there were also criticisms of the more politically and economically powerful AI&S. In 1960 state Member for Wollongong–Kembla, R. F. X. Connor, focused parliament's attention on the actions of AI&S. In an adjournment debate in the legislative assembly Connor pointed out that in 'the last four or five weeks this particular firm ... has seen fit to introduce a new industrial process in its open hearth furnaces ... as a result the smoke coming from the open hearth furnaces causes alarm and resentment and criticism, and a real danger to life and property'.[29] Connor's view is significant since it represents a dissident yet growing perception of industrial smoke as deleterious rather than a symbol of modernity and prosperity. In the following month Connor asked the chief secretary, C. A. Kelly, whether new experimental processes being trialled at Number 2 blast furnace at AI&S 'have caused acute distress to residents of the Wollongong–Kembla and Illawarra electorates by way of industrial pollution?'[30]

Kelly responded in vague terms, but the political controversy surrounding industrial pollution at the Port Kembla and Newcastle industrial centres was crucial in the passage of the *Clean Air Act*. This was the first major legislative response to post-war pollution control. Developments at Port Kembla were local expressions of changes that were occurring as residents responded to issues that manifested literally in their own backyards.

Beginning in the 1980s exhaustive studies by government organisations and university researchers probed the links between industry and health. Regarding lead, evidence that emerged in the 1980s and early 1990s established a relationship between exposure and adverse physiological and neurological outcomes. Exposure of children can adversely affect growth and development. In 1989 the Wollongong Lead Study sampled 83 Port Kembla children and found their average blood lead levels were 16.9 micrograms per decilitre. This figure was well above the national goal, subsequently defined in 1993 by the National Health and Medical Research Council, of 10 micrograms per decilitre. A 1994 study found that children living in Port Kembla were more likely to have respiratory problems like wheezing and chest coughs, while they appeared less susceptible to asthma.[31]

The list of epidemiological studies that focused on pollution and adverse health effects lengthened in the 1990s with concerns such as cancer and leukaemia joining blood lead levels and respiratory effects of airborne pollution. One innovative study used levels of school absenteeism as an indicator for general health, and found unusually high rates around industrial areas in the Illawarra. Because there were no clear reasons why the rates might vary across different suburbs, exposure to industrial pollution was postulated as one significant variant. High-school absenteeism in Corrimal, Port Kembla and Warrawong also correlated, to some extent, with high usage of pharmacy cough medicines and high rates of doctor visits.[32]

In 1996 concerns of a leukaemia cluster around the steel works emerged. Initial research suggested a link between benzene emissions from the coke ovens and the presence of abnormally high rates of leukaemia among young people in the Warrawong area.[33] A 1997 study by the Illawarra Public Health Unit concluded that benzene emissions in the area were lower than the UK standard of five parts per billion, and lower than the central business district in Sydney. A subsequent study published in the *Medical Journal of Australia* concluded that 'recent ambient air benzene concentrations in the Warrawong area represent a negligible leukaemia risk, and the estimated past benzene concentrations are too low to explain the large excess of leukaemia cases that occurred in 1989–1996'. The absence of monitoring data from before 1996, however, makes it impossible to exclude the role of 'intermittent and high transient benzene exposures'.[34] It is difficult to explain why benzene levels had not been monitored before 1996, given that the toxin had been identified as a possible carcinogen or cancer-causing agent from at least the 1970s.

As with all of these issues, independent agencies such as the Environment Protection Agency and the Illawarra Public Health Unit were perceived by sceptical resident and environmental groups to be close to the industry and government players. This undermined public confidence in the findings of this and other studies. In 2001 the Environment Protection Agency launched a major investigation into the nucleotide emissions, believed to have come from the BHP sinter plant. These emissions produced low-level radiation, and the effects on workers and nearby communities are presently under investigation.[35] The sinter plant was also a focus of concern because of ongoing emissions of dioxin. In 2001 BHP announced a major environmental upgrade of the sinter plant which it claimed would significantly reduce both dust and dioxin emissions.

Clearly the full extent of the environmental legacy of industrial society is being revealed in a gradual fashion. With further epidemiological research and improved monitoring equipment, often driven by community action, the true extent and effects of the historical burden of many years of unregulated emissions and dumping will be with Port Kembla and the region for many years to come. Regardless of the outcome of debates over the actual effects of industrial pollution on human health and quality of life, the barrage of publicity from the 1990s surrounding this issue has underlined it as a major disadvantage to industrial production. Moreover, particular protest groups, and perhaps even large numbers of local residents themselves, at least believed that they suffered at the hands of industry. Rather than signs of progress and wealth, chimneys and smoke plumes were symbols of environmental degradation, and threats to human health and quality of life.

Such developments represented fundamental challenges to the hegemony of industrial society. However, the extent to which this hegemony dissolved remains an open question. If the trajectory of economic, political and cultural changes outlined in this book continues, then perhaps industrial society is in inexorable decline. Certainly industry, once the motive force for the development of the locality of Port Kembla, has now more or less abandoned the locality. Industrial society rhetoric and its regional labour market entailed few interlocking relationships between industry and the locality. Furthermore, in the 1980s national politics became more heavily involved in the formal economy through the steel industry plan and political responses to retrenchment. Global influences diversified, and were amplified by policies such as the devaluation of the Australian dollar in 1983 that opened the Australian economy to the vicissitudes of the international money market. On the issue of pollution, however, one significant point stands out which suggests that the fundamental tenets of industrial society remain strong.

If industrial society had lost local support, it still maintained support from the state Labor government. Despite the development of environmentalism among lobby groups and even sections of the Council, state government and bureaucracy, the patterns of political and economic power had not altered significantly. In a controversial move the state Labor government under Premier Bob Carr passed legislation that effectively quashed a legal challenge to Southern Copper's development consent while it was going through the Land and Environment Court. After its closure in 1995, Southern Copper (formerly ER&S) had endeavoured to secure planning approval for its upgraded operations so as to make the plant more appealing to any potential buyer. The court challenge—in the name of Port Kembla resident Helen Hamilton, with backing from a group of local residents—had questioned the legitimacy of the development consent given to Southern Copper. These residents, who would form the core of IRATE in 1997, argued the extent of community consultation had been grossly deficient. The *Port Kembla Development (Special Provisions) Act 1997* simply asserted that the 'development consent is validated', that it was granted 'in accordance with the Principal Act and otherwise in accordance with law' and was deemed to be 'a valid development consent'.[36]

By 2001 the PKC smelter operated in a fundamentally different public environment from the one that prevailed in the first half of the century. There was close media scrutiny as well as determined and well-organised opposition by residents. Yet the bedrock of values that had supported industrial society still held sway in state parliament. *The Port Kembla (Special Provisions) Development Act* of 1997 was as powerful a symbol of state support as the original *Port Kembla Harbour Act* of 1898 that first initiated the industrial development of the port. Separated by a century, the historical contexts for these two Acts of parliament were fundamentally different, but the successful passage of both reflects the longevity and power of industrial society.

Conclusion

In 2001 PORT KEMBLA is a discrete suburban area whose houses and small commercial centre nestle alongside major industrial sites. As a child of industrial society, the town now sees its erstwhile parents focus on other places. Broken Hill Proprietary Company Ltd (BHP) diversified into oil and gas from the 1960s, and in 2001 merged with British company Billiton to become one of the world's largest resource companies. The Port Kembla steel works will be sold in mid-2002 as part of a public float of BHP Steel. In 1996 a Japanese consortium, known as PKC, purchased Port Kembla's oldest industry. This new company faces a difficult future operating close to a residential environment that has few links with the industry. MM, now the oldest continuously operating Port Kembla industry, has maintained its production levels, while the harbour has diversified to include a grain terminal. But the effects of the harbour trade and the other remaining industries radiate throughout the region, to a large degree leapfrogging Port Kembla.

The twentieth-century transformation of Port Kembla was wide-ranging and revolutionary. Within one generation the Illawarra's rural economy had been swept aside by a new industrial economy. In the formative period the effects of industrial society focused on Port Kembla itself. In the 1920s a town-centred labour market developed to meet the needs of local companies. New companies set up close to the boundaries of the town, creating a series of interlocking relationships between residents and industry. Such relationships lie at heart of the description 'industrial town'. Port Kembla people had significant economic, political and emotional investments in local industry. The health of industry, its successful operation and management, were central to the fate of the locality, while the amount of wages paid and the working conditions experienced in the formal economy shaped life opportunities for many men and a few women.

Industrial development created a commercial centre that became an important focus for local society, demonstrated by loyalty to local stores and the establishment of town-based organisations and services in the 1910s and 1920s. These conditions of Port Kembla's development, along with the social relations and cultural practices of town life, provided the town's inhabitants with a locally centred 'structure of feeling'.

The advent of industrial society and its initial focus on the one discrete locality created distinctive political and social effects. Two major responses, localist and class politics, emerged with characteristic political forms, and vied for dominance throughout the formative period. Localist politics was sustained by an ideology of local development and progress that divided the political and social world in terms of locals versus outsiders. In Port Kembla's case, local political groups like the Progress Association understood their principal rivals to be political and economic interests in Wollongong, the Wentworth trustees, and the farmers who dominated the Central Illawarra Council. This interpretation of regional politics from the Port Kembla perspective was not illusory, for these groups had their own political and economic agendas that often differed from the dominant interests of Port Kembla, but the focus on outsiders obscured Port Kembla-based conflict and division, creating an image of an apparently united town.

Opposed to the structures of locality and notions of local unity were divisions and conflicts based on class. Industrialisation brought to the town a three-tiered class structure—the middle class, petit-bourgeoisie, and working class—whose working conditions, wages and work patterns were worlds apart. These three classes formed the major divisions in local society that flowed through into local politics, and in some cases local culture. Class politics, expressed through class-based political organisations, revealed the class loyalties that localist politics and localism glossed over.

Working-class mobilisations at Port Kembla originated in the industrial workplaces of the town. From 1910 to 1920 industrial conflict between ER&S workers and management was an important forum for class politics, but class politics also tentatively embraced the town centre through the developing links between the working class and the petit-bourgeoisie, and the activities of such groups as the Political Labor League. In the late 1930s there was a more spectacular mobilisation of the working class through unions such as the WWF and the FIA. Class, then, represented a major challenge to the idea of a united town, but allegiances were often coexisting and contingent, ready to be activated in different historical contexts. Localist politics and class politics were not mutually exclusive political typologies, but rather interactive; they were related responses to industrialisation and its effects on local society.

Localist politics did not imply the absence of class. Indeed, it was a particular way of organising or managing class divisions. In specific circumstances local identity was mobilised to gloss over class conflict. However, the power of local identity was not simply the result of a cynical manipulation of local society by Port Kembla companies, or their local representatives, the middle class. ER&S in particular managed to tap into a pre-existing feeling that was the product of the conditions of Port Kembla's development and the experiences of town life, rather than the result of a company-constructed hegemony. After the late 1920s, localism was no longer politically valuable for Port Kembla industries, and AI&S and MM focused on the control and management of the workplace, paying little attention to the town itself.

Local allegiance was a powerful force among Port Kembla people, but the process of building local identity also involved a series of marginalisations and exclusions. Both class politics and localist politics were bounded by the idea of an active political subject as being male. Political organisations at Port Kembla were male-dominated, and their meeting places were usually male spaces such as hotels. Political conversation was often carried out in the industrial workplace, in hotels after work, or at the barber shop.

Furthermore, the vigorous social and political world created by locals was largely defined and organised by white townsmen. Koori people were on the edges of the town's civic and political life. Kooris did find employment at Port Kembla, but were clearly on the fringes of the labour market. Nonetheless, there is strong evidence that Kooris sought their own remedies to their particular problems. In the 1920s especially, Kooris embarked on a series of concerted campaigns to secure permanent occupation of many of their favoured sites in and around Port Kembla, though the loss of Hill 60 in 1942 was a major setback.

Port Kembla's transformation was wide-ranging; however, the degree to which the successful introduction of industrial society at Port Kembla was underpinned by the continuance of informal economic activities is striking. During the Great Depression, when the formal economy faltered, the informal economy saved many local families. These apparently 'preindustrial' patterns of household formation and survival were adapted and modified to merge with industrial society norms. While a focus on the historical experiences of men in the formal economy identifies rapid economic change, the persistence and ongoing importance of the informal economy suggests important adaptations from the region's older rural economy. As wage labour became increasingly dominant for men, women and children nonetheless continued to play crucial roles in the informal economy. This communicates a sense of historical change more attuned to the experiences of women and children.

There was also a gendered dimension to local attachment. Women, as both consumers and workers in the town's stores, played an important role in the creation of the cross-class site for local interaction in the main street.

A main street characterised by friendly social encounters is central to women's recollections. As the male-dominated formal economy region-alised and more men commuted both away from, and into, the town, women continued their involvement in local activities and sites. The formal economy also exposed men to the primary site of class conflict, the indus-trial workplace, while women were exposed to the key symbol of local cross-class identity, the main street.

After World War II, when industrial society reigned supreme, the industrial economy assumed monumental proportions as the steel works consumed more and more land, spreading out from Port Kembla towards Wollongong. This growth symbolically bridged the gap between these sep-arate urban areas, particularly once the old physical and psychological boundary between the two towns, Tom Thumb's Lagoon, was destroyed. Ultimately, industrialisation facilitated the regionalisation of the Illawarra. The expanding industrial economy soon overflowed the town-centred labour market of the 1920s, to become part of a larger regional labour market from the 1930s. The scale of the developments was such that their meanings and effects could no longer be contained within the one locality.

During the supremacy of industrial society from 1945 to 1970, the leading figures were regional labour leaders, Melbourne-based businessmen, and Canberra- or Sydney-based politicians. The split between the industrial struggles at AI&S and the locality of Port Kembla is a clear example of the removal of class politics from its local spatial context. At Port Kembla itself, fewer residents were engaged in their locality. With increasing mobility, lives were acted out on a regional stage, and commuting to work beyond one's place of residence became commonplace. The term Steel Town became increasingly irrelevant as the links between locality and industry unravelled and industrial society rhetoric denied reference to place altogether by emphasising technology, progress and growth. This process found its ulti-mate expression in the 1980s and 1990s when groups of Port Kembla resi-dents organised and protested against the operation of the town's oldest industry because of pollution concerns. By this time, Port Kembla was not an industrial town, but a residential area situated close to industry.

The informal economy continued into the post-war period and emerged as central to the lives and survival strategies of migrant groups. The tra-ditions of rural and small-town Macedonia and Italy continued to flourish in and around Port Kembla. Not only were these activities supplementing wage labour, but they also represented the recreation of country of origin culture in a new land. They were strategies that people maintained because they were holding on to a part of themselves and their cultures.

For the generations of Anglo-Australian residents who grew up in the formative period, and for the generations of migrant residents who arrived after 1947, industrial society placed demands on their social and kin networks. The broad patterns of commodification and the dominance of wage labour continued, yet the informal economy and relations of reciprocity were significant factors in the successful emergence of a mature industrial community in the post-war period. For all its modern technology, its plumes of smoke and steam and rhetoric of progress and efficiency, industrial society at Port Kembla relied heavily on familial, apparently 'small town' relationships and values that aided people's negotiation of the new industrial world. Migrant workers who staffed the post-war blast furnaces producing the new material of the modern age gorged on home-made bread and cheese to get them through another shift. Port Kembla's transformation was wide-ranging, but elements of the old persisted and indeed facilitated people's survival and quality of life.

The arrival of large numbers of migrants into Port Kembla and the surrounding suburbs led to major changes in the local social structure. Port Kembla society had successfully absorbed waves of migrants before 1945, but they were mostly Anglo-Celtic. After 1945 migrants with different cultural backgrounds and fewer points of access to established local organisations and networks built their own networks around locality and shared ethnicity. This created further distinctions and divisions within the locality, although migrant and Anglo Port Kembla shared the same space and enjoyed some areas of positive interaction.

From 1970 the declining level of manufacturing employment was the local manifestation of a major economic shift throughout the industrialised world. However, industrial society remained politically and economically powerful—the clearest example was the state Labor government's 1997 intervention to secure the continued production of the local copper smelter.

Worldwide recession and deindustrialisation affected many Australian, British and US industrial centres. Port Kembla's reliance on the one employer amplified its impact, decreasing any time-scale to that which pertained to the fortunes of one company. The economic fate of Port Kembla and the Illawarra during the supremacy of industrial society hinged on one firm alone. As the common saying in the Illawarra noted, 'If BHP sneezed then Wollongong caught a cold'. The dominance of AI&S and other BHP subsidiaries, and the narrow base of the regional economy by the 1960s, significantly heightened the impact of the decline once manufacturing investment slowed and retrenchments began in the 1970s.

The Port Kembla story has parallels with other Australian industrial towns. Newcastle, Australia's other major twentieth-century Steel Town, shared many of the industrial and labour movement experiences. Yet Port Kembla was no carbon copy of Newcastle, although they shared many features. Coal was important to both regions, and the traditions of the

British coalfields took a firm hold on regional working-class and labour politics, but Port Kembla changed much more rapidly in the post-war era. Not only did BHP target Port Kembla for the bulk of its capital expenditure and expansion, but the resulting labour demand shaped a more ethnically diverse population. By 1991 some 26.6 per cent of the Wollongong Statistical District's population were born overseas, including 9.2 per cent in Italy, 8.8 per cent in Yugoslavia, and 4.8 per cent in Macedonia. In the Newcastle Statistical District only 12.7 per cent of the population were born overseas, 7.4 per cent in Yugoslavia, 6.3 per cent in Italy and 4.2 per cent in Germany. Across New South Wales Wollongong was distinguished by having the highest numbers of overseas-born of any non-metropolitan local government area.[1]

A historical and human-centred perspective reveals that past lives and experiences shape the present. The past has a longevity that belies simplistic notions of 'rise and fall', 'old and new'. The 'old' economy has not disappeared; it is relocating to developing countries with lower labour costs and fewer impediments to capital accumulation. The experience of workers and nearby communities that characterised the growth of industrial society at Port Kembla is being repeated with local modifications in Mexico, Korea, Taiwan and elsewhere. As Korean industrial workers fight for union recognition and wage justice against large cartel-like companies and a repressive state, there are echoes of Port Kembla's past struggles. The frontiers of industrialisation have moved, though the central tenets of industrial society, together with our reliance on its products, remain.

The way the past shapes the present, regardless of overly simplified descriptions of all-embracing historical change, has relevance not only to debates about the future directions of economic change, but also to questions of heritage and preservation. If the past persists and informs the present in important ways, then the act of destroying factories, viable main streets, and nearby communities denies a part of ourselves and our future. From 1999 onwards such debates proceeded in Newcastle as steel making closed and large sections of the BHP works were demolished, and they will more than likely arise in the near future with respect to Port Kembla. The legacies of industrial society remain all around us and constitute a vital part of who we are.[2]

Industrial society, its future uncertain, is still present at Port Kembla. The locality still has one of the highest rates of manufacturing employment in the Illawarra. Industrial society is also present through the collective memories it generated. The significant changes in economy, society and culture in the post-war era did not erase the older forms of local belonging and identity. In fact such cultural forms were still available locally; they resurfaced in the political sphere in the 1950s, and again from the 1980s, in the protests over pollution. Old formative period skills and traditions of lobbying and coalition-building were reactivated. While the material conditions that underpinned the development of a self-sufficient locality at Port Kembla were altered, homogenised and regionalised, the 'idea' of Port Kembla has maintained a remarkable continuity. New ways of rebuilding the locality may concentrate less on reconstituting its infrastructure or improving its services and more on amplifying its cultural and symbolic meanings.

While the future remains unclear, the past is revealed in powerful and moving memories of generations of Port Kembla residents who experienced industrialisation. Their memories form a major part of the arguments presented here. The most significant theme common to all respondents is the way the locality infused the stories and narratives of collective memory. Such specific memories, a small number of which have been sampled in this book, highlight the way memory was sharpened by the peculiar, often mundane features, of the local environment. Closer examination reveals those features to be central components of local political and social history.

The oral record is a powerful reminder that people's lives were located within, and to some extent framed by, neighbourhoods, villages, towns and cities in what sociologist Anthony Giddens has called the realm of people's day-to-day 'practical and discursive consciousness'.[3] Oral history serves as a reminder that social life is constituted within places, however defined, and that the spatial component of any history is crucial.

Such memories of town and neighbourhood life have a dissonant quality when compared to the dominance of Wollongong in regional history narratives. While the blue-green Illawarra escarpment now frames a continuous ribbon of urban settlement along the coast, historians need to be mindful that how we see this coast and how we understand its history was a product of a remarkable series of political battles fought out across the twentieth century. To assume that the current arrangement was the only possible one and to adopt its labels is to overlook the geographical and historical diversity of this remarkable region.

Notes

Abbreviations

AA	Australian Archives
BHPBA	Broken Hill Proprietary–Billiton Limited Archives
CPD	*Commonwealth Parliamentary Debates*
ML	Mitchell Library, Sydney
MUA	Melbourne University Archives
nd	no date
NSWPD	*New South Wales Parliamentary Debates*
NSWPP	*New South Wales Parliamentary Papers*
NSWSA	New South Wales State Archives
NSWSL	New South Wales State Library
NSWV&P	*New South Wales Votes and Proceedings*
WPL	Wollongong Public Library
WUA	Wollongong University Archives

Introduction

[1] The name 'Kembla' itself derives from the Koori name for Mount Kembla, 'Dgenbella' or 'Djemba': Organ, *Illawarra and South Coast Aborigines 1770–1850*, Appendix 2 and 3.

[2] Angus, 'Locality and Universalization', pp. 15–32.

[3] Duggan, *The Impact of Industrialization*, pp. 32–9.

[4] Lois Bryson and Faith Thompson, *An Australian Newtown: Life and Leadership in a Working Class Suburb*, Penguin, Blackburn, Vic. 1972; R. A. Wild, *Bradstow: A Study of Status, Class and Power in a Small Australian Town*, Angus & Robertson, Sydney, 1974; H. G. Oxley, *Mateship in Local Organisation* (revised edn), Queensland University Press, St Lucia, 1978; and Dempsey, *Smalltown*. See also Wild's review of community studies, R. A. Wild, *Australian Community Studies and Beyond*, Allen & Unwin, North Sydney, 1981.

[5] Alan Walker, *Coaltown: A Social Survey of Cessnock*, Melbourne University Press, Carlton, 1945; Roy Kriegler, *Working for the Company: Work and Control in a Whyalla Shipyard*, Oxford University Press, Melbourne, 1980; and Metcalfe, *For Freedom and Dignity*.

[6] For example, a special issue of *Environment and Planning A*, vol. 23, 1991 was devoted to the 'locality debate'. Anthony Giddens has been influential in bringing these ideas into the social sciences generally. See his *Central Problems* and *Consequences of Modernity*.

7 An introduction to this work is Gregory and Urry, *Social Relations and Spatial Structures*. For a reaction from an Australian geographer to this work see Katherine Gibson, 'Considerations on Northern Marxist Geography: A Review from the Antipodes', *Australian Geography*, vol. 22, no. 1, 1991.
8 Doreen Massey, 'New Directions in Space' in Gregory and Urry, *Social Relations and Spatial Structures*, p. 12.
9 *Labour History* special edition, 'Labour History and Local History', no. 78, May, 2000.
10 My definition of 'locality' is influenced by Giddens' discussion of 'locales': *Central Problems*, p. 206.
11 'Illawarra' is a Koori word possibly meaning 'water far off' or 'a pleasant place'. See Organ, *Illawarra and South Coast Aborigines*, Appendix 2 & 3.

1 Port Kembla: The Global and the Local

1 *Australasian Agricultural Reporter* cited in *South Coast Times*, 8 February 1905; and R. V. Cardew, 'Urban Settlement in the Illawarra, 1890–1940' in Robinson, *Urban Illawarra*, pp. 89–115.
2 According to the definition of the Illawarra region used in this study, this figure includes the Shire of Bulli and the Municipalities of Central Illawarra, Illawarra North and Wollongong.
3 Information on these men comes from George Lindsay's obituary, *South Coast Times*, 8 November 1940, and for Thomas Armstrong, Evidence of Thomas Armstrong, 'Royal Commission on Food Supply and Prices', pp. 250–2; and Frances McCaffery Papers. John Brown's obituary is in *Illawarra Mercury*, 23 August 1912. On dairy farms generally see Dairies Supervision Act Book, 1886–1929.
4 *Sydney Morning Herald*, 26 July 1902; *Sands' Sydney and New South Wales Country Directory*, 1900; and Mitchell and Sherington, *Growing Up in the Illawarra*, pp. 64–6.
5 For the estimate of the number of miners in the Illawarra see Winifred Mitchell, The Miners of Southern New South Wales, p. 131; and T. A. Coghlan, *Wealth and Progress of New South Wales, 1900–1901*, Government of New South Wales, Government Printer, 1902, p. 414.
6 *Illawarra Mercury*, 23 April 1904; and C. N. Connolly, *Biographical Register of the New South Wales Parliament, 1856–1901*, Australian National University Press, Canberra, 1983, p. 342.
7 Parliamentary Standing Committee on Public Works, Deep-water Harbour at Port Kembla, p. 13.
8 Evidence of Charles Brynes (manager of Mount Pleasant Coal Company), p. 71; of Henry McCabe (manager of Mount Keira mine), pp. 100–3; and of Walter Evans (shipping manager), p. 3 [sectional committee], in Parliamentary Standing Committee on Public Works, Deep-water Harbour at Port Kembla; and Firth, The Industrialization of Wollongong, pp. 160–4.
9 *Illawarra Mercury*, 2 March 1883; and Select Committee on the Mt Kembla Coal and Oil Company's Railway Bill.
10 Parliamentary Standing Committee on Public Works, Deep-water Harbour at Port Kembla, p. 4.
11 B. R. Mitchell, *British Historical Statistics*, Cambridge University Press, Cambridge, 1988, pp. 524, 281.
12 Eric Hobsbawm, *Industry and Empire*, Penguin, Harmondsworth, Mddx, 1968, pp. 134–54. On the continental origins of some 'British' innovations see W. O. Henderson, *The Industrialization of Europe, 1780–1914*, Harcourt, Brace & World, New York, 1969, pp. 14–6.
13 Eklund, 'Managers, Workers and Industrial Welfarism', pp. 137–57.
14 Cochrane, *Industrialization and Dependence*, p. 11.
15 *Australians: Historical Statistics*, Fairfax, Syme & Weldon, Sydney 1987, pp. 193, 196.
16 *Census of the Commonwealth of Australia*, 1911, vol. 2, p. 303; and 1947, vol. 1, pp. 49, 56. All census figures quoted in this work are exclusive of Aborigines until the 1971 Census.
17 D. Patricia Hampton, *Retail Co-operatives in the Lower Hunter Valley*, Newcastle Region Public Library, Newcastle, 1986; Duncan Bythell, 'Class, Community and Culture—the brass band in Newcastle', *Labour History*, no. 67, November, 1994, pp. 144–55; and Leanne Blackley,

'"You didn't admit you were hard up": Working-class Notions of Moral Community', in Markey, *Labour and Community*, pp. 124–45.

[18] Janet McCalman, 'Class and Respectability in a Working-class Suburb' in Penny Russell and Richard White (eds), *Memories and Dreams: Reflections on Twentieth-Century Australia*, Allen & Unwin, Sydney, 1997, pp. 21–39; and Leanne Blackley, '"You didn't admit you were hard up"' in Markey, *Labour and Community*, pp. 124–45.

[19] W. David Lewis, *Sloss Furnaces and the Rise of the Birmingham District*, University of Alabama, Tuscaloosa, 1994, p. 49.

[20] Carl Bridge (ed.), *From Munich to Vietnam: Australia's Relations with Britain and the United States since the 1930s*, Melbourne University Press, Carlton, 1991, p. 4.

[21] David Brody, *Steelworkers in America: The Nonunion Era*, Harper Torchbooks, New York, 1969.

[22] Nora Faires 'Immigrants and Industry: Peopling the "Iron City"' in Hays (ed.), *City at the Point*, pp. 10–2.

[23] Graham, *Singing the City*, p. 7.

[24] Bodnar, *Immigration and Industrialization*, pp. 5–21.

[25] *Historical Statistics of the United States: Colonial Times to 1970. Part 1*, US Bureau of the Census, Washington, DC, 1975, pp. 8, 117; and *Australians: Historical Statistics*, pp. 8–9.

[26] Couvares, *The Remaking of Pittsburgh*, p. 1.

[27] *Illawarra Mercury*, 7 October 1899. Some of the descriptions in this section are based on Parish Maps of Wollongong, County of Camden, Land District of Wollongong, 1897 and 1907, WPL.

[28] St Stephen's Port Kembla, 'History', [no author, 1953?]. Another version of this story has the Reverend having to undress and wade across the lagoon. See *South Coast Times*, 8 March 1940.

[29] Interview with William Bailey, WPL; and photograph entitled 'Tom Thumb's Lagoon, 1890?', WPL.

[30] Lady Jane Franklin's diary cited in Krimhilde Henderson and Terry Henderson, *Early Illawarra: People, Houses, Life: An Australia 1838 Monograph*, History Project Incorporated, Canberra, 1983, p. 121.

[31] *Illawarra Mercury*, 12 March 1901.

[32] *Illawarra Mercury*, 30 June 1900.

[33] General Manager's Report, March 1900, p. 24 and Directors' Report, September 1901, p. 8 in *Mount Lyell Mining and Railway Company Ltd, Half Yearly Reports and Balance Sheets*, 1900–01, VSL.

[34] Lady Franklin cited in Henderson and Henderson, *Early Illawarra*, p. 121. Swamp oak and *Casuarina glauca* are the same tree, commonly found near wet marshy areas such as Tom Thumb's Lagoon. See Kevin Mills, 'The Clearing of Illawarra Rainforests: Problems in Reconstructing Pre-European Vegetation Patterns', *Australian Geographer*, vol. 19, no. 2, November 1988, pp. 230–40.

[35] Evidence of Archibald Campbell (Member for Illawarra) and of G. S. Yuill (Agent for the Southern Coal Company), Parliamentary Standing Committee on Public Works, Deepwater Harbour at Port Kembla, pp. 34, 23, respectively.

[36] See entry on W. C. Wentworth in A. G. L. Shaw and C. M. H. Clark (eds), *Australian Dictionary of Biography, vol. 1, 1788–1850*, Melbourne University Press, Carlton, 1967, pp. 582–9; and Notes on the Wentworth Family, Frances McCaffery Papers.

[37] B. T. Dowd, *The First Five Land Grantees and their Grants in the Illawarra*, Illawarra Historical Society, Wollongong, 1960, pp. 9–11.

[38] Mills, 'The Clearing of Illawarra Rainforests', p. 235.

[39] *Illawarra Mercury*, 12 May 1900; and St Stephen's, 'History'.

[40] Evidence of George Sinclair in Parliamentary Standing Committee on Public Works, Deepwater Harbour at Port Kembla, p. 241.

[41] *Illawarra Mercury*, 1 October 1894; and *Port Kembla Public School Centenary, 1890–1990*, Port Kembla, 1990, p. 9. See Appendix 2 in that publication for the attendance figures.

[42] St Stephen's, 'History'; and St Stephen's, Service Register, 12 March 1899.

[43] *Illawarra Mercury*, 6 August 1901; and *South Coast Times*, 27 July 1901.

44 Reports of water shortages at Port Kembla are in *Illawarra Mercury*, 7 September 1901, and Public Works Department, Annual Report for 1901, p. 126.

45 Evidence of Walter Evans, Parliamentary Standing Committee on Public Works, Wollongong Water Supply, p. 46.

46 Parliamentary Standing Committee on Public Works, Wollongong Water Supply, pp. 46–7; *South Coast Times*, 20 April 1901; and *The Coke Industry of New South Wales*, Department of Mines, Mineral Resources no. 23, Sydney, 1916.

47 Frances McCaffery Papers, WUA and Archibald Campbell Papers, Illawarra Historical Society Collection. Both men wrote of regional Aboriginal customs, language and religion around the turn of the century. The information on Port Kembla Kooris around 1900 is from Interview with Albert Rieck; and Organ, *Illawarra and South Coast Aborigines*, pp. 336, 342.

48 Jack Cummins cited in the *Daily Express*, 28 June 1972; and Joan Wakeman in *Noogaleek*, p. 9.

49 T. G. Rieck, 'As I Look Back' (unpublished memoirs of T. G. Rieck, nd, c. 1942), p. 2. Copy in possession of the author.

50 Report for 1904, p. 5.

51 *Illawarra Mercury*, 18 September 1969.

52 Interview with Carol Speechley.

53 Terry O'Toole, 'Under The Thumb': Race, Class and the State in the Housing Problems of Urban Blacks in Wollongong, BA (Hons) thesis, University of Wollongong, 1982, p. 89.

54 Coghlan, *Wealth and Progress*, pp. 8–11.

55 Interview with Albert Rieck.

56 Cardew, 'Urban Settlement in the Illawarra', p. 89.

57 This was a remnant of the open woodland that surrounded the Berkeley forest: Mills, 'The Clearing of the Illawarra Rainforests', p. 237.

58 T. G. Rieck, 'As I Look Back', p. 7.

59 Mitchell, The Miners of Southern New South Wales, pp. 53–4.

60 Photograph of Port Kembla, 1921, Tourist Bureau, Loc M7629, ML; and Photograph of Port Kembla, Tourist Bureau, Loc M7630, ML.

61 *Illawarra Mercury*, 19 March 1907.

62 Minutes of Directors' Meetings, ER&S Records, 15 February, 9 March 1907; and Peter Richardson, 'The Origins and Development of the Collins House Group, 1915–1951', *Australian Economic History Review*, vol. xxvii, no. 1, March 1987, p. 16.

63 J. W. Long, *The Early History of Mount Morgan, Dawson and Callide Valleys*, [Mount Morgan], 1962, p. 2.

64 Director's Report, Metal Manufactures, 21 June 1917; and Directors' and Manager's Reports, Metal Manufactures, 8 July 1918.

65 *MM Gazette* (21st Anniversary Issue), Port Kembla, 1939, pp. 7–8.

66 Photograph of Port Kembla, Corner of Darcy and Military Roads, 1916, Small Pictures File, ML.

67 Interview with Edith Neaves; Interview with Colin Warrington, Wollongong TAFE; and Mitchell, The Miners of Southern New South Wales, p. 107.

68 Port Kembla Subdivision Plans, ML.

69 *Census of the Commonwealth of Australia*, 1921, vol. 2, p. 71.

70 APB, Report for 1915, Appendix B, p. 11; and *Illawarra Mercury*, 13 February 1925.

71 *Illawarra Mercury*, 22 January, 15 August 1920; and Port Kembla Subdivision Plans, ML.

72 Parliamentary Standing Committee on Public Works, Proposed Transmission Line, p. 905.

73 *South Coast Times*, 28 January 1916.

74 Report of Inspector Wenholm to Chief Inspector, 'Septic tanks at Port Kembla and Great Eastern Hotels, Port Kembla', 19 August 1919, Board of Health, Health Inspection Branch.

75 *Illawarra Mercury*, 25 June 1920. The advertisements are in *Illawarra Mercury*, 21 May and 27 April 1920.

76 *Census of the Commonwealth of Australia*, 1921, vol. 2, pp. 4–9; and 1947, vol. 1, pp. 26–7.

77 A report on the conditions of the road is in *Illawarra Mercury*, 6 April 1939.

78 J. L. Sullivan, A Report of a Survey of Air Pollution in New South Wales, MA thesis, University of New South Wales, 1953, p. 183.

79 See Hoskins, *The Hoskins Saga*, ch. 7; and Bede Nairn and Geoffrey Serle (eds), *The Australian Dictionary of Biography, volume 8: 1891–1939*, Melbourne University Press, Carlton, 1981, pp. 371–3.

80 Minutes of Directors' Meeting, 1 October 1920, Hoskins Iron & Steel Pty Ltd, Minute Book Number 1, 1920–25, Hoskins Family Papers.

81 Details of the merger are in Firth, The Industrialization of Wollongong, pp. 332–57.

82 'Secondary Industry in the Illawarra Region' [1955], *Illawarra Regional Development Committee, Correspondence and Reports, 1945–1962.*

83 Firth, The Industrialization of Wollongong, p. 178; and 'Secondary Industry in the Illawarra Region' [1955], *Illawarra Regional Development Committee, Correspondence and Reports, 1945–1962.*

84 Young, 'Problems in the Urban Environment'; and Sullivan, A Report of a Survey, p. 47.

85 Bell, *Air Pollution from Metallurgical Industries.*

86 Interview with Heather Eklund.

87 Young, 'Problems in the Urban Environment', p. 2.

88 *Atlas of New South Wales*, Central Mapping Authority, Department of Lands, New South Wales, 1987, p. 114.

89 Interview with William Bailey, WPL; and *Illawarra Mercury*, 3 March 1939.

90 Davis, *Our Memories Your History*, p. 13.

91 Young, 'Problems in the Urban Environment', p. 2 .

92 For the effects of prevailing winds on pollution levels at Port Kembla see Crisp et al., 'The use of wind direction', pp. 243–60.

93 Vance Palmer, 'Battle', *Meanjin Papers*, no. 8, 1942, pp. 5–6. The population figure is from *South Coast Times*, 12 January 1940.

94 Shire of Central Illawarra, *Housing Report*, 1943. In 1934 the Central Illawarra Municipality became a Shire with its boundaries unchanged.

95 *Sydney Morning Herald*, 25 November 1937, 17 January 1938; and *Daily Telegraph*, 31 October, 11 November 1937.

96 Shire Clerk's Report, 24 April 1939, Central Illawarra Council Minutes.

97 Information on Spooner is in John Ritchie (ed.), *Australian Dictionary of National Biography, 1891–1939*, Melbourne University Press, Carlton, 1990, pp. 37–8.

98 Health Inspector's Report, 27 February 1940, Central Illawarra Council Minutes.

99 Davis, *Our Memories Your History*, p. 97.

1 Health Inspector's Report, 27 February 1939, and 18 November 1940, Central Illawarra Council Minutes; and *Illawarra Mercury*, 4 August 1933.

2 Shire President's Report for 1939 (Douglas McAuliffe), Central Illawarra Council Minutes.

3 Bath Manager's Report, 30 January 1940, Central Illawarra Council Minutes.

4 *Wise's Commercial Directory*, 1940.

5 Calculated from the Joint Commonwealth–State Electoral Roll, State Electorate of Illawarra, 1940, ML.

6 Electrical Engineer's Special Report, 20 May 1940; and Health Inspector's Report, 27 March 1939, Central Illawarra Council Minutes.

7 Health Inspector's Report, 22 May 1939, Central Illawarra Council Minutes.

8 Interviews with Ethel Combes and Ces Catterel.

9 O'Toole, 'Under the Thumb', p. 87.

10 APB, Annual Report for 1935–36, p. 3.

11 Interview with William Bailey, WPL; and O'Toole, 'Under the Thumb', p. 91.

12 Report, 13 March 1939, Central Illawarra Council Minutes.

13 Letter from J. P. Caddy (assistant manager, MM) to Colin Fraser (chairman of the Board of Directors, MM), 6 September 1939, 'MM Pty Ltd', Broken Hill Associated Smelters Pty Ltd Records.

14 *South Coast Times*, 28 June 1940.
15 *Illawarra Mercury*, 26 July 1940.

2 The Formal Economy to 1940

1 Interviews with Edith Neaves (granddaughter of George Neaves) and Morgan Simon.
2 Examples of a national focus are R. W. Connell and T. H. Irving, *Class Structure in Australian History: Documents, Narrative and Argument*, Longman Cheshire, Melbourne, 1980, as well as the national class structure project initiated by E.O. Wright and the Australian study which came from it. Wright, *Classes*; and Baxter, *Class Analysis*.
3 Nigel Thrift and Peter Williams, 'The Geography of Class Formation' in Thrift and Williams, *Class and Space*, p. 13.
4 Nicos Poulantzas, *Classes in Contemporary Capitalism*, Verso Press, London, 1978, p. 224; and Ralph Miliband, *Marxism and Politics*, Oxford University Press, London, 1977, pp. 22ff.
5 Anthony Giddens, *The Class Structure of Advanced Societies*, Hutchinson, London, 1973.
6 Poulantzas, *Classes in Contemporary Capitalism*, pp. 285–9.
7 *Illawarra Mercury*, 1 May 1914.
8 Spooner, *The History and Development*, p. 3; and Public Works Department Annual Reports, 1900–40.
9 Spooner, *The History and Development*, pp. 3–5.
10 General Manager's Report, March 1900, p. 24, Directors' Report, September 1901, p. 8, *Mt Lyell Mining and Railway Company Ltd, Half Yearly Reports and Balance Sheets*, State Library of Victoria.
11 *Illawarra Mercury*, 16 May 1903; and *South Coast Times*, 29 August, 26 September 1903.
12 Peter Sheldon, 'Public vs Private Employers in New South Wales Public Works, 1890–1910', *Australian Economic History Review*, vol. xxxiii, no. 1, March 1993, pp. 49–72.
13 *Illawarra Mercury*, 8 May 1906; and Piggin and Lee, *The Mt Kembla Disaster*.
14 G. Blainey, *The Peaks of Lyell* (3rd edn), Melbourne University Press, Carlton, 1967, p. 152.
15 *Port Heritage*, no. 2, 1990, p. 2.
16 *Illawarra Mercury*, 27 October 1908.
17 *Illawarra Mercury*, 30 June 1900; Report of the Coroner's Inquest, *Illawarra Mercury*, 8 September 1908; and *Illawarra Mercury*, 26 February 1909.
18 Public Works Department Annual Report for the year ended 30 June 1907, p. 58; *Illawarra Mercury*, 2 April 1907; J. P. O'Malley, *The Old Dapto Smelting Works* (2nd edn), Illawarra Historical Society, Wollongong, 1968; and G. Blainey, *The Rush That Never Ended: A History of Australian Mining*, Melbourne University Press, Carlton, 1963, pp. 277–8.
19 The *South Coast Times*, 5 September 1903, has that paper's opinion of the sulphuric acid plant, while another report from 4 March 1905 mentions German competition.
20 *Illawarra Mercury*, 8, 22 March 1907.
21 *Illawarra Mercury*, 1 March 1907; and O'Malley, *The Old Dapto Smelting Works*, p. 6.
22 *Australian Mining Standard*, 11 November 1908, p. 524.
23 Minutes of Directors' Meetings, 14 May 1909, ER&S Records. A report on the Mt Lyell contract is in Minutes of Directors' Meetings, 5 September 1910, ER&S Records, and *Australian Mining Standard*, 24 August 1910, pp. 195–6. The profit figure for 1912 is from Directors' Sixth Annual Report for the Year ended 31 October 1912, ER&S Records.
24 *Illawarra Mercury*, 9 February, 26 March 1909.
25 Calculated from the State Electoral Roll for Allowrie (Wollongong Division), 1912, ML.
26 Cochrane, *Industrialization and Dependence*, p. 79; and Colin Forster, 'Australian Manufacturing and the War of 1914–18', *Economic Record*, vol. 29, November 1953, pp. 211–30.
27 Rupert Lockwood, *War on the Waterfront: Menzies, Japan and the Pig Iron Dispute*, Hale & Iremonger, Sydney, 1987, pp. 49–54.
28 *South Coast Times*, 7 August 1914, editorial.
29 Minutes of Directors' Meetings, 31 August, 1915, ER&S Records.

30 Directors' Report for the Year ended 31 October 1915, ER&S Records.
31 Richardson, 'The Origins and Development of the Collins House Group, 1915–1951', pp. 16–17; and Cablegram from W. M. Hughes (Prime Minister [then in Paris]) to W. A. Watt (Acting Prime Minister), 12 April 1919, Prime Minister's Department—Metals, Brass and Copper Works, Port Kembla, Item no. 1919/2410, CRS A2, AA.
32 *MM Gazette* (Coming of Age Number), June 1939, pp. 14–16.
33 Forster, *Industrial Development in Australia, 1920–1930*, p. 266.
34 *Illawarra Mercury*, 30 June, 8 September 1908; and 26 February, 2 March 1909.
35 *Illawarra Mercury*, 11 June 1915; *South Coast Times*, 16 April 1915; and *Illawarra Mercury*, 3 March 1920.
36 Pan-Pacific Science Congress, Australia, 1923, *Guide Book to the Excursion to the Illawarra District*, Government Printer, Sydney, 1923, pp. 27–8.
37 Evidence of George Sloan (president, South Coast branch of the Waterside Workers' Association), 'Report together with Minutes of evidence relating to the proposed Duplication of the Coaling Plant at No. 1 jetty, Port Kembla', Parliamentary Standing Committee on Public Works, *NSWPP*, vol. 3, 1927, p. 3.
38 Interview with William Bailey, WPL.
39 Minutes of Directors' Meetings, 6 September 1917, ER&S Records.
40 *Illawarra Mercury*, 26 July 1912.
41 Evidence of James Perry (president, Port Kembla branch AWU), Parliamentary Standing Committee on Public Works, Railway from Moss Vale to Port Kembla, p. 17; and *Illawarra Mercury*, 9 July 1926.
42 *Illawarra Mercury*, 30 June 1903.
43 William Davies (MLA for Wollongong), *NSWPD*, 1929–30, vol. 121, p. 2893.
44 Calculated from the State Electoral Roll for Wollondilly, 1924, ML.
45 'Skill' is a problematic concept and recent research has shown it represents a measure of political power as much as an objective assessment of the abilities of a worker. For a discussion see Raelene Frances, *The Politics of Work: Gender and Labour in Victoria, 1880–1939*, Cambridge University Press, Cambridge, 1993, pp. 3–5.
46 E. A. White, 'Electrolytic Refining and Smelting at Port Kembla, New South Wales', *Australian Institute of Mining Engineers Transactions*, vol. 15, pt 1, 1911, p. 243.
47 NSW Board of Trade, Inquiry into the Living Wage—South Coast, 1920, pp. 130, 137.
48 The ER&S Award was published in the *Illawarra Mercury*, 9 January 1912.
49 Firth, The Industrialization of Wollongong, p. 18.
50 ER&S Staff as at 20 June 1928, Broken Hill Associated Smelters Pty Ltd Records.
51 Port Kembla report by E. A. White, Broken Hill Associated Smelters Pty Ltd Records.
52 Report and Statements of Account for the year ending 25 May 1927, Metal Manufactures Pty Ltd.
53 *Census of the Commonwealth of Australia*, 1921, vol. 1, p. 666.
54 *Census of the Commonwealth of Australia*, 1921, vol. 1, pp. 662–6.
55 NSW Board of Trade, Inquiry into the Living Wage, p. 314.
56 Minutes of Directors' Meetings, 17 January 1913 (company housing), 11 November 1918 (Employees' Co-operative Scheme), ER&S Records; *Illawarra Mercury*, 26 January 1918 (Recreation Club); and *Illawarra Mercury*, 2 January 1919 (Provident Fund).
57 Minutes of Directors' Meeting, 20 February, 27 March 1914, ER&S Records.
58 The term 'paid workforce' does not quite capture the situation of the petit-bourgeoisie, who are more accurately described as 'self-employed'.
59 State Electoral Roll, District of Wollongong, 1906, ML; and Letter from J. J. Middleton to Postmaster-General, 30 August 1908, Port Kembla Post Office Files.
60 *Illawarra Mercury*, 11 February 1908; and Letter from J. J. Middleton to Deputy Postmaster-General, 28 December 1908, Port Kembla Post Office Files.
61 *Illawarra Mercury*, 19 September 1913.
62 Interview with John Philpot; and obituary of J. T. Philpot, *South Coast Times*, 15 November 1940.

63 *Illawarra Mercury*, 2, 5, 16 and 19 May 1911.

64 Notes on McCaffery Family, Francis McCaffery Papers; and *South Coast Times*, 9 January 1914.

65 Edith Neaves, Handwritten Memoirs, 1991, copy in possession of the author.

66 State Electoral Roll, Electorate of Wollondilly, 1924, ML.

67 Interview with Sarah Drury.

68 AWU Minute Book, 15 April 1924; *New South Wales Industrial Gazette*, vol. xi, 30 November 1930, p. 817; and Reports and Statements of accounts for the year ended 31 March 1933, Metal Manufactures Pty Ltd.

69 Interview with Sarah Drury.

70 Interview with Edith Neaves.

71 Thomas Collins, Pupil Teacher Report, Memo to Chief Inspector [nd], Port Kembla School Files.

72 Letter from Joseph Robinson (mayor, Central Illawarra) to Under Secretary, Department of Public Instruction, 12 September 1908, Port Kembla School Files.

73 Letter from Port Kembla Progress Association to Under Secretary, Department of Public Instruction, 21 August 1913, Port Kembla School Files.

74 Memo from Inspector to Chief Inspector, 24 August 1918, Port Kembla School Files.

75 Department of Public Instruction to Mrs T. Bourke, 5 September 1919, Port Kembla School Files.

76 Desley Deacon, *Managing Gender: The State, the New Middle Class and Women Workers, 1830–1930*, Oxford University Press, Melbourne, 1990, especially Chapter 8.

77 *Census of the Commonwealth of Australia*, 1933, Census Bulletin no. 9, p. 9. These figures also probably underestimate women's participation in the formal economy.

78 *Illawarra Mercury*, 7 January 1927, editorial.

79 *South Coast Times*, 11 September 1925; and Annual Report for the Year ended 30 September 1925, *Mt Lyell Mining and Railway Company*, State Library of Victoria.

80 William Davies (MLA for Wollongong), *NSWPD*, 1928, vol. 113, p. 995.

81 G. Blainey, *The Peaks of Lyell* (3rd edn), Melbourne University Press, Carlton, 1967, p. 216.

82 J. W. Long, *The Early History of the Mt Morgan, Dawson and Callide Valleys*, [Mt Morgan?], 1962.

83 Eklund and Murray, *Copper Community*; Richardson, 'The Origins and Development of the Collins House Group, 1915–1951', pp. 3–29; and Blainey, *The Peaks of Lyell*, pp. 260–1.

84 Directors' Report to the Shareholders [early 1928], ER&S Records.

85 Letter from J. P. Caddy to Colin Fraser, 4 January 1932, MM Pty Ltd 1928–1932, Sir Colin Fraser Papers, Broken Hill Associated Smelters Collection.

86 Reports and Statement of Account for Year ended 31 March 1930, Metal Manufactures Pty Ltd.

87 Forster, *Industrial Development in Australia*, p. 226.

88 Richardson, *The Bitter Years*, p. 31; and William Davies (MLA for Wollongong), *NSWPD*, 1924, vol. 96, pp. 409–16.

89 *Illawarra Mercury*, 17 June 1927.

90 Minutes of Directors' Meetings, Hoskins Iron and Steel Company Ltd, 10 February 1927, BHPBA Ref. S24/1. The Hoskins family had made their fortune in the metalworking trade in Sydney in the late nineteenth century and moved into iron and steelmaking at Lithgow in 1908. See Nairn and Serle, *Australian Dictionary of Biography*, pp. 371–3; and Hoskins, *The Hoskins Saga*, Chapter 4.

91 Hoskins, *The Hoskins Saga*, pp. 93, 97.

92 Hughes, *The Australian Iron and Steel Industry*, p. 107.

93 *BHP Review*, June 1937.

94 Davis, *Our Memories Your History*, p. 86.

95 Hughes, *The Australian Iron and Steel Industry*, p. 107.

96 Cochrane, 'Australian Iron and Steel Company Port Kembla, 1935–1939', p. 63.

97 Forster, *Industrial Development in Australia*, p. 143.

98 Minutes of AI&S Directors' Meetings, 23 August 1929, BHPBA Ref. S24/1.

99 Murray and White, *The Ironworkers*, p. 70.

1 Organiser's Report Book, 1928, D169/15, South Coast Trades and Labour Council Records.

2 Interview with Ces Catterel.

3 *Illawarra Mercury*, 5 February 1932; and *South Coast Times*, 29 January 1932.

4 Home purchases and rents (Employees), D21/9/25, Metal Manufactures Records.

5 Richardson, *The Bitter Years*, p. 46; and Sheila Gray, *Newcastle in the Great Depression* (2nd edn), Newcastle History Monographs No. 11, Newcastle Region Public Library, Newcastle, 1989, pp. 11–16.

6 *Census of the Commonwealth of Australia*, 1933, vol. 1, pp. 137–42.

7 *New South Wales Industrial Gazette*, vol. xxxviii, April 1930, p. 893.

8 Letter from Colin Fraser to W. S. Robinson, 26 June 1930, ER&S—Miscellaneous; and Letter from E. A. White to Colin Fraser, 20 June 1928, Port Kembla Report 1928, Sir Colin Fraser Papers, Broken Hill Associated Smelters Pty Ltd Records.

9 General Manager's reports for the years ending 31 March 1931, 31 March 1934, Metal Manufactures Pty Ltd.

10 F. A. Bland, 'Unemployment Relief in Australia', *International Labour Review*, vol. xxx, July–December 1934, pp. 45–7.

11 Central Illawarra Council Minute Book, 5 May 1933.

12 *New South Wales Industrial Gazette*, vol. xlviii, December 1935, pp. 1601–2.

13 Statement showing the details of employees who were engaged on construction at the works of Australian Iron & Steel Ltd (labouring gang only) during the twelve months ended 31 May 1935, AI&S, Port Kembla Industrial Department—Correspondence File, Industrial Relations, BHPBA Ref. W2/131/3. The pence on both figures have been excluded. The basic wage during that time was £3 7s 6d, except for the last six weeks when it was raised to £3 8s 6d.

14 *South Coast Times*, 4 October 1940.

15 Preston, *If I Remember Rightly*, p. 38.

16 Card Index to Publicans' Licences.

17 Interview with Colin Warrington, Wollongong TAFE.

18 Health Inspector's Report, 11 October 1937, Central Illawarra Council Minute Book.

19 General Superintendent's Report for the year ended 1 November 1938, 1/100/2/9/3, Broken Hill Associated Smelters Pty Ltd Records; and 'Select Committee Upon the Employment of Youth in Industry–Progress Report, South Coast', *NSWPP*, vol. 4, 1940, Appendix 16.

20 The 1935 workforce figure and economic conditions generally at MM are based on Reports and Statements of Account for Year ended 31 March, 1931–35, Metal Manufactures Pty Ltd, WUA. The 1939 figure is from *Sydney Morning Herald*, 19 January and 17 December 1940.

21 The employment figures at the end of 1940 were Commonwealth Rolling Mills (586), and John Lysaght (685): 'Select Committee Upon the Employment of Youth in Industry—Progress Report, South Coast', *NSWPP*, vol. 4, 1940, Appendix 16; Department of Trade, *Australia's Iron and Steel Industry*; and *Lysaght Venture*, p. 38.

22 Calculated from the Joint Commonwealth–State Electoral Roll, State Electorate of Illawarra, 1930 and 1940, ML.

23 ER&S Port Kembla Letters Inwards September–December, 1937, Unprocessed ER&S Records, Group 5, Number 2, Broken Hill Associated Smelters Collection.

24 List of Open Hearth Second and Third Hands, 6 November 1939, Port Kembla Industrial Department—Correspondence Files, FIA, BHPBA Ref. W2/71/4.

25 Cochrane, 'Australian Iron and Steel, Port Kembla', pp. 62–8.

26 Cochrane, 'Australian Iron and Steel, Port Kembla', pp. 63, 74.

27 Port Kembla Industrial Department—General Correspondence File, BHPBA Ref. W2/78/1–5.

28 Chris Wright, 'Taylorism Reconsidered: The impact of scientific management', *Labour History*, no. 64, May 1993, pp. 34–49.

29 Memo from Production Superintendent to Cecil Harold Hoskins (general manager), 19 September 1940, Staff—19 February 1940 to 17 August 1940, BHPAW2/111/4 and generally Staff—12 March 1937 to 17 August 1940, BHPAW2/111/1–4. Insight into dual labour

markets and the labour process are in Richard C. Edwards, *Contested Terrain: The Transformation of Work in the Twentieth Century*, Basic Books, New York, 1979.

30 *Sydney Morning Herald*, 20 July, 22, 24 August 1934; and Sheridan, 'A Case Study in Complexity: The Origins of the 1945 Steel Strike in New South Wales', *Labour History*, no. 41, November 1981, p. 90.

31 Memo from V. R. Petney (industrial officer) to Cecil Harold Hoskins (general manager), 10 December 1938, Staff, 12 March 1937–22 December 1937, BHPBA Ref. W2/111/1.

32 Memo from V. R. Petney to Cecil Harold Hoskins, 10 December 1938, Staff, 22 February 1938–15 December 1938, BHPBA Ref. W2/111/2.

33 Australian Iron & Steel Limited, Port Kembla—Segregation of Labour, 19 December 1941, Port Kembla Industrial Department—Correspondence Files, BHPBA Ref. W2/49/3.

34 *Sydney Morning Herald*, 25 October 1940; and Keys and Wilson, *The Urban Illawarra*, p. 5.

3 The Informal Economy to 1940

1 *South Coast Times*, 19 May 1916.

2 Evidence of James Sloan (stevedore, Port Kembla) and Patrick Mulhall (silver mill assistant, ER&S), Parliamentary Standing Committee on Public Works, Northern Breakwater at Port Kembla, pp. 22–7.

3 State Electoral Roll for Illawarra, 1903, ML; Report of the Government Land Valuer (circa February 1915), Port Kembla School Files; and Wentworth Family Legal Papers.

4 M. Hutton, Reading the Rural Landscape in the Central Illawarra, MA thesis, University of Sydney, 1987, pp. 49–54, 97.

5 Arthur Cousins, *The Garden of New South Wales*, Producers' Co-operative Distributing Society, Sydney, 1948, p. 113. The importance of unpaid domestic labour to farming is covered by Marilyn Lake, *The Limits of Hope: Soldier Settlement in Victoria, 1915–1938*, Oxford University Press, Melbourne, 1987, pp. 177–9.

6 *Illawarra Mercury*, 11 February 1899; and *South Coast Times*, 7 February 1903.

7 Letter from Inspector Burton to Secretary, Postmaster-General's Office, 19 July 1907, Port Kembla Post Office Files.

8 *Illawarra Mercury*, 29 October 1904.

9 Interview with Joe Hill and Steve Wade, WPL.

10 *Census of the Commonwealth of Australia*, 1901, vol. 1, p. 480; and 1911, vol. 3, p. 2032.

11 *Illawarra Mercury*, 1 March 1912.

12 *Illawarra Mercury*, 8 March 1907.

13 *Illawarra Mercury*, 19 November 1912.

14 *Illawarra Mercury*, 29 November 1911; and *South Coast Times*, 12 March 1915.

15 Interview with William Bailey, WPL.

16 A report of the drowning of Modesta Cappalleto, an Italian fisherman, in this area is in *Illawarra Mercury*, 21 January 1927.

17 Davis, *Our Memories Your History*, p. 15; and Interview with William Bailey, WPL.

18 David Potts, 'A Positive Culture of Poverty Represented in Memories of the 1930s Depression', *Journal of Australian Studies*, no. 26, May 1990, pp. 3–14.

19 *Illawarra Mercury*, 3 February 1928.

20 *South Coast Times*, 3 February 1928.

21 Davis, *Our Memories Your History*, p. 27.

22 Those living in flats, boarding houses and camps were exceptions. Also, some residents of Military and Darcy Road did not have vegetable gardens because regular flooding in their street washed gardens away. Evidence of James Perry (labourer, ER&S), NSW Board of Trade, Inquiry into the Living Wage, pp. 155–60. The size of blocks of land at Port Kembla is covered in Evidence of W. L. Weber (real estate agent), NSW Board of Trade, Inquiry into the Living Wage, p. 56.

23 Interviews with Sarah Drury, Ethel Combes, and Heather Eklund.

[24] Robin Walker's article on life in the industrial suburbs of Sydney in 1913 makes no mention of activities such as growing vegetables, rabbiting or even fishing to supplement working-class incomes. See Robin Walker, 'Aspects of Working-Class Life in Industrial Suburbs, 1913', *Labour History*, no. 58, May 1990, pp. 36–47. The situation in Richmond, a suburb of Melbourne, is covered in McCalman, *Struggletown*, pp. 120–9.

[25] Peter Cochrane, 'The Wonthaggi Coal Strike, 1934', *Labour History*, no. 27, 1974, p. 14 ; and John Merritt, 'The Federated Ironworkers' Association in the Depression', *Labour History*, no. 21, 1971, p. 52.

[26] NSW Board of Trade, Inquiry into the Living Wage, pp. 70–6, 144. Lodgers are mentioned on pp. 110–16.

[27] Concluding address by Mr Croft (advocate for the AWU and other unions), NSW Board of Trade, Inquiry into the Living Wage, p. 372.

[28] As Lydia Morris (*The Workings of the Household*, Polity Press, Cambridge, 1990, pp. 17, 21) argues, the household cannot be treated as a 'consensually operating unit . . . In fact, both power within the household and material resources may be differentially distributed'.

[29] NSW Board of Trade, Inquiry into the Living Wage, p. 131.

[30] *Illawarra Mercury*, 5 August 1921.

[31] For example in March 1927 Council began charging campers on the reserve one shilling rental and 'caution[ed] them against timber cutting and such or prosecution will follow': Central Illawarra Council Minute Book, 9 March 1927.

[32] Central Illawarra Council Minute Book, 18 April 1928.

[33] The unimproved capital value of land in 'A Riding' in the Central Illawarra Shire (which included Port Kembla and its surrounding suburbs, Windang, Steeltown, Lake Heights, Berkeley and Warrawong) grew from £322 505 in 1934 to £852 030 in 1943: Shire of Central Illawarra, Information Sheet, July 1944, Central Illawarra Council Finance Committee Minute Book.

[34] *Illawarra Mercury*, 1 April 1921.

[35] *South Coast Times*, 22 February 1935.

[36] *South Coast Times*, 22 February 1935.

[37] See *Illawarra Mercury*, 15 May 1931; and *South Coast Times*, 21 April 1933.

[38] This feeling of crisis is best evoked by Andrew Moore in *The Secret Army and the Premier: Conservative Paramilitary Organisations in New South Wales, 1930–32*, New South Wales University Press, Kensington, NSW, 1989, ch. 3.

[39] NSW Board of Trade, Inquiry into Living Wage, p. 160.

[40] *Census of the Commonwealth of Australia*, 1921, vol. 2, p. 71; and 1933 Census Bulletin, no. 2, p. 4.

[41] *New South Wales Statistical Register*, 1916–17, p. 142; 1927–28, p. 21; and 1934, pp. 553–62.

[42] Stuart Macintyre alludes to this tension in his *The Oxford History of Australia, Volume 4: The Succeeding Age, 1901—1942*, Oxford University Press, Melbourne, 1986, p. 279.

[43] Preston, *If I Remember Rightly*, p. 38.

[44] Transcript of Interview with Len Ewart, Wollongong TAFE.

[45] *New South Wales Industrial Gazette*, 30 December 1940, vol. lix, no. 3, p. 415.

[46] Interviews with Iris Jenks and Sarah Drury.

4 The Structures of Locality, 1900 to 1920

[1] *Illawarra Mercury*, 10 October 1914; and Reports of the Quarterly Meeting and Business Papers of the Sydney District of the Manchester Unity Independent Order of Oddfellows, July 1915, ML.

[2] *South Coast Times*, 18 December 1914.

[3] Letter from Inspector Burton to Secretary, Postmaster-General's Office, 19 July 1907, Port Kembla Post Office Files.

[4] *South Coast Times*, 24 May 1902.

[5] St Stephens, 'History', St Stephen's Records.

6 Illawarra Catholic Sesquicentenary Committee, *The Catholic Church in the Illawarra, 150 Years, 1838–1988*, Wollongong, 1989, p. 96.
7 Letter from A. E. Tomkinson (Acting Inspector) to Postmaster-General's Office, 5 September 1907, Port Kembla Post Office Files.
8 *Illawarra Mercury*, 14 June, 8 November 1907; and *NSWPD*, 1907 vol. 27, pp. 758, 1518–19.
9 *Illawarra Mercury*, 7 February 1908.
10 *Illawarra Mercury*, 24 January 1908. A map of the area in 1908 shows the school and the 'workmen's camp site' to the north of the school: Fixed defences at Port Kembla, Department of Defence, Correspondence Files, 1913–17, CRS A2023, A116/2/4, AA.
11 Letter from P. N. Prott (Postmaster Wollongong) to Postmaster-General's Office, 4 April 1908, Port Kembla Post Office Files.
12 *South Coast Times*, 3 July 1909.
13 *South Coast Times* (Supplement), 24 September 1951; and Illawarra Catholic Sesquicentenary Committee, *The Catholic Church in the Illawarra*, pp. 96–8.
14 *Illawarra Mercury*, 8 January 1915.
15 *South Coast Times*, 5 March 1915.
16 *Illawarra Mercury*, 12 June 1914.
17 *Illawarra Mercury*, 18 July 1913.
18 Sergeant Noble's comments before the Special Licensing Court, *Illawarra Mercury*, 5 May 1911.
19 The Port Kembla Hotel was completed in early 1915, but the Licensing Court refused a liquor licence. It traded as a boarding house and restaurant until 1917.
20 *Illawarra Mercury*, 27 February 1914; and Interview with Bob Rees. The Rees family eventually moved to Port Kembla to live in 1918.
21 *Illawarra Mercury*, 24 September 1920.
22 Port Kembla Subdivision Plans, ML.
23 *Sands' Sydney and New South Wales Country Directory*, 1920, ML.
24 *Census of the Commonwealth of Australia*, 1921, vol. 2, p. 71.
25 Port Kembla Subdivision Plans, ML.
26 Report of the Government Land Valuer (circa February 1915), Port Kembla School Files; and Wentworth Family Legal Papers.
27 Alfred Edden (MLA for Kahibah), *NSWPD*, vol. 1, 1898, p. 360.
28 Report of the Government Land Valuer (circa February 1915), Port Kembla School Files.
29 *Illawarra Mercury*, 29 January 1909.
30 Council's concern over the costs of government subdivision is reported in *Illawarra Mercury*, 16, 23 March 1909. The comments by the Minister for Public Works come from *Illawarra Mercury*, 12 February 1907.
31 *Sydney Morning Herald*, 7 August 1908.
32 Criticism of land companies was evident in comments by the Minister for Public Instruction, A. C. Carmichael, in 'Transcripts of meeting between A. C. Carmichael and residents of Port Kembla in regard to the site for a new school', 17 February 1915, Port Kembla School Files. Details of the government subdivision were outlined by M. F. Morton (MLA for Allowrie), in *NSWPD*, vol. 65, 1916, pp. 2273–4; and Port Kembla Subdivision Plans, ML.
33 *Illawarra Mercury*, 8 March 1907.
34 NSW Board of Trade, Inquiry into Living Wage, p. 314.
35 A total of 97 electors gave their address as 'Port Kembla' and so could not be placed in streets.
36 Evidence of Ted Livermore (labourer), NSW Board of Trade, Inquiry into Living Wage, pp. 142–5.
37 Evidence of Eleanor Allan (music teacher), NSW Board of Trade, Inquiry into Living Wage, pp. 126–36.
38 *Census of the Commonwealth of Australia*, 1921, Census Bulletin Number 20, p. 6.
39 *Illawarra Mercury*, 29 March 1912.
40 *South Coast Times*, 12 March 1915.

[41] *Illawarra Mercury*, 14 May 1920.

[42] *Illawarra Mercury*, 22 January 1920.

[43] *Illawarra Mercury*, 26 March 1909.

[44] Annex to the Application for Establishment of a Public School, 15 February 1890, Port Kembla School Files.

[45] *Illawarra Mercury*, 14 February 1902.

[46] *Illawarra Mercury*, 12 July 1907.

[47] *Illawarra Mercury*, 1 March 1907.

[48] Kylie Tennant, *The Battlers*, Angus & Robertson, Sydney, 1971, p. 389.

[49] Interviews with Colin Warrington and Len Ewart, Wollongong TAFE; and Sid Hayes and Len Ewart, 'The Remarkable Story of D'arcy Road Sportspersons' in Davis, *Our Memories Your History*, pp. 38–54.

[50] Interview with Edith Neaves; and Interview with Colin Warrington, Wollongong TAFE.

[51] *Illawarra Mercury*, 12 February 1907, editorial.

[52] *Sydney Morning Herald*, 22 August 1910.

[53] Advertisement for the third subdivision of the Wentworth estate, *South Coast Times*, 26 February 1915; and Advertisement for the first subdivision of the Steeltown estate, *South Coast Times*, 31 August 1928.

[54] For example, John Lack, *A History of Footscray*, Hargreen, Melbourne, 1991, p. 108; and Nancy Cushing, 'Creating the "Coalopolis": Perceptions of Newcastle, 1797–1940', Paper given to the National Conference of the Australian Society for the Study of Labour History, Newcastle, 24 June 1993.

[55] *Illawarra Mercury*, 4 March 1921.

[56] *Illawarra Mercury*, 5 April 1923.

[57] *South Coast Times*, 28 November 1924.

[58] *Sydney Morning Herald*, 4 February 1927.

[59] *Illawarra Mercury*, 15 September 1911, 3 June 1927.

[60] *Illawarra Mercury*, 22 November 1929.

[61] *Illawarra Mercury*, 8 July 1899.

[62] *Illawarra Mercury*, 7 March, 26 September 1913.

[63] Comments by Mr Dunne, *Illawarra Mercury*, 15 March 1918.

[64] *South Coast Times*, 2 January 1931.

[65] Interview with Avis Bright, WUA.

[66] *Illawarra Mercury*, 8 November 1929.

[67] Interview with William Bailey, WPL.

[68] St Stephen's Marriage Registers, 21 April 1920 to 4 April 1931.

[69] Interviews with Bob Rees, Ces Catterel, and William Bailey, WPL.

[70] *Illawarra Mercury*, 26 March 1920.

[71] *South Coast Times*, 17 April 1924; and *Illawarra Mercury*, 20 January 1922.

[72] *South Coast Times*, 3 January 1918, 11 January 1919.

[73] *The Oddfellow* (journal of the Grand United Order of Oddfellows), 15 August 1926.

[74] *The Oddfellow*, 15 November 1926. On the interpretation of farewells and welcomes I have benefited from A. P. Cohen, *The Symbolic Construction of Community*, Routledge, London, 1989, pp. 50–8.

[75] Interview with Hazel Parkes and Lee Forrester, Wollongong TAFE.

[76] R. J. Sampson, 'Local Friendship Ties and Community Attachment in Mass Society: A multi dimensional model', *American Sociological Review*, vol. 53, no. 5, October 1988, pp. 766–74; and T. Stovall, 'Friends, Neighbours and Communists: Community Formation in Suburban Paris during the early Twentieth Century', *Journal of Social History*, vol. 22, no. 2, 1989, pp. 237–54.

[77] St Stephen's Marriage Registers, 21 April 1920 to 5 May 1927 and 2 July 1927 to 4 April 1931.

[78] Len Ewart, 'Port Kembla Rugby League Football Club: The Club's History' in Davis, *Our Memories Your History*, pp. 55–6.

[79] Reports of a police raid on a billiards room in Wentworth Street are in *Illawarra Mercury*, 11, 18 May 1923.

[80] *Australian Boy Scout Association—South Coast and Tablelands Area*, Annual Reports nos 7 and 8, 1931, 1932, ML.

[81] *Illawarra Mercury*, 13 February 1931.

[82] Interview with Edith Neaves.

5 Class, Locality and Politics, 1900 to 1930

[1] *Illawarra Mercury*, 18 May 1906, 29 June 1906.

[2] *Illawarra Mercury*, 8 October 1907.

[3] *Illawarra Mercury*, 21 August, 1 September 1908; and State Electoral Roll for Wollongong 1909, Port Kembla Polling Place, ML.

[4] *Illawarra Mercury*, 21 August 1919; and *South Coast Times*, 5 September 1919.

[5] Letters received by the Council from the Progress Association, Central Illawarra Council Minute Book, 14 October 1908–10 October 1917.

[6] *Illawarra Mercury*, 10 October 1908.

[7] Parliamentary Standing Committee on Public Works, Deep-water Harbour at Port Kembla, p. 14.

[8] Evidence of Henry McCabe (mayor of Wollongong), Parliamentary Standing Committee on Public Works, Deep-water Harbour at Port Kembla, p. 213.

[9] *Illawarra Mercury*, 26 November 1912.

[10] *Illawarra Mercury*, 13 May 1927.

[11] *South Coast Times*, 6 November 1925.

[12] G. H. Knibbs, *Local Government in Australia*, Commonwealth Bureau of Census and Statistics, Melbourne, 1919, pp. 232, 238. The *Women's Legal Status Act 1918* allowed women to stand for office. The *Local Government Act 1919* extended voting rights to all owners, occupiers and lessees, but this effectively excluded many women: Larcombe, *The Advancement of Local Government*, p. 395.

[13] *New South Wales Statistical Register*, 1901, p. 8.

[14] Central Illawarra Council Minute Book, 10 April 1907.

[15] Firth, The Industrialization of Wollongong, p. 8.

[16] *Illawarra Mercury*, 18 July 1913. A bail yard is part of a milking shed that holds the cow's head in place.

[17] *South Coast Times*, 17 May 1918.

[18] *Illawarra Mercury*, 13 September 1929.

[19] For example, Shipp's comments at the Progress Association meeting: *South Coast Times*, 8 February 1924.

[20] *Sydney Morning Herald*, 4 February 1927.

[21] *South Coast Times*, 24 June 1927.

[22] 'Transcripts of meeting between A. C. Carmichael and residents of Port Kembla in regard to the site for a new school', 17 February 1915, Port Kembla School Files.

[23] *South Coast Times*, 26 February 1915.

[24] *Illawarra Mercury*, 29 August 1908.

[25] Minutes of Directors' Meetings, ER&S Records, 21 April 1916.

[26] Memo from Senior Inspector to Chief Inspector, 23 October 1917, Port Kembla School Files.

[27] Letter from J. A. Henry (headmaster) to Department of the Education, 25 November 1918, Port Kembla School Files. More details on the company's role in local primary and technical education can be found in Geoffrey Sherington, 'Families and State Schooling in the Illawarra, 1840–1940' in M. R. Theobald and R. J. W. Selleck (eds), *Family, School and State in Australian History*, Allen & Unwin, Sydney, 1990, pp. 129–30.

[28] Minutes of Directors' Meetings, ER&S Records, 26 November 1912. An 'honorarium' is an honorary reward recognising professional services for which no price can be set.

[29] *South Coast Times*, 7 February 1919.

30 *South Coast Times*, 25 April 1919.

31 *Illawarra Mercury*, 2 January 1920.

32 *South Coast Times*, 7 March 1919.

33 'Transcripts of meeting between A. C. Carmichael and residents of Port Kembla in regard to the site for a new school', 17 February 1915, Port Kembla School Files.

34 *Illawarra Mercury*, 8 June 1915.

35 *South Coast Times*, 16 July 1915; and [Port] Kembla Rifle Range, 1915–18, Department of Defence—Correspondence Files, MP367/1/577/5/521, AA.

36 *Illawarra Mercury*, 30 December 1910.

37 *Illawarra Mercury*, 25 July 1911; and Minutes of Directors' Meetings, ER&S Records, 27 July 1911.

38 *Australian Mining Standard*, 27 July 1911.

39 *Australian Mining Standard*, 14 December 1911.

40 Managing Director's Fifth Annual Report for the year ending 31 October 1911, ER&S Records.

41 Minutes of Directors' Meetings, 7 November 1916, ER&S Records.

42 Minutes of Directors' Meetings, 17 January 1917, ER&S Records.

43 Interview with Colin Warrington, Wollongong TAFE.

44 *South Coast Times*, 15 August 1919.

45 *Illawarra Mercury*, 22 October 1926.

46 *Illawarra Mercury*, 7 March, 2 May 1913.

47 *Illawarra Mercury*, 27 June 1913.

48 *Illawarra Mercury*, 23 May 1913.

49 *Illawarra Mercury*, 11 July 1913.

50 *Illawarra Mercury*, 9 August 1912.

51 *Illawarra Mercury*, 23 September 1913.

52 *South Coast Times*, 14 August 1914.

53 AWU Minute Book, 12 December 1917.

54 Post-war inflation is outlined by Stuart Macintyre in *The Oxford History of Australia, Volume 4: The Succeeding Age*, p. 183.

55 *South Coast Times*, 3 January 1919.

56 *South Coast Times*, 7 March, 6 June, 7 May 1920.

57 *South Coast Times*, 25 April 1919; and generally AWU Minute Book, 1919–20.

58 AWU Minute Book, 12 February 1920; and Turner, *Industrial Labour and Politics*, pp. 199–200.

59 Connell and Irving, *Class Structure*, p. 205; and Turner *Industrial Labour and Politics*, p. 194.

60 *Illawarra Mercury*, 15 September 1911.

61 *Illawarra Mercury*, 23 January, 3 April 1914.

62 Connell and Irving, *Class Structure*, p. 198; and Love, *Labour and the Money Power*.

63 *South Coast Times*, 16 January 1920.

64 *Illawarra Mercury*, 2 January 1920; and *South Coast Times*, 16 January 1920.

65 *Illawarra Mercury*, 12 March 1920.

66 *Illawarra Mercury*, 13 February 1920; *South Coast Times*, 27 February 1920; and AWU Minute Book, 8, 19 February 1924.

67 Connell and Irving, *Class Structure*, pp. 191–2; and Peter Cochrane, 'The Wonthaggi Coal Strike, 1934', *Labour History*, no. 27, 1974, pp. 19–20.

68 *South Coast Times*, 23 December 1921.

69 Wollongong Benevolent Society, *Annual Reports for 1920 and 1921*, ML.

70 Jim Hagan, *A History of the A.C.T.U.*, Cheshire, Melbourne, pp. 18–25.

71 Preamble to the WIUA, NSW Trades and Labour Congress, cited in Robin Gollan, *Reformists and Revolutionaries: Communism and the Australian Labour Movement, 1920–1950*, Allen & Unwin, Sydney, 1975, p. 8.

72 Gollan, *Reformists and Revolutionaries*, p. 10.

73 Gollan, *Reformists and Revolutionaries*, pp. 8–10.

74 AWU Minute Book, 21 October 1918.

75 *Worker*, 24 July 1919.

76 AWU Minute Book, 22 September 1922.

77 AWU Minute Book, 9 January 1923.

78 *Worker*, 15 May 1919. The AWU's approach to the OBU is outlined by Verity Burgmann in *Revolutionary Industrial Unionism: The Industrial Workers of the World in Australia*, Cambridge University Press, Melbourne, 1995, pp. 258–61.

79 Gollan, *Reformists and Revolutionaries*, p. 12. The political suppression of the IWW should not be overlooked as a factor that also disempowered the radical interpretation of the OBU: Frank Cain, 'The Industrial Workers of the World: Aspects of its Suppression in Australia, 1916–1919', *Labour History*, no. 42, May 1982, pp. 54–62.

80 AWU Minute Book, 2 January 1922.

81 *Illawarra Mercury*, 13 March 1925.

82 *Illawarra Mercury*, 4 June 1920.

83 *South Coast Times*, 14 January 1921.

84 *Illawarra Mercury*, 25 March 1921.

85 Green and Cromwell (*Mutual Aid*, pp. 214–16) argue that to calculate the number of people covered by friendly society benefits, the membership should be multiplied by four to include 'dependants'. In 1923 the Manchester Unity Independent Order of Oddfellows had 187 members and the Grand United Order of Oddfellows had 28 members (*Manchester Unity Journal*, 1 October 1923; and *The Oddfellow*, 15 April 1923.) Port Kembla's population in 1923 was 2115: Police Census reported in *Illawarra Mercury*, 25 December 1925.

86 *Australian Triple Links*, 1 July 1929.

87 Registry of Co-operative and Friendly Society Subvention Registers.

88 *Manchester Unity Journal*, 1 October 1923; and *The Oddfellow*, 15 March 1925.

89 The formation of the Independent Order of Rechabites is reported in *South Coast Times*, 7 January 1927. The list of members is from Registry of Co-operative and Friendly Society Subvention Registers. McCann was president of the Progress Association in 1924, while Simon was president in 1920 and 1926. Humble was active in the Port Kembla Ratepayers' Association in the 1930s.

90 *Illawarra Mercury*, 17 February 1922.

91 Wollongong Council was eventually successful with the Mount Keira properties, which became part of the municipality in early 1924: *Illawarra Mercury*, 10 March 1924. The Wollongong Council's initial moves on this issue, and its designs on Port Kembla, are in *Illawarra Mercury*, 19 December 1921, 16 February 1922.

92 The state seat of 'Wollongong', which Davies had represented from 1917 to 1920, had a name change to 'Wollondilly' from 1920 to 1927, after which it was changed back to 'Wollongong' until 1930, when it was renamed 'Illawarra'.

93 *Illawarra Mercury*, 14 November 1924.

94 *Illawarra Mercury*, 2 March 1923.

95 *South Coast Times*, 8 February 1924.

96 Griffith, 'The Growing Militancy of the South Coast Branch of the Waterside Workers' Federation', pp. 38–9.

97 Interview with Walter Bailey, WUA.

98 Griffith, The Growing Militancy of the South Coast Branch of the Waterside Workers' Federation, p. 37.

99 *Illawarra Mercury*, 6 May 1921.

1 Comments by William Davies (MLA for Wollondilly), *Illawarra Mercury*, 24 March 1922.

2 *Illawarra Mercury*, 24 March, 7 April 1922.

3 *Illawarra Mercury*, 24 March, 15 May 1922.

4 *Illawarra Mercury*, 24 June 1926. The 44-hour week had been introduced by the state government led by Premier J.T. Lang at the beginning of the year, but due to a technicality in their award the FEDFA claimed they were working 48 hours and being paid for only 44.

⁵ *Illawarra Mercury*, 16 July 1926; and Richardson, *The Bitter Years*, pp. 14, 24.

⁶ *Illawarra Mercury*, 23 August 1929; and Miriam Dixson, 'The Timber Strike of 1929', *Historical Studies: Australia and New Zealand*, vol. 10, no. 40, May 1963, pp. 479–92.

⁷ *Illawarra Mercury*, 16 August 1929.

⁸ This interpretation is informed by Mary Douglas, *Purity and Danger: An analysis of the concepts of pollution and taboo*, Routledge & Kegan Paul, London, 1978, especially ch. 7.

⁹ *Illawarra Mercury*, 30 August 1929.

¹⁰ Minutes of Directors' Meetings, 21 April, 6 October 1926, 19 March 1928, ER&S Records.

¹¹ Central Illawarra Council Minutes, 14 July 1926; and *Illawarra Mercury*, 16 March 1928.

¹² *Illawarra Mercury*, 4 March 1930.

¹³ *Illawarra Mercury*, 24 January 1930.

6 Kooris and Port Kembla, to the 1970s

¹ Heather Goodall, A History of Aboriginal Communities in New South Wales, PhD thesis, University of Sydney, 1982, p. 156; and Henry Reynolds, *With the White People: The Crucial Role of Aborigines in the Exploration and Settlement of Australia*, Penguin, Ringwood, Vic., 1990, pp. 131–9.

² See P. J. Hughes, 'Prehistoric Population Change in South Coastal New South Wales' in Sandra Bowdler (ed.), *Coastal Archaeology in Eastern Australia*, Department of Prehistory, Research School of Pacific Studies, ANU, Canberra, 1982, pp. 16–28.

³ Hughes, 'Prehistoric Population Change', p. 28; and Josephine Flood, 'Man and Ecology: The Highlands of South Eastern Australia' in Nicolas Peterson (ed.), *Tribes and Boundaries in Australia*, Australian Institute of Aboriginal Studies, Canberra, 1976, p. 32.

⁴ Evidence of Koori place-names is fragmentary and not always recorded in ways that indicate correct pronunciations. For instance, Port Kembla can be Nitoka or Nihorka; Tom Thumb's Lagoon, Tuckulung or Mangau; and Red Point, lllowra or Illara: Organ, *Illawarra and South Coast Aborigines 1770–1850*, Appendixes 2 & 3.

⁵ Eades, *The Dharawal and Dhurga Languages*; and Organ, *Illawarra and South Coast Aborigines, 1770–1850*, pp. xli–xliii. Eades argues that the linguistic evidence for 'Wodi Wodi' is slim, but the Illawarra Kooris now identify themselves as Wodi Wodi or Wadi Wadi.

⁶ Organ, *Illawarra and South Coast Aborigines, 1770–1850*, pp. 94–100; and Liston, *Campbelltown*, p. 24.

⁷ Tony Dingle, *Aboriginal Economy: Patterns of Experience*, McPhee/Gribble, Fitzroy, 1988, p. 4.

⁸ R. H. Mathews 'Ethnological Notes on the Aboriginal tribes of NSW and Victoria', *Journal of the Royal Society of New South Wales*, vol. 38, 1904, pp. 253–4.

⁹ Anne Blackwell, 'Bowen Island: Further Evidence of Economic Change and Intensification on the south coast of New South Wales' in Bowdler, *Coastal Archaeology*, pp. 46–51.

¹⁰ Helen Ross, Australian Aboriginal perceptions of dwellings and living environments, PhD thesis, University of London, 1983; and Peterson, *Australian Territorial Organisation*.

¹¹ Organ, *Illawarra and South Coast Aborigines, 1770–1850*, p. xli.

¹² Bain Attwood, *The Making of the Aborigines*, Allen & Unwin, Sydney, 1989; Dianne Bell, *Daughters of the Dreaming*, McPhee Gribble/Allen & Unwin, Melbourne, 1983; and Richard Broome, *Aboriginal Australians*, Allen & Unwin, Sydney, 1982. The spiritual significance of Illowra comes from Interview with Carol Speechley.

¹³ Liston, *Campbelltown*, pp. 19–24; and Keith Willey, *When the Sky Fell Down: The Destruction of Tribes of the Sydney Region*, Collins, Sydney, 1979.

¹⁴ *Sydney Gazette*, 28 September 1816, cited in Mitchell and Sherington, *Growing Up in the Illawarra*, p. 3.

¹⁵ Organ, *Illawarra and South Coast Aborigines, 1770–1850*, pp. 101–4.

¹⁶ Goodall, A History of Aboriginal Communities in New South Wales, especially Chapter 2; and Peter Read, 'A Double Headed Coin: Protection and Assimilation in Yass, 1900–1960' in Bill Gammage and Andrew Markus (eds), *All that Dirt: Aborigines, 1938*, An Australia 1938 Monograph, Canberra, 1982, pp. 9–28.

[17] Aborigines' Welfare Board, Annual Report for the Year Ended 30th June 1944, *NSWPP*, vol. 2, 1945–46.

[18] APB, *Reports*, 1894–99.

[19] *New South Wales Aborigines' Advocate*, 23 July 1901, and generally 1901 to 1908.

[20] *Illawarra Mercury*, 31 April, 3 July 1899. Johnson was born on the Clarence River and moved to the Illawarra with a white family, the Westons. He was given a breastplate with the inscription 'King of the Illawarra Tribe' at the Wollongong Show by Archibald Campbell (member for Illawarra) in 1896. He died at Minnamurra in 1906 aged seventy-two: *Illawarra Mercury*, 1 February 1896; and *Town and Country Journal*, 21 November 1906.

[21] APB, *Reports*, 1894–1905; and *Illawarra Mercury*, 22 July, 14 October 1899.

[22] *New South Wales Aborigines' Advocate*, 23 July 1901; and *Illawarra Mercury*, 3 July 1900.

[23] *New South Wales Aborigines' Advocate*, 23 March 1903; and APB, Report for 1904, p. 4.

[24] Peter Read, *A Hundred Years War: The Wiradjuri people and the state*, Australian National University Press, Canberra, 1988, p. 4.

[25] Organ, *Illawarra and South Coast Aborigines, 1770–1850*, pp. 336–7, 342.

[26] Report on the Fisheries of New South Wales for the Year 1910, *NSWPP*, vol. 3, 1911, p. 720; and Interviews with Albert Rieck, Joe Hill and Steve Wade, WPL, and Bruce Halcrow.

[27] *Noogaleek, Belonging to Me: An Aboriginal Oral History*, Wollongong TAFE, Wollongong, 1984, p. 16.

[28] 'The Economic Life of Mixed Blood Aborigines', p. 183; and *La Perouse, the Place, the People and the Sea*, pp. 7, 27.

[29] Interviews with Dick Henry and Carol Speechley; and *La Perouse, the Place, the People and the Sea*, pp. 7, 27.

[30] *Illawarra Mercury*, 29 January 1901.

[31] *South Coast Times*, 7 February, 21 March 1930; and Interview with Joe Hill and Steve Wade, WPL.

[32] *La Perouse, the Place, the People and the Sea*, p. 7.

[33] 'Wollongong' in this case probably includes Port Kembla as well: APB, *Report for 1901*, p. 3; and *New South Wales Aborigines' Advocate*, 23 July 1901.

[34] *Noogaleek, Belonging to Me*, pp. 8–9.

[35] Interview with Dick Henry.

[36] Interview with Joe Hill and Steve Wade, WPL; and Interview with Albert Rieck.

[37] Goodall, A History of Aboriginal Communities in New South Wales, pp. 71–83.

[38] APB, *Report for the Year Ended 30th June 1939*, p. 4

[39] Aborigines' Welfare Board, Annual Reports for the Years Ended 30th June 1958–1959, *NSWPP*, vol. 1, 1960–61, pp. 6, 9.

[40] APB, *Report for 1901*, p. 3; and *Report for 1904*, p. 5.

[41] APB, *Report for 1905*, pp. 3–4.

[42] *New South Wales Aborigines' Advocate*, 30 May 1904.

[43] *Australian Mining Standard*, 22 January 1914; and *Illawarra Mercury*, 8 May 1914.

[44] APB, *Report for 1915*, Appendix B, p. 11; *Illawarra Mercury*, 13 February 1925; Dolly Henry in *Noogaleek, Belonging to Me*, p. 46; Interview with Ursula Lindsay; and *South Coast Times*, 11 July 1919.

[45] *Illawarra Mercury*, 22 November 1912.

[46] Miller, *Koori*, pp. 138–42; and Read, *A Hundred Years War*, pp. 56–9.

[47] *Illawarra Mercury*, 22 February 1918.

[48] Interview with Jean Payne, Wollongong TAFE.

[49] Town Clerk's Report 12 December 1929, Central Illawarra Council Minute Book.

[50] Evidence of Reverend William Morley, Select Committee on the Administration of the Aborigines' Protection Board, *NSWPP*, vol. 7, 1938–40, pp. 609–73

[51] *Annual Report of the Association for the Protection of Native Races*, 1930, p. 7, ML.

[52] Central Illawarra Council Minute Book, 13 November 1929.

[53] The APB's views and figures are quoted in the Town Clerk's Report, 12 December 1929, Central Illawarra Council Minute Book.

54 *APB*, Report for 1904, p. 5.

55 Interview with Albert Rieck; and Edith Neaves in Preston, *If I Remember Rightly*, p. 34.

56 Joan Wakeman in *Noogaleek, Belonging to Me*, p. 10; Interview with Joe Hill and Steve Wade, WPL; Interview with Ursula Lindsay; and Bell, 'Economic Life', p. 181.

57 *La Perouse, the Place, the People and the Sea*, p. 81.

58 *Noogaleek, Belonging to Me*, p. 9.

59 Interview with Walter Bailey, WPL.

60 Information taken from Council debates reported in *Illawarra Mercury*, 10 June 1927.

61 Letter from Office of the Aborigines' Protection Board to Department of Defence, Canberra, 3 October 1929, SP344/1 Box 42 Port Kembla Part 1, Department of Defence, AA.

62 Memo from Major SOES to Supervising Engineer (fortifications) Department of Interior, 31 August, 1938, MOUNT 7/1 Item No. D573, AA.

63 Sgt J. Fletcher to Acting Director-General Works, Department of the Interior, 16 February, 1940, MOUNT 7/1 Item No. D573, AA.

64 Dan McNamara and Bob West, *Port Kembla—a living history*, Port Kembla, 1998, p. 87.

65 Interview with Dick Henry, p. 2; *Noogaleek, Belonging to Me*; and Interview with Morgan Simon; and Mavis King in Preston, *If I Remember Rightly*, p. 54.

66 Interview with Ces Catterel.

67 'Survey into Living Conditions of Aboriginal People from Wollongong to the Victorian Border', December 1961, South Coast Trades and Labour Council Records.

68 *South Coast Times*, 12 March 1962.

69 Goodall, *Invasion to Embassy*, pp. 308–9

70 Report for the Minister for Aboriginal Welfare on the workings of the Aborigines Act, 1969, p. 6, Report for the Year Ended 30th June 1970, *NSWPP* (second session), vol. 1, 1971–72.

71 Aborigines' Welfare Board, Annual Report for the Year Ended 30th June 1965, p. 12, *NSWPP* (third session), vol. 1, 1965.

72 Interview with Ursula Lindsay.

73 James Wallace, Statistical Study of Aborigines in the Illawarra, Economics Department, University of Wollongong, 1976, p. 4.

74 Report By Reverend T. Fox, Catholic Presbytery, Fairy Meadow, 30 October 1974, reproduced in Wallace, Statistical Study of Aborigines in the Illawarra, Appendix 2.

75 Justice J. French, National Native Tribunal Determination, In the matter of the Native Title Act of 1993 and in the matter of the Wadi Wadi peoples Native Title Determination Application, NN94/9, 15 February 1995, accessed through www.austlii.edu.au/cgi-bin/ ...TA/1995/5.html (1 September 2001).

7 The Challenges to Locality, 1890 to 1947

1 Mitchell and Sherington, *Growing Up in the Illawarra*, p. 66.

2 A copy of the timetable is in *Illawarra Mercury*, 12 September 1920.

3 NSW Board of Trade, Inquiry into Living Wage, p. 314.

4 Cardew, 'Urban Settlement in the Illawarra, 1890–1940' in Robinson (ed.), *Urban Illawarra*, p. 95.

5 Interview with Colin Warrington, Wollongong TAFE.

6 *South Coast Times*, 25 April 1924.

7 For example a Council resolution setting motor car speed limits at 15 miles per hour in town areas is at Central Illawarra Council Minutes, 14 May 1924; and Mitchell and Sherington, *Growing Up in the Illawarra*, p. 91.

8 Interviews with Bob Rees and Edith Neaves; and Peter Spearritt, 'Cars for the People' in Ann Curthoys, A. W. Martin and Tim Rowse (eds), *Australians from 1939*, Fairfax, Syme & Weldon, Sydney, 1987, p. 119.

9 *South Coast Times*, 19 April 1918; and *Historical Notes on the Port Kembla, Unanderra and Moss Vale Branches*, Public Transport Commission, Sydney, 1977, pp. 66–7.

10 *South Coast Times*, 13 March 1918; and *Illawarra Mercury*, 15 March 1918.

11 Fairley's comments were reported in *Illawarra Mercury*, 15 March 1918; and Evidence of Robert Shipp, Parliamentary Standing Committee on Public Works, Railway from Moss Vale to Port Kembla, p. 23.

12 Central Illawarra Council Minutes, 11 January 1928; Housing Report, 1943, Central Illawarra Council Committee Minute Book; and *Census of the Commonwealth of Australia*, 1947, vol. 1, p. 510.

13 *BHP Review*, vol. xiii, October 1936; and K. Barwick-Hooke, *Berkeley and Surrounding Districts, Glimpses into the Past and Present*, Illawarra Historical Society, Wollongong, 1988, p. 369.

14 Barwick-Hooke, *Berkeley and Surrounding Districts*, p. 369; and *Census of the Commonwealth of Australia*, 1947, vol. 1, pp. 550–2.

15 On the understanding of Cringila as a suburb of Port Kembla see letter from J. Kelly (store-keeper at Cringila) to W. M. Hughes (at the time federal Member for North Sydney), 25 July 1938, Port Kembla Post Office, Item no. GA37/2383, SP439/3, AA.

16 *Illawarra Mercury*, 25 April 1934.

17 *Sydney Morning Herald*, 6 August 1936.

18 Spooner, *The History and Development of Port Kembla*, p. 17.

19 Spooner, *The History and Development of Port Kembla*, pp. 17–18; and H. E. Maiden, *The History of Local Government in New South Wales*, Angus & Robertson, Sydney, 1966, p. 275.

20 See Illawarra Regional Development Committee, Minutes of Meetings 1945–60, B1/1/1, WUA; Background Notes—Regional Organisation in NSW, B1/3/1, WUA; and Illawarra Regional Planning Authority, *Annual Reports*, 1952–59, WPL.

21 Central Illawarra Council Minute Book, 8 August 1934; and Shire of Central Illawarra, Information Sheet, July, 1944, Central Illawarra Council Minutes of Finance Committee.

22 *Illawarra Mercury*, 8 March, 14 and 26 July 1946.

23 Peter Sheldon, 'Local Government to 1947' in Hagan and Wells (eds), *A History of Wollongong*, p. 112.

24 Peter Sheldon, 'Local Government since 1947' in Hagan and Wells (eds), *A History of Wollongong*, pp. 115–117.

25 The implications of the removal of political power from localities in the United Kingdom is covered by Duncan and Goodwin, *The Local State*, ch. 1.

26 Cited in *Illawarra Mercury*, 22 December 1898.

27 C. N. Connolly, *Biographical Register of the New South Wales Parliament, 1856–1901*, Australian National University Press, Canberra, 1983, p. 41.

28 *Illawarra Mercury*, 10 December 1898.

29 *Illawarra Mercury*, 4 January 1900, editorial.

30 *Illawarra Mercury*, 22 April 1917, editorial. Musgrave remained in charge of the paper until his death in 1943.

31 *Illawarra Mercury*, 22 April 1917.

32 *Sydney Morning Herald*, 9 December 1898.

33 *NSWPD*, 1898, vol. 1, p. 360.

34 Newcastle harbour was, at times, treacherous, but extensive government work had improved conditions considerably by the late nineteenth century. In contrast, the coal trade in the Illawarra, before the development of Port Kembla, had relied on open, inadequately sheltered jetties at Bulli and Coalcliff, and the small harbour at Wollongong: Robin Gollan, *The Coalminers of New South Wales: A History of the Union, 1860–1960*, Melbourne University Press, Carlton, 1963, p. 12.

35 *Newcastle Morning Herald*, editorials, 3 December 1897, 9 November 1898.

36 *South Coast Times*, 29 March 1902.

37 *Illawarra Mercury*, 24 September 1904, editorial.

38 *Illawarra Mercury*, 19 March 1920.

39 *Illawarra Mercury*, 4 April 1930; and *South Coast Times*, 27 January 1933.

40 Wollongong and District Citizens' Association, *Annual Report for 1920–21*, MSS 113/1, WPL.

41 Secretary's Report, Minutes of Annual Meeting, 26 February 1920, Wollongong and District Citizens' Association, MSS 113/1, WPL.

[42] Obituary of J. F. Beatson by S. R. Musgrave, *Illawarra Mercury*, 6 May 1927.

[43] Letter from H. R. Lee (secretary, South Coast Water Supply Advisory League) to Wollongong and District Citizens' Association, 26 August 1925, in Wollongong and District Citizens' Association, Correspondence, MSS 113/2, WPL.

[44] An article by H. R. Lee in *Illawarra Mercury*, 11 March 1927, gives details of the public and private lobbying for the railway.

[45] Evidence of H. R. Lee in 'Select Committee on the Industrial Conciliation and Arbitration Bill', *NSWPP*, 1930–32, vol. 5, pp. 77–83.

[46] *Illawarra Mercury*, 14 March 1930.

[47] *Illawarra Mercury*, 16 July 1926; and Richardson, *The Bitter Years*, pp. 14, 24.

[48] Richardson, *The Bitter Years*, p. 54.

[49] For example, the company contributed £500 to the National Party funds for the 1930 State election: Minutes of AI&S Directors' Meetings, 24 September 1930, BHPBA Ref. S24/1.

[50] *MM Gazette* (21st Anniversary Issue), Port Kembla, 1939, p. 9.

[51] *Illawarra Mercury*, 12 March 1932.

[52] *BHP Journal*, no. 2, 1978, pp. 54–5.

[53] *South Coast Times*, 21 April 1933.

[54] By August 1934 ward Number 1 (consisting principally of Port Kembla and the nearby towns of Windang and Berkeley) had arrears in rates totalling £5137: Financial statement for 1934, Central Illawarra Council Minute Book, 8 August 1934.

[55] *South Coast Times*, 4 August 1933.

[56] William Davies (MLA for Wollongong), *NSWPD*, 1929–30, vol. 121, p. 2893.

[57] Davis, *Our Memories Your History*, p. 30.

[58] Calculated from the State Electoral Roll for the District of Illawarra, 1940, ML.

[59] *Illawarra Mercury*, 29 January 1932; and Richardson, *The Bitter Years*, pp. 71–4.

[60] *Illawarra Mercury*, 15 May, 3 July 1931.

[61] *Illawarra Mercury*, 22 May 1931.

[62] *Illawarra Mercury*, 15 May 1931.

[63] Wollongong District Court, Plaint and Minute Books, 7/9960 (1920 to 1926) & 7/9961 (1926 to 1931), NSWSA.

[64] Interview with John Philpot, Wollongong TAFE.

[65] Minutes of the New Guard's Executive Council indicate that in October 1931 there was no separate branch at Port Kembla, and the combined membership of the localities of Wollongong and Port Kembla amounted to only thirty: Minutes of the Executive Council, 15 October 1931, in 'New Guard Movements', Premier's Department Special Bundles, 9/2459, NSWSA. Beyond a few hints in oral history interviews, there is little evidence to suggest that the New Guard was very active at Port Kembla.

[66] Letter from J. P. Caddy to Colin Fraser, 5 November 1931, 'MM Ltd, 1928–1932', 1/127/27, Broken Hill Associated Smelters Pty Ltd Records.

[67] Trevor Mathews, 'The All for Australia League' in Robert Cooksey (ed.), *The Great Depression in Australia* (Labour History special edition), no. 17, November 1970, pp. 136–47.

[68] Richardson, *The Bitter Years*, pp. 173–4; and Merritt, 'A History of the FIA', p. 174.

[69] F. H. Rickleman to Colin Fraser, 12 September 1933, Reports and comments on Kembla works by D. Yates and F. H. Rickleman, 1/84/3, Broken Hill Associated Smelters Pty Ltd Records.

[70] Griffith, The Growing Militancy of the South Coast Branch of the Waterside Workers, p. 63.

[71] *The Red Blast* (Issued by the Communist Party), no. 15, 28 August 1934, copy in AI&S Port Kembla, Industrial Department—Correspondence File, Industrial Relations, BHPBA Ref. W002/131/002.

[72] Industrial Report for the six months ending 13 October 1936, AI&S Port Kembla, Industrial Department—Industrial Reports, BHPBA Ref. W002/080/001; and Tom Sheridan, 'A Case Study in Complexity: The Origins of the 1945 Steel Strike in New South Wales', pp. 87–109.

[73] Sheridan, 'A Case Study in Complexity', pp. 90–3.

[74] Griffith, The Growing Militancy of the South Coast Branch of the Waterside Workers, p. 63.

[75] Murray and White, *The Ironworkers*, p. 94.

[76] Half Yearly Industrial Report for the period ending 31 May, 1938, AI&S, Port Kembla, Industrial Department, BHPBA Ref. W002/080/003.

[77] Half Yearly Industrial Report for the period ending 31 May, 1940, AI&S, Port Kembla, Industrial Department, BHPBA Ref. W002/080/005. The labour process and union mobilisation at AI&S is covered by Cochrane, 'Australian Iron and Steel Company Port Kembla, 1935–39', pp. 61–77.

[78] Details of the dispute are enumerated by Griffith, The Growing Militancy of the South Coast Branch of the Waterside Workers, Chapter 5; and John White, 'Port Kembla Pig Iron dispute', *Labour History*, no. 37, November 1979, pp. 63–77.

[79] Griffith, The Growing Militancy of the South Coast Branch of the Waterside Workers, pp. 72–6.

[80] Lockwood, *War on the Waterfront*, chs 11–15; and L. Richardson, 'Dole Queue Patriots' in Robert Cooksey (ed.), *The Great Depression in Australia* (Labour History special edition), no. 17, November 1970, pp. 204–14.

[81] Richardson, *The Bitter Years*, pp. 194–200.

[82] Lockwood, *War on the Waterfront*, p. 141.

[83] Lockwood, *War on the Waterfront*, pp. 151–2, 160.

[84] Summary of Interview between Minister for Labour and Industry (Mr Dunningham), Under Secretary of Department (Mr Bellmore) and Mr Burgess (Industrial Officer), 25 July 1936, AI&S Port Kembla, Correspondence Files—Department of Labour and Industry, BHPBA Ref. W002/064/001.

[85] *Illawarra Mercury*, 27 March 1936.

[86] *Illawarra Mercury*, 9 August 1940.

[87] Interview with Morgan Simon.

8 Industrial Society Supreme, 1945 to 1970

[1] John Steinke, *Wollongong Statistical Handbook, No. 2*, Department of Economics, University of Wollongong, p. 81.

[2] Geoffrey Bolton, *The Oxford History of Australia, Volume 5, 1942–1988: The Middle Way*, Oxford University Press, Melbourne, 1990, p. 177.

[3] Bulletin No. 33, 27 May 1949, Bulletins January 1948–August 1957, BHPBA Ref. PE26/1–98.

[4] Bulletin No. 11, 12 July 1948, Bulletins January 1948–August 1957, BHPBA Ref. PE26/1–98; and Chairman's address (Colin Syme), *Report of the 101st Ordinary General Meeting of Broken Hill Proprietary Company Ltd*, no page numbers, BHPBA.

[5] Hughes, *The Australian Iron and Steel Industry*, p. 153.

[6] Jack Beale, *NSWPD* (fifth session), 25 October 1955, p. 1247.

[7] Hughes, *The Australian Iron and Steel Industry*, pp. 156–7; and 'Port Kembla's Decade of Development', *BHP Review*, vol. 36, no. 6, October 1959, pp. 14–15.

[8] Eklund and Murray, *Copper Community*, pp. 45, 52–6.

[9] NSW Parliament, *Australian Iron & Steel Limited Agreement Ratification Act, 1936*; and *Port Kembla Inner Harbour Construction and Agreement Ratification Act, 1955*.

[10] NSW Parliament, *Port Kembla (No. 6) Jetty Act, 1953*; and *Port Kembla Inner Harbour (further construction) Act, 1961*.

[11] The plan is referred to in J. C. Steinke, 'Future Prospects of the Port Kembla Shopping Centre: A Report to the Illawarra Regional Development Committee', Illawarra Regional Development—Commercial Activity Port Kembla 1966–69, D116/1/3/4, WUA.

[12] *Illawarra Mercury*, 26 June 1946.

[13] NSW Parliament, *Port Kembla Inner Harbour Construction and Agreement Ratification Act 1955*, No. 43.

[14] R F. X. Connor, *NSWPD*, 12 October 1961, p. 1519.

[15] *Census of the Commonwealth of Australia*, 1961, vol. 1, pp. 98–9.

[16] *New South Wales Industrial Gazette*, vol. 31, 31 October 1951, pp. 72–80.

[17] Segregation of wages employees as at 28th March 1967, ER&S Records.

[18] Half yearly report for period ending 30 November 1948, AI&S Port Kembla Steel Works, Industrial Department, General Correspondence Files, Industrial Reports Half Yearly, November, 1948, BHPBA Ref. W002/081/001; and Half Yearly report for period ending 31 May 1968, AI&S Port Kembla Steel Works, Industrial Department, General Correspondence Files, Industrial Reports Half Yearly, May, 1968, BHPBA Ref. W002/081/019.

[19] James Jupp, *Arrivals and Departures*, Cheshire–Lansdowne, Melbourne, 1966, p. 46.

[20] John Steinke, *Wollongong Statistical Handbook, No. 2*, p. 80.

[21] Jabubowicz, *Immigrant Parents and Port Kembla Schools*, section 6.3(a).

[22] Mendo Trajcevski, 'Macedonian Pioneers in the Illawarra—Interview with Angele Brglevski', *Compass*, Newsletter of the Macedonian Welfare Association, 1994?

[23] Interview with Tome Kokalevski, Neda Kotsofski and Trajanka Mangovsky.

[24] Immigration Advisory Council, *Inquiry into the Departure of Settlers from Australia—Final Report July 1973*, Australian Government Publishing Service, Canberra, 1973, p. 12.

[25] David Cox, 'The welfare needs of migrants', *Commission of Inquiry into Poverty: Welfare of Migrants*, Australian Government Printing Service, Canberra, 1975, pp. 11–12.

[26] Interview with Mendo Trajcevski.

[27] Year of Client Arrival, 1951–2000, Macedonian Welfare Association, Port Kembla. Document supplied by the Association.

[28] Interview with Tome Kokalevski, Neda Kotsofski and Trajanka Mangovsky.

[29] Interview with Paul Wand, p. 10.

[30] Colin Warrington in Davis, *Our Memories Your History*, p. 33.

[31] Davis, *Our Memories Your History*, p. 1.

[32] *Illawarra Mercury*, 27 August, 8 October 1957.

[33] For example, Ray Markey and Andrew Wells, 'The Labour Movement in Wollongong' in Hagan and Wells (eds), *A History of Wollongong*, pp. 81–100.

[34] *Labor News*, vol. 6, no. 8, 8 June 1949, p. 3.

[35] Lever Tracy and Quinlan, *A Divided Working Class*, pp. 168–170; and FIA Wollongong/Port Kembla/South Coast Branch, Correspondence, General: November 1944 to November 1949, D196/1, WUA.

[36] Lever Tracy and Quinlan, *A Divided Working Class*, pp. 168–70; and Murray and White, *The Ironworkers*, p. 229.

[37] 'Immigration Planning Council visits Port Kembla', *BHP Review*, vol. xxix, June 1952.

[38] Half yearly report for period ending 30 November 1968, AI&S Port Kembla Steel Works, Industrial Department, General Correspondence Files, Industrial Reports Half Yearly, BHPBA Ref. W002/081/020.

[39] Foreman's Daily report: L. Sutton Machine Shop foreman, 16 April 1964, AI&S Industrial Office, D216, WUA. The names of both the worker and foreman have been changed.

[40] AI&S—Port Kembla: Suspensions and Dismissals—Flat Products Shops, 1957 to 31 March 1961, AI&S Industrial Office, D216, WUA.

[41] AI&S, Port Kembla Steel Works, Industrial Department, General Correspondence Files, Industrial Matters—General, 12 January 1945–20 December 1945, BHPA Ref. W002/078/010.

[42] Memo from N. Akhurst to General Manager, 2 December 1968, AI&S, Port Kembla Steel Works, Bonus Payments at AI&S—General, 1968, BHPBA Ref. W002/052/028.

[43] Report on events leading up to and including the interview with Mr. C. Stevens on 12 May 1966, AI&S, Port Kembla Steel Works, Industrial Department, General Correspondence Files, Labour—Sinter Plant and Ore Handling, 4 January 1966–6 March 1967, BHPBA Ref. W002/179/013. The name of the worker has been changed.

[44] Half yearly report for period ending 31 May 1954, AI&S, Port Kembla Steel Works, Industrial Department, General Correspondence Files, Industrial Reports Half Yearly, BHPBA Ref. W002/081//006.

[45] Half yearly report for period ending 31 May 1954, Half Yearly report for period ending 30 November 1954, and Half Yearly report for period ending 31 May 1958, AI&S, Port Kembla Steel Works, Industrial Department, General Correspondence Files, Industrial Reports Half Yearly, BHPBA Ref. W002/081//006, W002/081//010.

46 Open Hearth Department—Walk Off Following Disciplinary Action, 8 August 1957, AI&S, Port Kembla Steel Works, Industrial Department, General Correspondence Files, Labour—New Australians, 27 February 1957–8 August 1957, BHPBA Ref. W002/089/009.

47 AI&S Port Kembla Steel Works, Industrial Department, General Correspondence Files, Labour—New Australians, 4 January 1950–2 February 1951, BHPBA Ref. W002/089/002.

48 Memo to General Manager 10 July 1954, AI&S, Port Kembla Steel Works, Industrial Department, General Correspondence Files, Labour—New Australians, 4 January 1954–2 February 1955, BHPBA Ref. W002/089/006.

49 *Action!*, Leaflet of the Ironworkers Rank and File Vigilance Committee, December 1960?, AI&S, Port Kembla Steel Works, Union and Political Publications, 1960, BHPBA Ref. W002/101/020.

50 Metcalfe, 'Mud and Steel', pp. 1–16.

51 Turnbull, *Commemorating the official opening by the Prime Minister of Australia, the Rt. Hon. R. G. Menzies, C.H., Q.C., of the hot strip mill.*

52 *South Coast Times*, 1 September 1955; and *Illawarra Mercury*, 30 August 1955.

53 R. F. X. Connor, *NSWPD* (second session), 23 September 1953, p. 779.

54 *Directors' Report for the year Ending 31 May 1970*, Broken Hill Proprietary Company Ltd, pp. 9–12, BHPBA.

9 The Dissolution of Industrial Society? 1970 Onwards

1 *Policies for Development of Manufacturing Industry, A Green Paper, Volume one*, Australian Government Publishing Service, Canberra, 1975, p. 1.

2 *BHP Annual Report for the year Ending 30 May 1972*, p. 8; and 'Managing Director's Review of Operations', *BHP Annual Report for the Year Ending 31 May 1975*, BHPBA.

3 Schultz, *Steel City Blues*, p. 36.

4 Donaldson, *Is There a Crisis in the Steel Industry?*

5 Commonwealth of Australia, *Appropriation Act (No. 2) 1983–84*, No. 87 of 1983, Schedule 2; *Appropriation Act (No. 2) 1984–85*, No. 171 of 1984, Schedule 2 Question on Notice: Steel Industry Assistance; and *CPD*, House of Representatives, 19 August 1986 (Questioner: The Hon B. J. Conquest: Responder: The Hon B. O Jones), p. 64.

6 *Sydney Morning Herald*, 20 March 2001; and *Australian*, 20 March 2002.

7 Eklund and Murray, *Copper Community*, pp. 71–89.

8 Illawarra Regional Information Service, *1986 Census of Population and Housing—Small Area Comparisons, No. 1 Population and Housing Growth*, Wollongong, 1989, p. 2.

9 Illawarra Regional Information Service, *A Statistical Guide to the Illawarra*, Wollongong, 1998.

10 Australian Bureau of Statistics, *Population and Housing Collection District Summary Data (NSW)* (postcode area 2505), 1976 and 1981; and Illawarra Regional Information Service, *1986 Census of Population and Housing—Census Data: Small Area Comparison: Statistical Data Series No. 6*, Wollongong, 1989, p. 18.

11 Australian Bureau of Statistics, *Population and Housing Collection District Summary Data (NSW)* (postcode area 2505), 1976; and Illawarra Regional Information Service, *1986 Census of Population and Housing—Census Data: Small Area Comparison: Statistical Data Series No. 6*, Wollongong, 1989, p. 14.

12 Illawarra Regional Information Service, *1986 Census of Population and Housing—Census Data: Small Area Comparison: Statistical Data Series No. 2*, Wollongong, 1989, p. 6.

13 *Australian Story*, 'Every Breath You Take', ABC Television, 3 June 1999.

14 *Policies for Development of Manufacturing Industry, A Green Paper, Volume One*, Australian Government Publishing Service, Canberra, 1975, p. 72.

15 Illawarra Regional Information Service, *Census Data: Small Area Comparison: Statistical Data Series No. 3*, Wollongong, 1981, p. 50.

16 Year of Client Arrival, 1951–2000, Macedonian Welfare Association, Port Kembla. Figures supplied by the association.

17 Mr Landa, Minister for Housing, *NSWPD*, 7 November 1961, p. 1286.

[18] J. C. Steinke, *Future Prospects of the Port Kembla Shopping Centre*, Economics Department, University of Wollongong, p. 7.

[19] Interview with Mendo Trajcevski.

[20] J. C. Steinke, *Future Prospects of the Port Kembla Shopping Centre*, Economics Department, University of Wollongong, p. 7.

[21] Davis, *Our Memories Your History*, pp. 95–6.

[22] *Daily Mercury*, 9 August, 1969.

[23] *Green Left Weekly*, 2 June 1999.

[24] Wollongong City Council, *Port Kembla No Loitering/Disorderly Behaviour Policy Trial—Evaluation Report*, Wollongong, December 1999; and Wollongong City Council, *Port Kembla Safety Program, September 2000*, Wollongong, 2000.

[25] G. Mitchell, Company, Community and Governmental Attitudes and their Consequences to Pollution at Port Kembla, with special reference to the ER&S company, 1900 to 1970, Ph.D. thesis, University of Wollongong, 1981, pp. 82–3.

[26] *Illawarra Mercury*, 16 November 1945.

[27] *Illawarra Mercury*, 11 February 1959.

[28] A. Bell, *Air Pollution from Metallurgical Industries: The Effects on Health of the Residents of East Port Kembla*, Director, Division of Occupational Health, NSW, 1961.

[29] R. F. X. Connor, *NSWPD* (third session), 25 August 1960, p. 88.

[30] R. F. X. Connor, *NSWPD* (third session), 7 September 1960, p. 352.

[31] *NSW EPA State of the Environment Report*, 1997, http://www.epa.nsw.gov.au/soe/97/ (August 2001); and I. A. Kreis et al., *Illawarra Child Blood Lead Study*, Wollongong, Illawarra Environmental Health Unit, 1994, p. 4.

[32] Chris Illert and Daniela Reverberi, 'The Ills of the Illawarra: Industrial Pollution and School Absenteeism', *Search*, vol. 25, no. 4, May 1994, pp. 101–3.

[33] *Illawarra Leukaemia Cluster Investigation Report*, Leukaemia Investigation Steering Committee for the Illawarra Area Health Service and NSW Health Department, Illawarra Public Health Unit, Wollongong, 1997.

[34] Victoria J. Westley-Wise et al., 'Investigation of a Cluster of Leukaemia in the Illawarra Region of New South Wales, 1989–1996', *Medical Journal of Australia*, 1999, vol. 171, pp. 178–83.

[35] *Illawarra Mercury*, 4 April, 2001.

[36] NSW Parliament, *Port Kembla Development (Special Provisions) Act 1997*, No. 40, section 4.

Conclusion

[1] *People of New South Wales: Statistics from the 1991 Census*, Ethnic Affairs Commission, Sydney, 1994, pp. 190–2, 207–9, 15.

[2] Graham, *Singing the City*.

[3] Giddens, *Central Problems in Social Theory*, p. 71.

Select Bibliography

Commonwealth Government Sources

Attorney-General's Department, File of papers, Refusal by Port Kembla waterside workers to load pig iron for Japan, A432 Item No. 1938/827, 1938.

Australian Federal Police (New South Wales branch), Intelligence Report—Port Kembla, C320, 1939.

Defence, Department of, Correspondence Files, Defence of Port Kembla 1909–13, A2023 A116/2/4.

——, Correspondence Files, Suspicious Lights at Port Kembla, 1917, MP367/1 Item No. 512/3/200.

——, Port Kembla Fortifications part one, SP344/1 Box 42.

Postmaster-General's Office, Port Kembla Post Office Files, SP32, Item No. 32.

New South Wales State and Local Government Sources

Aborigines' Protection Board, Register of Aboriginal Reserves, 1861–99, 2/8349.

Board of Health, Dairies Supervision Act Book, 1886–1929, 5/5867.

——, Health Inspection Branch, Sanitary Inspection Files—Central Illawarra and Port Kembla, 1918–30, 8/1359.

——, Register of Licensed Private Hospitals, 1910–28, 5/5856–63.

——, Register of Noxious Traders Licensed, 1925–38, 5/5870–71.

——, Noxious Trades Book, 1894–1927, 5/5872.

Card Index to Publicans' Licences, 1927–37, 3/7886.

Central Illawarra Council and Greater City of Wollongong Council Records, WPL.

Dapto Court of Petty Sessions Small Debts Register, 1911–38, 7/9951–53.

Locality Index to Friendly Societies and Trade Union Register, 1929, 8/1135.1.

New South Wales Attorney-General's Department, Special Files, Protests by Various Organisations at the treatment of demonstrations by Unemployed, 1933–34, 5/7787.1.

——, Special Files, Remissions, Fines and Sentences imposed on Workers for Participating in unauthorised public meetings in Wollongong, 1930–32, 5/7783.3.

New South Wales Board of Trade, Inquiry into the Living Wage—South Coast, 1920, 2/5780.

Port Kembla School Files, 5/17372.5 to 17374, 1890–1939.

Premier's Department, Special Bundles—New Guard Movements, 9/2459, 1931–1932.

Public Works Department, Special Bundles—Port Kembla, Notes by E. S. Spooner, 7/5883.

——, Special Bundles—Extracts from Annual Reports re Harbour Works Tweed Heads to Port Kembla, 7/7582, 1898–1940.

Registry of Co-operative and Friendly Societies, Subvention Registers, 7/10558–10577, 1932.

Wollongong Local Court Records, 7/9959, 7/9960–9976, 6/4441–4448, 7/9921–9950.

Wollongong District Court, Minutes of Judgements, 1920–56, 7/9958.

Government Publications and Reports

Aborigines' Protection Board, *Annual Reports*, 1889–1939.

Aborigines' Welfare Board, *Annual Reports*, 1940–68.

Handbook of Port Kembla. New South Wales Department of Public Works, Sydney, 1925.

Historical Notes on Port Kembla, Unanderra and Moss Vale Branches, Public Transport Commission, Sydney, 1977, ML.

Parliamentary Standing Committee on Public Works, 'Report together with Minutes of Evidence, Appendices and Plans relating to the Proposed Construction of a Deep-water Harbour at Port Kembla', *New South Wales Legislative Assembly Votes and Proceedings*, 1897, vol. 7, pp. 37–344.

——, 'Report together with Minutes of Evidence, Appendices and Plans relating to the Proposed Extension of the Northern Breakwater at Port Kembla', *New South Wales Parliamentary Papers*, 1912, vol. 2, pp. 5–50.

——, 'Report together with Minutes of Evidence, Appendices and Plans relating to the Proposed Railway from Moss Vale to Port Kembla', *New South Wales Parliamentary Papers*, 1923, vol. 2, pp. 447–529.

Report on the Fisheries of New South Wales for the Year 1910, *New South Wales Parliamentary Papers*, 1911, vol. 3, pp. 685–720.

Royal Commission on Railway Decentralisation, 1911, *New South Wales Parliamentary Papers*, 1911, vol. 2, part 1, pp. 31–360.

Select Committee on the Mt Kembla Coal and Oil Company's Railway Bill, *New South Wales Parliamentary Papers*, 1880–81, vol. 2, pp. 1031–2.

Spooner, E. S. *The History and Development of Port Kembla*. Government Printer, New South Wales, 1938.

The Coke Industry of New South Wales. Descriptive notes by the Department of Mines, Mineral Resources no. 23, Sydney, 1916.

Other Archival Sources

Association for the Protection of Native Races, *Annual Reports*, 1911, 1930, 1932–35, 1938, ML.

Australian Workers' Union, Central Branch, *Annual Reports and Balance Sheets*, 1916–31, ML.
Broken Hill Associated Smelters Pty Ltd Records, 1928–40, MUA.
BHP–Billiton Records, 1927–70, BHPBA.
Hoskins Family Papers, MSS 361, ML.
Illawarra Planning Authority, *Annual Reports*, 1952–60, WPL.
Illawarra Regional Development Committee, *Records and Reports, 1945–1970*, WUA.
Metal Manufactures Pty Ltd Records, WUA.
Southern Copper Collection (formerly ER&S collection), MUA.
W. S. Robinson Papers, MUA.
South Coast Trades and Labour Council Records, WUA.
St Michael's, Wollongong, Anglican Church Records, ML.
St Stephen's, Port Kembla, Anglican Church Records, WUA.
Wentworth Family Legal Papers, MSS 7, 1890–1948, ML.
Wollongong and District Citizens' Association, MSS 113, 1919–27, WPL.
Wollongong Benevolent Society, *Annual Reports*, 1912–23, ML and WPL.

Interviews by the Author

Ces Catterel, 16 October 1991

Ethel Combes, 15 August 1991

Sarah Drury, 26 May 1991

Heather Eklund, 29 January 1992

Bruce Halcrow 3 July 2000

Olive Halcrow 3 July 2000

Iris Jenks, 17 July 1992

Bill King, 15 May 1991

Tome Kokalevski, Neda Kotsofski and Trajanka Mangovsky, 13 June 2001

Ursula Lindsay, 12 June 1991

Danny McNamara 12 December 2000

Edith Neaves, 21 June 1991

Bob Rees, 16 August 1991

Albert Rieck, 6 June 1990

Gordon Rodwell, 11 June 1991

Morgan Simon, 3 June 1991

Mendo Trajcevski, 13 June 2001

Paul Wand, 7 December 2000

Books, Articles and Theses

Atkinson, Alan. *Camden: Farm and Village Life in Early New South Wales*. Oxford University Press, Melbourne, 1988.
Baxter, Janeen, et al. *Class Analysis and Contemporary Australia*. Macmillan, South Melbourne, 1991.
Bell, A. *Air Pollution from Metallurgical Industries: The Effects on the Health of Residents of East Port Kembla*. Division of Occupational Health, New South Wales Department of Health, Sydney, 1961.
Bell, James. 'The Economic Life of Mixed Blood Aborigines on the South Coast of NSW'. *Oceania*, vol. 26, 1955–56, pp. 181–5.
Blainey, Geoffrey. *The Steel Master: A Life of Essington Lewis*. Sun Books, Melbourne, 1981.
Bland, F. A. 'A Note on Regionalism'. *Australian Geography*, vol. 4, no. 8, 1944, pp. 212–16.
Bodnar, John. *Immigration and Industrialization: Ethnicity in an American Mill Town, 1870–1940*. University of Pittsburgh Press, Pittsburgh, Pa, 1977.
Bowman, Margaret (ed.). *Beyond the City: Case Studies in Community Structure and Development*. Longman Cheshire, Melbourne, 1981.

Briton, J. N. *The Growth of Port Kembla*. Department of Geography, University of Sydney, Sydney, 1963.

Capell, A. 'Aboriginal Languages on the South Central Coast of New South Wales'. *Oceania*, vol. 41, 1970, pp. 20–7.

Cochrane, Peter. *Industrialization and Dependence: Australia's Road to Economic Development*. University of Queensland Press, St Lucia, Qld, 1980.

——. 'Australian Iron & Steel Company Port Kembla, 1935–1939'. *Labour History*, no. 57, November 1989, pp. 61–77.

Cohen, A. P. *The Symbolic Construction of Community*. Routledge, London, 1989.

Cooke, Philip. *Back to the Future: Modernity, Post Modernity and Locality*. Unwin Hyman, London, 1990.

Cousins, Arthur. *The Garden of New South Wales*. Producers' Co-op Distributing Society, Sydney, 1948.

Couvares, F. G. *The Remaking of Pittsburgh: Class and Culture in an Industrializing City, 1877–1919*. State University of New York Press, Albany, NY, 1984.

Cox, Kevin, and Mair, Andrew. 'From Localised Social Structures to Localities as Agents'. *Environment and Planning A*, vol. 23, 1991, pp. 197–213.

Crago, E. A., and Lowndes, A. G. 'Port Kembla and its Harbour'. *Australian Geographer*, vol. 1, part 3, 1929, pp. 50–7.

Crisp, P. T., Archibold, O. W. and Crisp, E. A. 'The Use of Wind Direction Data to Predict Pollution Dispersal around the Port Kembla Industrial Area, New South Wales'. *Australian Geographical Studies*, vol. 22, no. 2, October 1984, pp. 243–60.

Davis, Wayne (ed.). *Our Memories Your History: An Oral History of Port Kembla*. Wollongong College of Technical and Further Education, Wollongong, NSW, 1984.

Dempsey, Ken. *Smalltown: A Study of Social Cohesion and Belonging*. Oxford University Press, Melbourne, 1991.

Department of Trade. *The Australian Steel Industry*. Commonwealth of Australia, Melbourne, 1958.

Donaldson, Michael. *Time of Our Lives: Labour and Love in the Working Class*. Allen & Unwin, Sydney, 1991.

Donaldson, Michael et al. *Is There a Crisis in the Steel Industry?* Wollongong Workers' Research Centre, Wollongong, NSW, 1981.

Dowd, B. T. *The First Five Land Grantees and their Grants in the Illawarra*. Illawarra Historical Society, Wollongong, NSW, 1960.

Duggan, E. P. *The Impact of Industrialization on an Urban Labor Market: Birmingham, England, 1770–1860*. Garland, New York, 1985.

Duncan, Stuart, and Goodwin, Martin. *The Local State and Uneven Development: Behind the Local Government Crisis*. Polity Press, Oxford, 1991.

Eades, D. K. *The Dharawal and Dhurga Languages of the New South Wales South Coast*. Australian Aboriginal Research and Regional Studies no. 8, Institute of Aboriginal Studies, Canberra, 1976.

Eardley, G. H. 'The Making of Port Kembla', Parts 1 and 2. *Illawarra Historical Society Bulletin*, November 1976, pp. 77–9, and March 1977, pp. 14–16.

Edwards, R. C. *Contested Terrain: The Transformation of Work in the Twentieth Century*. Basic Books, New York, 1979.

Egloff, B. J. *Wreck Bay: An Aboriginal Fishing Community*. Australian Institute of Aboriginal Studies, Canberra, 1981.

Eklund, Erik. ' "We Are of Age": Class, Locality and Region at Port Kembla, 1900 to 1940'. *Labour History*, no. 66, May 1994, pp. 72–85.

——. 'Managers, Workers and Industrial Welfarism: Management Strategies at ER&S, Port Kembla and the Sulphide Corporation, Cockle Creek, 1895–1929'. *Australian Economic History Review*, vol. 37, no. 2, July 1997, pp. 137–57.

——. 'Memories of Place: Local History and Oral Evidence'. *The Oral History Association of Australia Journal*, no. 19, 1997, pp. 73–7.

——. 'The "Place" of Politics: Class and Localist Politics at Port Kembla, 1900–1930'. *Labour History*, no. 78, May 2000, pp. 94–115.

Eklund, Erik and Murray, Maree. *Copper Community: A History of the Electrolytic Refining and Smelting Company of Australia Ltd and Southern Copper Ltd, Port Kembla*. University of Wollongong Press, Wollongong, NSW, 2000.

Ellis, M. H. *Metal Manufactures: A Golden Jubilee History*. Harbour Press, Sydney, 1966.

Firth, Beverly. The Industrialization of Wollongong with special reference to Australian Iron & Steel Pty Ltd, 1926–1976. PhD thesis, Macquarie University, 1986.

Forster, Colin. *Industrial Development in Australia, 1920–1930*. Australian National University Press, Canberra, 1964.

Foster, John. *Class Struggle and the Industrial Revolution: Early Industrial Capitalism in Three English Towns*. Weidenfeld & Nicolson, London, 1974.

Giddens, Anthony. *Central Problems in Social Theory, Action and Structure and Contradiction in Social Analysis*. Macmillan, London, 1979.

——. *The Consequences of Modernity*. Polity Press, Stanford, Calif., 1990.

Goodall, Heather. 'Land in Our Own Country: The Aboriginal Land Rights Movement in South East Australia, 1860–1914'. *Aboriginal History*, vol. 14, no. 1–2, 1990, pp. 1–24.

——. *Invasion to Embassy: Land in Aboriginal Politics in New South Wales, 1770–1972*. Allen & Unwin, Sydney, 1996.

Graham, Laurie. *Singing the City: The Bonds of Home in an Industrial Landscape*. University of Pittsburgh Press, Pittsburgh, Pa, 1998.

Gray, Ian. *Politics in Place: Social Power Relations in an Australian Country Town*. Cambridge University Press, Cambridge, 1991.

Green, David and Cromwell, Lawrence. *Mutual Aid or Welfare State: Australia's Friendly Societies*. Allen & Unwin, Sydney, 1984.

Gregory, David and Urry, John (eds). *Social Relations and Spatial Structures*. Macmillan, Hampshire, 1985.

Griffith, Gary. The Growing Militancy of the South Coast Branch of the Waterside Workers' Federation, 1930–1939. BA (Hons) thesis, University of Wollongong, 1980.

Hagan, Jim, and Wells, Andrew (eds). *A History of Wollongong*. University of Wollongong Press, Wollongong, NSW, 1997.

Harvey, David. *Limits of Capital*. Basil Blackwell, Oxford, 1982.

Hays, Samuel P. (ed.). *City at the Point: Essays on the Social History of Pittsburgh*. University of Pittsburgh Press, Pittsburgh, Pa, 1988.

Hosgood, C. P. ' "The Pygmies of Commerce" and the Working Class Community: Small Shopkeepers in England, 1870–1914'. *Journal of Social History*, vol. 22, no. 3, 1989, pp. 439–60.

Hoskins, Cecil. *The Hoskins Saga*. Halstead Press, Sydney, 1969.

Hoskins, Donald. *The Ironmaster: The Life of Charles Hoskins 1851–1926*. University of Wollongong Press, Wollongong, NSW, 1995.

Hughes, Helen. *The Australian Iron and Steel Industry, 1848–1962*. Melbourne University Press, Carlton, Vic., 1964.

Illert, Chris and Reverberi, Daniela. 'The Ills of the Illawarra: Industrial Pollution and School Absenteeism'. *Search*, vol. 25, no. 4, May 1994, pp. 101–3.

Jabubowicz, Andrew. *Immigrant Parents and Port Kembla Schools: Multiculturalism and the School Environment*. Centre for Multicultural Studies, University of Wollongong, NSW, 1980.

Johnson, Louise. 'Making Space for Women—Feminist Critiques and Reformulations of the Spatial Disciplines'. *Australian Feminist Studies*, no. 9, Autumn 1989, pp. 31–50.

Johnston-Liik, E. M., Liik, George and Ward, R. S. *A Measure of Greatness: The Origins of the Australian Iron and Steel industry*. Melbourne University Press, Carlton, Vic., 1998.

Keys, C. L. and Wilson, M. G. A. *The Urban Illawarra: A Social Atlas, Census 1981*. Illawarra Regional Information Service, Wollongong, NSW, 1984.

Kreis, I. A. et al. *Illawarra Child Blood Lead Study*. Illawarra Environmental Health Unit, Wollongong, NSW, 1994.

La Perouse, the Place, the People and the Sea: A Collection of Writing by the Aboriginal Community. Aboriginal Studies Press, Canberra, 1988.

Lack, John. 'Residence, Workplace, Community: Local History in Metropolitan Melbourne'. *Australian Historical Studies*, vol. 19, April 1980, pp. 16–40.

Larcombe, F. A. *A History of Local Government in New South Wales, vol. 3: The Advancement of Local Government in New South Wales 1906 to the Present*. Sydney University Press, Sydney, 1978.

Lee H. H. 'A Medical History of Wollongong'. *Medical Journal of Australia*, no. 10, 3 September 1955, pp. 353–5.

Lever, William and Bailly, Antoine (eds). *The Spatial Impact of Economic Changes in Europe*. Avebury, Aldershot, 1996.

Lever Tracy, Constance and Quinlan, Michael. *A Divided Working Class: Ethnic Segmentation and Industrial Conflict in Australia*. Routledge & Kegan Paul, London, 1988.

Lockwood, Rupert. *War on the Waterfront: Menzies, Japan and the Pig Iron Dispute*. Hale & Iremonger, Sydney, 1987.

Love, Peter. *Labour and the Money Power: Australian Labour Populism, 1890–1950*. Melbourne University Press, Carlton, Vic., 1984.

Lysaght Venture. Stewart Howard and Associates, Sydney, 1955.

McCaffery, Frank. *The History of Illawarra and its Pioneers*. Frank McCaffery, Kiama, NSW, 1922.

McCalman, Janet. 'Class and Respectability in a Working Class Suburb'. *Australian Historical Studies*, vol. 19. no. 74, April 1980, pp. 90–103.

——. *Struggletown: Portrait of an Australian Working-Class Community*. Penguin, Ringwood, Vic., 1984.

McCarty, J. W. 'Australian Regional History'. *Australian Historical Studies*, vol. 18, no. 70, April 1978, pp. 88–105.

McDonald, T. A., and Wilson, M. G. A. *Illawarra Healthy Cities Project*. Wollongong, NSW, 1990–91.

Markey, Ray. *The Making of the Labor Party in New South Wales, 1880–1900*. New South Wales University Press, Kensington, NSW, 1988.

——. (ed.). *Labour and Community: Historical Essays*. University of Wollongong Press, Wollongong, 1999.

Mathews, R. H. 'Ethnological Notes on the Aboriginal Tribes of New South Wales and Victoria', *Journal of the Royal Society of New South Wales*, vol. 38, 1904, pp. 203–381.

Merritt, John. A History of the Federated Ironworkers' Association, 1909–1952. PhD thesis, Australian National University, 1967.

Metcalfe, Andrew. *For Freedom and Dignity: Historical Agency and the Class Structures of the Coalfields of New South Wales*. Allen & Unwin, Sydney, 1988.

——. 'Mud and Steel: The Imagination of Newcastle'. *Labour History*, no. 64, May, 1993, pp. 1–16.

Mitchell, Winifred. The Miners of Southern New South Wales: A History of the Union to 1900. MA thesis, University of New England, 1964.

Mitchell, Winifred and Sherington, Geoffrey. *Growing up in the Illawarra: A Social History, 1834–1984*. University of Wollongong, Wollongong, NSW, 1984.

Murray, Robert and White, Kate. *The Ironworkers: A History of the Federated Iron-workers' Association of Australia*. Hale & Iremonger, Sydney, 1982.

Noogaleek, Belonging to Me: An Aboriginal Oral History. Wollongong Technical and Further Education, Wollongong, NSW, 1984.

Organ, Michael (comp. and ed.). *Illawarra and South Coast Aborigines, 1770–1850*. Aboriginal Education Unit, University of Wollongong, NSW, 1990.

Organ, Michael et al. *Illawarra and South Coast Aborigines, 1770–1900*. Report for the Australian Institute of Aboriginal and Torres Strait Islander Studies, Wollongong, NSW, 1993.

Peterson, Nicolas. *Australian Territorial Organisation*. Oceania Monograph no. 30, University of Sydney, 1986.

Piggin, Stuart. *A History of the Christian Churches in the Illawarra*. University of Wollongong, Wollongong, NSW, 1984.

Piggin, Stuart and Lee, Henry. *The Mt Kembla Disaster*. Oxford University Press, South Melbourne, 1992.

Pleck, Elizabeth. 'Two Worlds in One: Work and Family'. *Journal of Social History*, vol. 10, no. 2, 1976, pp. 178–95.

Policies for Development of Manufacturing Industry, A Green Paper, volume one. Australian Government Publishing Service, Canberra, 1975.

Port Kembla: A Social Survey. Social Studies Department, University of Sydney, 1945.

Port Kembla Public School Centenary, 1890–1990. Port Kembla, NSW, 1990.

Pratt, A. C. 'Discourses of Locality'. *Environment and Planning A*, vol. 23, 1991, pp. 257–66.

Preston, Denise (ed.). *If I Remember Rightly: An Oral History of Port Kembla*. Wollongong City Council, Wollongong, NSW, 1988.

Reiger, Kerreen. *Family Economy*. McPhee/Gribble, Ringwood, Vic., 1991.

Rich, D. C. *The Industrial Geography of Australia*. Methuen, North Ryde, NSW, 1986.

Richardson, Len. *The Bitter Years: Wollongong during the Depression*. Hale & Iremonger, Sydney, 1984.

Richardson, Peter. 'The Origins and Development of the Collins House Group, 1915–1951'. *Australian Economic History Review*, vol. 27, no. 1, March 1987, pp. 3–29.

Rickard, John. *Class and Politics: New South Wales, Victoria and the Early Commonwealth, 1890–1910*. Australian National University Press, Canberra, 1976.

Robinson, Ross (ed.). *Urban Illawarra*. Sorrett, Melbourne, 1977.

Schultz, Julianne. *Steel City Blues: The Human Cost of Industrial Crisis*. Penguin, Ringwood, Vic., 1985.

Sheridan, Tom. 'A Case Study in Complexity: The Origins of the 1945 Steel Strike in New South Wales'. *Labour History*, no. 41, November 1981, pp. 87–109.

Shields, John (ed.). *All Our Labours: Oral Histories of Working Life in Twentieth Century Sydney*. New South Wales University Press, Sydney, 1992.

Silverman, C. J. 'Neighboring and Urbanism: Commonality versus Friendship'. *Urban Affairs Quarterly*, vol. 22, no. 2, December 1986, pp. 312–28.

Stacey, Margaret. 'The Myth of Community Studies'. *British Journal of Sociology*, vol. 20, no. 2, 1969, pp. 134–47.

Steinke, J. C. *Future Prospects of Port Kembla Shopping Centre: A Report to the Illawarra Regional Development Committee*. Economics Department, Wollongong University College, NSW, [1969?].

Thompson, E. P. *The Making of the English Working Class*. 2nd edn, Pelican, Harmondsworth, 1968.

Thrift, Nigel and Williams, Paul (eds). *Class and Space: The Making of Urban Society*. Routledge & Kegan Paul, London, 1988.

Turnbull, Clive. *Commemorating the Official Opening by the Prime Minister of Australia, the Rt. Hon. R.G. Menzies, C.H., Q.C., of the Hot Strip Mill and Other Major Plant Extensions at the Australian Iron & Steel Ltd. Kembla works, N.S.W., on Tuesday, August 30, 1955*. Broken Hill Proprietary Company/Speciality Press, Melbourne, 1955.

Turner, Ian. *Industrial Labour and Politics: The Dynamics of the Labour Movement in Eastern Australia, 1900–1921*. Australian National University Press, Canberra, 1965.

Tweedale, Geoffrey, *Steel City: Entrepreneurship, Strategy and Technology in Sheffield, 1743–1993*. Clarendon Press, Oxford, 1995.

Urry, John. 'Localities, Regions and Social Class'. *International Journal of Urban and Regional Research*, vol. 5, 1981, pp. 455–74.

Walker, Jill. 'The Production of Exchange Values and Employment in the Home'. *Australian Feminist Studies*, no. 9, Autumn 1989, pp. 51–84.

Westley-Wise, Victoria J., et al. 'Investigation of a Cluster of Leukaemia in the Illawarra Region of New South Wales, 1989–1996'. *Medical Journal of Australia*, 1999, vol. 171, pp. 178–83.

White, John. 'Port Kembla Pig Iron Dispute'. *Labour History*, no. 37, November 1979, pp. 63–77.

Wollongong City Council. *Port Kembla No Loitering/Disorderly Behaviour Policy Trial: Evaluation Report*. Wollongong, December 1999.

——. *Port Kembla Safety Program, September 2000*. Wollongong, 2000.

Wright, Chris. 'The Formative Years of Management Control'. *Labour History*, no. 55, November 1988, pp. 55–70.

Wright, E. O. *Classes*. Verso Press, London, 1985.

Young, Ann R. M. 'Problems in the Urban Environment: Pollution in the Wollongong–Shellharbour Area'. *Wollongong Studies in Geography*, no. 15, Department of Geography, University of Wollongong, NSW, 1984.

Index